MW00880032

"I have read dozens of Peace Co
of service on the individual writ￼
contains not just the memories ￼
one hundred. It is therefore that much more authoritative."

—Robert E. Gribbin, III
Ambassador to Rwanda and Central African Republic
Peace Corps Volunteer—Kenya

"Randy Hobler has written the best memoir of a Peace Corps experience that I have ever read. His amazingly detailed book instantly grips the reader by putting Libya in its properly rich and unique historical perspective. Everyone should read this book, to enjoy its humor as well as its insights. Bravo to Randy Hobler for all the hard work and writing talent that has resulted in this unparalleled but eminently readable chronicle of a time and place lost forever."

—Niels Marquardt
Former Ambassador to Equatorial Guinea, Cameroon, Madagascar and the Union of the Comoros
Peace Corps Volunteer—Zaire and Rwanda

"Reading the book, I found myself laughing more times than I could count. Bravo for telling this story in a way that is accessible and entertaining!"

—Cameron Hume
Ambassador to South Africa, Indonesia and Algeria
Peace Corps Volunteer—Libya

"A *magnum opus*!" I must remark that the level of detail in terms of time, places and people is remarkable. This book does remind one how living in utter simplicity has beauty and how uncluttered time leads to clarity."

—Nicholas Craw
Peace Corps Director, 1973—1974

"At its best, the story telling was fun and engagingly told with a fond memory that lacked rancor about the struggles of drinking water with colored worms and finding scorpions in their shoes. Telling the story nearly 50 years later gives this memoir the feel of a saga."

—Paul Sully
Country Director, Peace Corps Jamaica

"As the first American ambassador posted to Libya in 36 years, I found this epic tome by Randy Hobler to be a veritable and precious treasure trove of Libyan history, politics and culture, of the individual experiences of Peace Corps volunteers and an exciting piece of storytelling that rivals any academic enterprise. It is a book full of joy, tears and knowledge that could only be found in Hobler's telling. Thank you, Randy for this amazing journey."

—Gene Cretz
Ambassador to Libya and Ghana

"Hobler kept a detailed diary while including the accounts of more than 100 fellow volunteers. This group approach enables him to cover every aspect of the Peace Corps experience, whether the exotic food they pretended to enjoy, the old motorbikes forever dying on them in the middle of the desert, or Hobler's own challenges of maintaining a budding long-distance relationship. These vivid memories, via Hobler's novelistic eye, take you into the thick of this extraordinary adventure."

—Tom Seligson
Author of six books, two of which sold to Hollywood,
and an 11-year CBS documentary producer

"Randolph Hobler's account of Ghaddafi's rise to power and the impact on ordinary Libyans is fascinating. His updates, addressing Libya's current descent into disorder, heartbreaking. As in Ondaatje's *The English Patient*, Hobler introduces us to an 'international sand club' of interesting personalities living fully in a unique place and time."

—Edmund Hull
Ambassador to Yemen
Peace Corps Volunteer—Tunisia

"A bittersweet wonder. The book is 'about' the author's Peace Corps epoch in Libya but is, of course, ultimately about youth, the passage of time—and about love. This colorfully detailed account of Hobler's life during a period of extraordinary change—his own and that of his adoptive country—is an edifying, emotionally nourishing journey. His naturally sympathetic depiction of a place and people most Americans reflexively regard as savage and violent is bridge-building. A completely immersive read!"

—Jeff Wing
Columnist, *The Santa Barbara Sentinel*
Content/Feature Writer, Procore Technologies
Resident, Libya 1968–1970

"Having served as US Ambassador to Libya from 2013-2015 following the attack on our mission in Benghazi that took the lives of Ambassador Chris Stevens, I was intrigued by the penetration of these young, idealistic Americans into the cities, towns and villages across the vastness that is Libya, their resourcefulness, and most of all their engagement with a broad spectrum of Libyans. The photographs are an added treat. I wish this book had been available prior to my own engagement."

—Deborah Jones
Ambassador to Libya
Peace Corps Volunteer—Afghanistan

"Randolph Hobler has produced a fascinating study of the unique experience of Peace Corps Volunteers in Libya before and during Muammar Qadhafi's 1969 coup d'état. As a former Peace Corps Volunteer myself, I can attest that he deals humorously and accurately with the fumbling efforts of the early Peace Corps to select effective volunteer candidates and then to cope with the chaos which often accompanied their deployment in a land which then had little experience of Americans."

—Dane Smith
Ambassador to Guinea and Senegal
Peace Corps Volunteer—Ethiopia

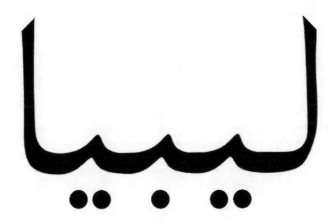

"Libya" in Arabic. Even though in Arabic it reads right to left, you can equally well read it left to right.

The only country name that's a visual palindrome.

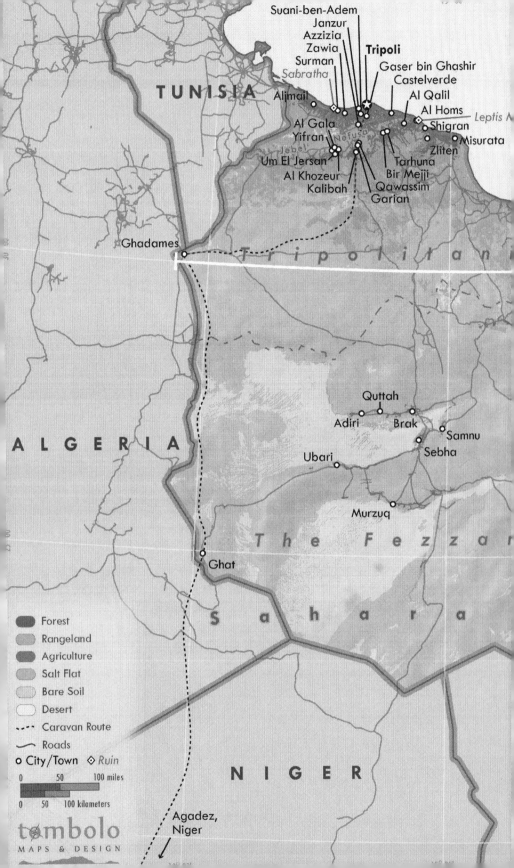

e d i t e r r a n e a n   S e a

Cyrene Ayn
Al Beida Habbun
Farzougha   As Derna
Daryanah   El Merj Safsaf
Ganfuda   Benghazi   Tobruk
Sidi Khalifa

Ajedabia

5 mi

Aujila

E G Y P T

B Y A

C y r e n a i c a

825 mi

Al Taj

D e s e r t

S U D A N

H A D

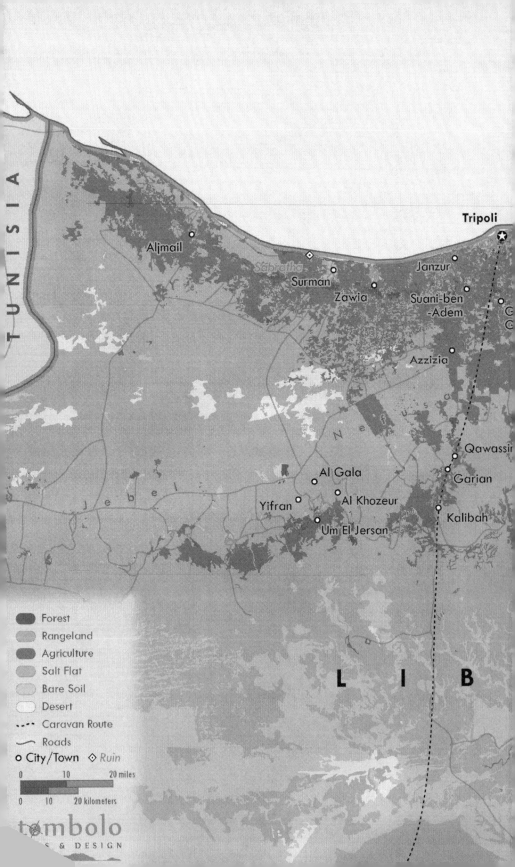

Tripoli ★

Ajmail ○

Sabratha ◇

Surman ○

Zawia ○

Janzur ○

Suani-ben -Adem ○

Azzizia ○

Qawassir ○

Garian ○

Al Gala ○

Al Khozeur ○

Yifran ○

Kalibah

Um El Jersan ○

TUNISIA

N e ... u ...

J e b e l

L I B

Forest
Rangeland
Agriculture
Salt Flat
Bare Soil
Desert
Caravan Route
Roads
○ **City/Town** ◇ *Ruin*

0   10   20 miles
0   10   20 kilometers

t๏mbolo
S & DESIGN

15° 00'

Mediterranean

Sea

Castelverde

Al Homs
◇ *Leptis Magna*

Al Qalil

Shigran

Tarhuna

Mejji

Zliten

Misurata

Tripolitania

101 Arabian Tales

How We All Persevered in Peace Corps Libya

RANDOLPH W. HOBLER

ISBN: 979-8-6981-6219-3 (sc)
ISBN: 978-1-7167-1130-5 (hc)
ISBN: 978-1-7168-1165-4 (e)

Because of the dynamic nature of the Internet, any web addresses or links contained in this book may have changed since publication and may no longer be valid. The views expressed in this work are solely those of the author and do not necessarily reflect the views of the publisher, and the publisher hereby disclaims any responsibility for them.

Lulu Publishing Services rev. date: 08/20/2020

This book is dedicated to the villagers

of Al Gala and Um El Jersan, Libya

for their heartfelt generosity, unstinting hospitality

and deep human goodness.

*"The only real voyage is not an approach to landscape but a viewing
of the universe with the eyes of one hundred other people."*

—Marcel Proust

Forethoughts

In a book of recollections, I suppose I should make mention of my earliest one. One that will forward-relate to Libya, I promise. At the tender age of three, I'd managed to develop a right inguinal hernia. So, on October 14, 1949 my parents trundled me off to the Children's Hospital of Philadelphia. I vividly remember lying on the operating table and watching as a brown rubber ether mask bore down upon my face just before I went under. The surgeon who operated on me subsequently performed no less than 17,000 hernia operations. And 35 years later, Dr. C. Everett Koop became U.S. Surgeon General under President Ronald Reagan. Clearly, I should get credit for giving him such a great start.

Although I was one of the first Baby Boomers, none of us knew we were Boomers until some demographer bestowed that moniker upon us 31 years later in 1977. I was born March 28, 1946, a mere three months after the very first Boomer—Kathleen Casey-Kirschling—came into this world at one second past midnight on January 1, 1946. The boom was an explosion of the pent-up desires of millions of war-weary GI's coming home to millions of war brides and fiancées-to-be. In 1945 there were 2,858,000 births in the U.S. In 1946 this skyrocketed up 20% to 3,426,000. (The "boom" continued until midnight December 31, 1964.)

In my case, my father, Herbert Hobler, a B-29 navigator, married my mother, Mary Randolph (whence my first name) in San Antonio, Texas, before shipping out to Tinian in the South Pacific (the very island from which the Enola Gay lifted off toward Hiroshima). In mid-1945 he returned stateside and around June 28, 1945 I was conceived in Van Nuys,

California. In 1946, 70 other baby boys were born across the country, little knowing they would converge in Clearfield, Utah in 1968, joining 38 other young men—born between 1942-1945 and 1947-1948—to bond as Libya II Peace Corps volunteers-in-training.

My life has been littered with uncanny coincidences, to which, of course, I ascribe myself credit for emanating some kind of mystical force field that attracts them to me. (I'm not talking ordinary, run-of-the-mill, everyday coincidences like "Gee, I was thinking of Bill yesterday, and wow, I saw him today!") I fancy myself as some sort of Prince of Coincidence. A kind of Smarty-Pants of Happenstance. A Long Oddsfellow. We're talking hard numbers. Non-causal, i.e. independent relationships between events. The simultaneity of multiple events, each with highly remote odds. I will belabor the reader only this initial example of many, in this book, as all readers retain a repertory of coincidental stories.

So. My father's best buddy in the Army Air Corps was B-29 blister gunner Thurman "Wally" Walling.

My father, Herbert Hobler and Wally Walling on Tinian

On June 6, 1945, he died when his plane—the Dauntless Dotty, a B-29 superfortress— crashed at 3:06 AM, just after take-off, on the tiny, remote island of Kwajalein in the South Pacific, sinking down 6,000 feet. Wally was en route to Hawaii for Rest and Recreation. A casualty of War.

Now, this was not any old B-29, but the very first B-29 from the Marianas to bomb Japan in the war. That's 1 out of 3,490 B-29's. Wally was 1 of 200 friends my father might have known at the time. In 2005, one of my close friends from elementary school, John Sheehan, a Jesuit priest, just happened to be assigned to Kwajalein. So, I've got say, conservatively, 1 out of 400 friends. And the chances of Father Sheehan being on Kwajalein in any year from 1945 to 2005 is 1 in 60 years. Now, how many Jesuits were there in the world in 2005 who might have been assigned to Kwajalein? Well, that's 1 out of 12,000. And the topper is there were three dive bombers who crashed on Kwajalein in WWII. Their type out of 286 U.S. planes? "SBD Dauntless." 1 out of 286. So, the math: you multiply the denominators and the chances of all this happening are 1 in 1.4 trillion.

The arc of my personal story propels this memoir from Wally's death in 1945 25 years forward to bookend at the very last page of this book.

A trifecta confluence of simultaneous coincidences inspired this book. The first fecta: Out of the blue in late 2016 my sister Debbie sent me an article she espied by a writer for her local *Santa Barbara Sentinel*—Jeff Wing. A charming, witty, self-deprecating teenage memoir ("Gaddafi's Rise and my Libyan Little League Fall") it chronicled Jeff's lucklessness with girls and baseball. Turns out this Air Force brat was in Libya at the exact same time as I (1968—1969) and so lived through the Ghaddafi (my spelling, but you can choose 17 other variations) Revolution.

The second fecta? Around the same time, while surfing the Internet I chanced upon a book published in 2012 by one of our fellow Libyan Peace Corps volunteers, Dennis "Wild Thing" Carlson, entitled *Volunteers of America: The Journey of a Peace Corps Teacher*. I immediately ordered and devoured it. It was compelling to compare my Libyan experience to his. (Sadly, Dennis died in 2015.)

The third fecta: After years of built-up double-guilt, I bravely decided to tackle Herodotus. (It's one of the 50 *Great Books*—Plautus, Aristotle, Copernicus, Aquinas, etc.—that forms the spine [no pun intended] of the University of Chicago's undergraduate curriculum. All the books any truly well-educated person must read, according to Robert Hutchins, the president of the University of Chicago in the '30s and '40s.) When my grandfather asked what I wanted to inherit, I said *The Great Books*, which I had always admired on his bookshelf, with their rich brown leather bindings and embossed gold titles. Not to mention their promise of deep wisdom. So, the first guilt is that since he died in 1974, I've walked past these books virtually every day without having read a one, feeling increasingly guilty betraying my grandfather's bequest. The second guilt? I've always felt my own education was severely lacking in not having read those classics.

So, of all the opportunities from 1974 to 2016 that I could have read Herodotus, I dove into his histories in the exact same time frame as reading Dennis' book and Jeff's article. "Dove" makes it seem too easy. "Trudged through Herodotus" is more like it.

Erroneously, I had assumed Herodotus was some kind of Latin poet, but soon learned he was a Greek historian who lived about 500 B.C.E. His take on Libya was it was "A tract which is wholly sand." However, my curiosity was piqued when he wrote that Libya is "surrounded on four sides by water." I thought "That can't be. Libya borders water only on its north side, facing the Mediterranean. Maybe, back when, there were some large dried-up rivers or lakes encircling Libya?"

It took only scant Google-image minutes to ferret out that the ancients used the name "Libya" to describe the entire continent of what is now Africa. How great Libya's loss of prestige—from whole continent to mere nation! Here's how the ancients mapped Libya in the day:

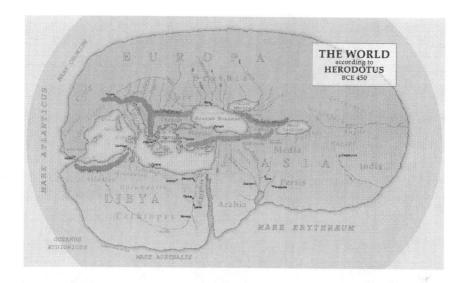

500 B.C.E. Herodotus: Libya as all of Africa

But wait! Bonus coincidence! I wanted to know what the origin of "Africa" itself was. Turns out that the "-ica" suffix indicates a place name (e.g. "Attica," "America," "Thessalonica," "Billerica"). The "Afri" core of the word comes from Berber "Ifra," which comes from a small town in Libya, "Yifran." Yifran is a town I've visited some 50 times as it is just six miles from my Libyan village of Al Gala.

No sooner had I launched into laying the groundwork for my book than yet another coincidence kicked in. For 47 years, in response to their persistent requests to sign up, I'd been telling the Peace Corps Association how glad I would be to present my Peace Corps experiences to a school group. They finally took me up on it—in December 2016. I got an e-mail from Fairleigh Dickinson University asking me to present to their International ESL class (English as a Second Language—what I taught in Libya). I duly presented to them on December 23, 2016. In parallel, I had been reaching out to my fellow RPCV's (Returned Peace Corps Volunteers) to solicit material for this book. My first interviewee was Angus Todd. Since he lived nearby, we had dinner just four days later, on December 27, 2016. Most appropriately, we chose a restaurant in New York City—Jean Claude—where the owner was an Algerian who speaks French, Arabic, English and

Berber, all among my languages. Angus shared some wonderful stories. And, it turns out Angus himself is who? A Fairleigh Dickinson grad.

Another remarkable coincidence? As part of my book research, I had dinner with fellow Libya Peace Corps colleague Richard Massey outside Washington, DC. He just happened to mention that he's been hosting young adults from countries all over the world for years. Then, two years later, he mentioned he was hosting a young man from Libya, of all places. His name was Ali Said ElSeddick, a Michigan State grad going for his Ph.D. at M.I.T. When I got in touch with Ali, he happened to mention that he knew a young Libyan woman named Malak El Taeb. Then it just happened that Malak's family is from the very village where I lived. What are the chances of that, given that there are over 300 towns and villages in Libya? After 50 years of radio silence, if you will, I was, thanks to Malak, able to hook into Facebook Libya and tap into an avalanche of information. Reciprocally, I e-mailed photographs of my fifth-grade students in Al Gala (see Appendix) generating enormous excitement in the village, culminating with a formal invitation for me to visit from the mayor.

As source material for this memoir, beyond the memories cradled in my cranium, there is my ever-faithful diary, which remembers so many long-forgotten specifics and so frequently corrects my misremembrances. There is also the much more detailed journal that I kept for a key portion of my time in Libya. And, there are my archivist-intensive family members—my parents, my grandparents and my sister Mary Bassett—who slavishly saved detailed letters I'd sent to them from Libya and providentially returned them to me decades later.

Important are the recollections I've solicited from my fellow Libya II (1968—1969) RPCVs. These volunteers include those who trained with me at Clearfield, Utah as well as the married couples and single women who simultaneously trained in Bisbee, Arizona. I've cast a wider net to include stories of volunteers from Libya I (1966-1968) and from Libya III (1969) trainees who never got to serve in Libya due to the Ghaddafi Revolution. Beyond the perspective of fellow volunteers, I've interviewed field staff and one Libya desk jockey from the day in the State Department and an Air Force radio DJ from Wheelus Air Base in Tripoli. The totality of this amounts to a collective memoir reflecting a multi-prismed kaleidoscope of experiences. Total interviews conducted? 101.

With respect to any direct quotations, I have only included actual dialogue where for whatever reason—the drama, the humor—I or my interviewees retain a vivid memory. Also, I have made no assumptions about facts—either my own or those of my interviewees. Always skeptical, I dutifully fact-checked hundreds of items, including storks in Istanbul, plane fares in the Middle East, aquifers in Libya and details of Hubert Humphrey's visit to Salt Lake City.

In the short 15 months that this book covers for my piece of the memoir, I have experienced tales and travails—including three close calls—plus journeys to Utah, New Mexico, Arizona, Libya, Tunisia, Algeria, Italy, France, Spain, France again, Monaco, Italy again, France again, the UK, Greece, Turkey, Lebanon, Syria, Egypt, and oh, yes, Sandusky, Ohio.

Please join me on a journey through the eyes of 101 American Peace Corps volunteers. A journey through the fascinations of an exotic culture; through history—ancient and recent; through copings, struggles, gratifications large and small; through laughter, surprise and astonishment; through dangers, predations and revolution; through romance and tragedy; through misunderstandings, miscues, misadventures, misjudgements and mischief; through incompetencies, cruelties; through moments of breathtaking beauty; through the bonding of Libyans and Americans; and through my own personal journey in the thick of it all.

Berbers, Bombs and Bob Hope

In the middle of an English lesson, I cast my eyes over my class of 36 restless Libyan 5th-grade boys. All wore white shawls swathed across their bodies in a variety of configurations. All wore tight-fitting red felt caps. Their faces varied from black to white. Most were swarthy like Arabs, but with a mix of Berber that had accumulated over the centuries. The classroom was adobe. It had no electricity. Open windows with no screens. Instead of a blackboard, a wall painted black. The grayish-brown desks were rough-hewn, two-to-a-student, without drawers. The door was well worn and splintered. It was time to introduce a new English word, the noun "knife." To illustrate, I decided to draw the pocket-knife out of my pocket.

Me: "Knife."

Class: "Knife."

Me: "This is a knife."

Class: "This is a knife."

On to the prepositions. I placed the knife on my table. "Where is the knife?"

"The knife is on the table!"

At this point I suddenly had a "Should I or shouldn't I?" moment. "Knife" reminded me of a Bowie knife, (a very large knife like that in *Crocodile Dundee*) which in turn reminded me of *The Adventures of Jim Bowie* show on 1950s television. In the opening credits of the show, the hero cocks his arm and flings a Bowie knife through the air. It's rendered in slow motion, with a dramatic helicopter-rotor phht, phht, phht sound. The knife then slams point-first-perfectly into a tree trunk, with a zonk effect followed by a sproing-sproing effect as the knife vibrates in place.

1

I put the knife in my hand. "Where is the knife?"

"The knife is in the hand!"

Do I dare open up the knife and replicate the opening credits of *The Adventures of Jim Bowie?* There's that ratty old door fifteen feet to my left. It wouldn't hurt the door. I put the knife on my head. "Where is the knife?"

"The knife is on the head!"

I was not a knife expert. I was not Jim Bowie. I never even played mumblety-peg as a kid. At best I did a little whittling or used a knife to cut string. If it worked, how great would that be? But if it failed, what a humiliation!

I put the knife under the table. "Where is the knife?"

"The knife is under the table!"

What the hell. I opened the knife. In one motion, I cocked my arm and swiveled to the left. Taking dead aim, I released the knife tumbling through the air. Ka-ching! It penetrated the door. It zonked. It sproinged. Not missing a beat, I said, "Where is the knife?"

The students didn't answer. They were slack-jawed in amazement. A little louder, I said, "Where is the knife?" Still frozen. Even louder, I repeated, "Where is the knife?" Then in full-throated unison, they roared out a sentence they had never before uttered: "THE KNIFE IS IN THE DOOR!"

Behind my little anecdote above were three giants upon whose shoulders we stood. One, John F. Kennedy, bequeathed upon us the inspiration of the Peace Corps. Two, Noam Chomsky, the father of modern linguistics bequeathed upon us the principle that all languages can be taught the same way. Three, John Rassias, immersive foreign language pioneer who trained thousands around the world, bequeathed upon us the indefatigable energy, verve and drama to make classrooms come alive.

Before we Boomers forayed off as Libya II, Libya I—the first Peace Corps contingent in Libya and the smallest one in Peace Corps history—showed up for training on June 23, 1966 at Princeton University. I was living in Princeton at the time, often strolling through the campus, totally unaware—until 50 years later—that I might well have passed some of these Libya I trainees on Princeton's paths. Of all the dorms on campus, they happened to end up rooming in 1939 Hall. John F. Kennedy originally joined Princeton in the class of 1939. And, until I just checked

my diary for July 1, 1966, I didn't know that I was to go to a movie—
Arabesque (How perfect!)—with a friend, Jack Seifert, who showed up in
Clearfield, Utah, for our Libya II training two years later. It turns out that
Santa Barbara Sentinel reporter Jeff Wing was born on June 23rd. And for
yet another coincidence, just nine days before the Libya I trainees arrived,
Norman Rockwell graced the cover of *Look Magazine* with a spiritually
uplifting painting of President John F. Kennedy gazing to the future beside
eight young inspired Peace Corps volunteers.

**Rockwell traveled to Ethiopia to meet and
photograph six of these volunteers**

Libya I was to be a peace initiative unique in the otherwise on-and off
military-intensive relationship of the U.S. with Libya going back 219 years.
Libya is permanently enshrined in our oldest military hymn—the stirring
Marine Hymn—whose second line refers to "the shores of Tripoli." This was
a reference to Barbary pirates raiding U.S. shipping in the Mediterranean,
culminating in the First Barbary War (1801-1805) under Jefferson.
("Barbary" refers to "Berbers," the original inhabitants of Libya, who lived
there over a thousand years before the Arabs, arrived in 643 A.D.)

The signal event of this war was the spectacular explosion of the USS Intrepid in Tripoli harbor, carrying 100 barrels of gunpowder and 150 fixed shells that had been cannonaded by the pirates, on September 4, 1804. It would not be the first time that explosions figured in U.S.-Libya relations.

1804: USS Intrepid explosion in Tripoli Harbor

Courtesy National Archives, photo no. 208-LU-25F-10

In the second Barbary War, in 1805, eight U.S. marines and 500 Greek, Arab and Berber mercenaries marched 500 miles from Alexandria, Egypt to Derna, Libya, with the U.S. forces prevailing. The historic importance? This was the first time the United States flag was raised in victory on foreign soil.

Fast forward to 1942 when Field Marshal Erwin Rommel, nicknamed "The Desert Fox," heading up his Afrika Corps, captured Tobruk, Libya. (Coincidence: *rommel* means "sand" in Arabic.) U.S. B-24 and B-25 bombers subsequently bombed Tobruk, Benghazi and the oil fields.

The only interlude where the U.S. could say to Libya, "We come in peace" was the small slice of historical time from 1945-1969 when peace befell Libya and the U.S. The country was a British and French (the Fezzan area only) protectorate from 1945 until Christmas Eve, 1951 when it won its independence as a constitutional monarchy, headed by King Idris.

At the time, many Libyan towns and cities were in rubble. Benghazi alone had suffered over a thousand air raids. 400,000 Libyans had died in the conflict. Libya was the poorest country in the world, with an average annual income of $30 per person. The Libyan citizenry was 94% illiterate. The first university was only opened in 1955. And only 16 Libyans (count 'em) had university degrees. Its export economy was threadbare: the major export was scrap iron from salvaged war materiel, followed by salt and esparto grass, used for making high-grade paper and bank notes. Other exports included olives, hides and skins, wool, tuna fish, sponges and citrus fruits. In 1953, this prompted the United States Agency for International Development (USAID) to arrive in Libya, providing highway construction, electric power generation, harbor improvements, irrigation projects, initiating fly control and malaria eradication programs, rehabilitating wells, developing municipal water supplies and building many schools.

While no U.S. presidents have deigned to set foot upon Libyan soil—I mean sand—two vice-presidents have. Vice-President Richard Nixon visited Libya twice—in 1953 and in 1957.

March, 1957: Richard Nixon greeting shopkeepers in Tripoli

In 1954, five American oil companies began drilling for oil in Libya. Under current conditions, it would be folly to shoot a feature film in Libya, but in the peaceable 1950s, five were shot on location in Libya.

This included four British films: *The Desert Rats* with Richard Burton, *Sea of Sand*, directed by Richard Attenborough, *The Black Tent* with Donald Pleasance and *Ice Cold in Alex*, starring Anthony Quayle. Having second thoughts, perhaps, about the incongruity between the title and a climate that was the hottest on earth, in their infinite wisdom the producers re-released the film in the U.S. with the title *Desert Attack*, ditching the movie poster's romantic visuals for America-appropriate blood and guts. Finally, for American audiences, there was *Legend of the Lost*, starring John Wayne and Sophia Loren.

1956: John Wayne and Sophia Loren in Leptis Magna

The director was lost, indeed, when it came to costumes. They forced the Libyan extras to don turbans over their usual red *caboose* hats. So strongly did Hollywood believe that all Arabs wear turbans that they ignored the reality right in front of them. (And 63 years later, some Americans stubbornly persist in their "ugly American" ignorance by attacking and sometimes even killing turban-wearing Indian Sikhs, mistaking them for Arabs.)

In January, 1958, among the dozen oil companies drilling and exploring in Libya, it was Esso that first discovered oil, in Bir Ziltan, about 50 miles west of Tripoli. And many U.S. companies flourished in Libya in the 1950s.

On May 22, 1962, Vice-President Lyndon Johnson visited Wheelus Air Base outside Tripoli for just one hour.

Lyndon Johnson jawbones with Libyans

During WWII, Wheelus had been used by the Luftwaffe. After the war, it became a training base for F-4, B-36 and F-100 fighter pilots, who used the Sahara Desert as a practice bombing range. It was the largest U.S. military facility outside the U.S.: fully 20 square miles and at its height housing 15,000 troops. The hospital there was the largest U.S. military hospital outside the U.S.

Bob Hope trekked to Wheelus for his 1963 Christmas show, cracking jokes about the climate. "It's really dry here. I asked for a dry Martini in the Officer's Club and they handed me an olive pit and a pinch of dust."

**Christmas Time, 1963: Bob Hope joking
with troops at Wheelus Air Base**

These peaceful relations culminated with the arrival of Peace Corps Libya I and II serving from 1966-1969. Relations turned sour once Ghaddafi took over. On December 2, 1979, the U.S. Embassy in Tripoli was torched. In 1986, President Reagan retaliated for the Libyan bombing of a Berlin discotheque in which two American servicemen were killed and 79 injured. He launched Operation El Dorado Canyon on April 15 when 60 tons of munitions were dropped aiming at the elimination of Ghaddafi.

A Tomahawk missile destroys Ghaddafi force vehicles

On to the Arab Spring in 2011: as Libyans rose up against Ghaddafi, U.S., British and French naval forces fired hundreds of missiles on Libya, as part of Operation Odyssey Dawn. The U.S. rained 110 Tomahawk missiles down upon Ghaddafi's army. Combined NATO forces flew some 26,000 sorties in Libya, all in support of the rebels. This military effort ceased upon the ignominious death of Ghaddafi. (More coincidences: Ghaddafi was born and was killed in the city of Sirte, Libya. In Homer's Odyssey, written around 750 B.C.E., according to a number of Homeric scholars, Odysseus was shipwrecked on the shoals of Sirte. And in the classic myth of Jason and the Argonauts, where else should they shipwreck but on those very same shoals!) On the heels of that, of course, was the horrific attack on the U.S. diplomatic compound in Benghazi in 2012 that resulted in the killing of Ambassador Christopher Stevens. Since then, Libya has been in a constant state of tribal civil war.

So, in the 219-year relationship between the U.S. and Libya, only 23 years or 11% of that time, was there an oasis of peace. A *Pax Libyca* from 1945 to 1969. It was one brief, shining moment, that was (if you will) Camel-ot.

■

Our generation of three contingents of Libya volunteers, born between 1940 and 1949, lived through those pacific years as children, and from 1966 through 1969 as young adults, became their own force for peace.

Dangers and Daggers

When the Libya I trainees plopped themselves down on the Princeton campus, all they knew about why they were there was that King Idris of Libya wanted every child in Libya to learn English. That given the lack of professional schools in Libya, they could learn overseas, then return to serve their country as doctors, lawyers, engineers and so forth, according to Martin Sampson (Cornell '66) a Libya I volunteer and later an Associate Director for Libya II. In fact, they never knew, until this writing, the full slate of real reasons why the U.S. was in Libya. It was, by no means, a foregone conclusion.

A countervailing matrix of circumstances involving multiple players and political forces behind the scenes led to the Peace Corps' entry into Libya, starting in 1964. First, an educational crisis. Although Libya had been flush with oil money for six years, school participation remained abysmal. Only 629 students graduated from high school in 1964. And college? Only 130. This, in turn left a virtual vacuum of desired American influence in Libya. According to new Libyan Ambassador David Newsom, "We are down to less than 10 Americans out of 2,500 foreign specialists in this country." The U.S. State Department extended feelers to U.S. foundations and to petroleum companies operating in Libya about funding English teachers.

For two years, none of these initiatives panned out. But traction was finally attained as reflected in a cablegram to the State Department on February 1, 1966, reading, "The government of Libya has requested a representative of the Peace Corps to visit Libya for discussions." Libyan and Peace Corps staff hammered out an agreement for 30 Peace Corps volunteers to teach English. The Peace Corps had just four months to scramble to put together a program. And they had ambitious plans—to expand from 25 volunteers to 400 in two years, and to augment this with educational television throughout the country.

When Alan Frank, just out of Duke University, was accepted to train for Libya, the Peace Corps Alan—no athlete he—imagined the training would include swinging from vines in a jungle somewhere. Faced with going to an Arab country he said, "Even though I was Jewish, I was too naïve to think that perhaps that was not a good idea." The trainees were a mix of 19 single men, two single women and two married couples—at the time, the smallest Peace Corps contingent in history. The project director, Kenneth Crawford, was doing graduate work at UCLA and had spent time in Libya at the American Wheelus Air Force Base in military intelligence. He spoke Arabic and was even fluent in Berber. Mornings and afternoons, the trainees studied Arabic, memorizing dialogues the Libyan staff (mostly Libyans doing graduate work in the U.S., whom Martin Sampson described as being very bright) composed in shopkeeper language. For Jack Doyle, who had gone to Boston Latin School (before going on to Northeastern) where the language learning method was rote memorization with no speaking or hearing a language, his work at the Princeton language lab was inspirational. "It captivated me." Unfortunately, Crawford directed the Libyan teachers *not* to teach the Arabic alphabet. Hunh? Learning to read a language is critical to reinforce any aural training you've received.

The trainees were taught TEFL (Teaching English as a Foreign Language, a close variation of ESL—English as a Second Language) by Harold and Rosemary Ames, who had taught in Tripoli, Libya. Harold was, according to trainee Franklin "Pancho" Huddle, (fresh out of Brown) "the ultimate of mild-mannered men, a self-effacing man who loved his country." This belied his actual behavior as a Special Forces ski warrior in Italy in WWII. A take-charge woman, Rosemary was the aunt of recent Secretary of Defense James Mattis. The Libya I volunteers practiced TEFL in Trenton on non-English-speaking Puerto Rican children. Dr. Othman Shemisa, a Libyan from Benghazi taught Libyan culture and Arabic, as did four of his Libyan colleagues, Suleiman Ma'ana, Ibrahim Felfel, Mohammed Abu Gassa and a colleague who was a World-Cup level soccer player. (Othman went on to teach in Bisbee for Libya II and for Libya III.)

Princeton, 1966, Libya I: Othman Shemisa, Ibrahim Felfel, unidentified, Mohammed Abu Gassa and Anis Ishtewi.

A towering figure in Middle Eastern studies, Gustave von Grunebaum, who sported a Ph.D. in Oriental Studies from the University of Vienna, imparted useful insights on Middle Eastern culture but knew little about Libya. Princeton provided psychologists who administered psychology tests, conducted interviews and feedback sessions and psychological screening. Their opinions weighed heavily on whether a trainee would, in Peace-Corps speak be "deselected" (not "let go," "failed," "weeded out" or "washed out"). Back in 1963 the expression began as "Selected Out," an oxymoron if ever I met one. The most memorable of the psychologists was a wacko who, while interviewing, lifted hand-weights and was constantly sharpening his pencil. On the center of his desk sat a large round holder stuffed with about 40 perfectly sharpened number 2 pencils. (Upon leaving the program, trainee and *artiste extraordinaire* Phillip Denney Brown (UC Davis) left his legacy on a 4' x 6' blackboard: an elaborate multi-colored chalk drawing of an Indian fakir, in guru garb, lying on a bed of sharpened pencils). Despite the available strong Middle East program at Princeton, the Peace Corps failed to leverage this resource one whit.

While there were no demanding physical challenges, it was a mental grind. Alan Frank remembers the mid-boards (a mid-training review of the volunteers) when "people from Peace Corps Washington came and were pretty rough on some of the trainees." Individuals were criticized by standards the trainees found to be ridiculous: "This one's too creative," "That one's too abrasive," "This one's on the periphery of the group," "That one loses his temper," and best of all, "This one's too Italian."

Marcus Wood (Ohio State) was touched by John F. Kennedy's idealism. He was further motivated by the idea of being a part of the first Peace Corps contingent in a country. So, he took on the toughest location in Libya—the Fezzan (meaning "rough rocks" in Berber), deep in the Sahara Desert. (By the by, Sahara means "desert" in Arabic, so when you say "Sahara Desert" you're repeating yourself.) While he considered that overall it was a "beautiful program," after the fact he felt the cultural training should have alerted the trainees to the existence and implications of tribes in Libya.

By the end of training, seven volunteers had been deselected. Two trainees—including Chuck Mizelle (Berkeley)—were illegally drafted into the armed services, despite holding a Peace Corps exemption. And the two single women—Karen Southard (St. Lawrence) and Colleen Ehart (University of Denver)—were summarily informed at the very end of training that due to the difficulties and dangers faced by single women in Libya they would *not* be going. This was especially crushing for Karen who was known for being a linguistic genius with a great memory and exceptional talent. The Ameses had worked hard to get them to teach in girls' schools in Libya, but the Libyan government pulled the plug. Why were they invited to train in the first place? Once there, why did whoever was in charge of the program wait until the women had gone through months of training before cutting them off? Surely the American staffers who had lived in Libya and the Libyans themselves knew that unmarried Western women living alone in Libya would have problems. Any single woman walking about without a husband with her—despite being dressed modestly—would be considered a prostitute and suffer abuse. Colleen ended up going to Tunisia for the Peace Corps and married a Tunisian.

Little did the remaining 18 trainees (Caucasian except for one Japanese-American, Bill Tsukida (San Francisco State College) and one

African-American, Peter Mayberry (King's College) know how events would unfold once they found themselves in-country.

When the 18 Libya I volunteers showed up for orientation in Tripoli, they were first welcomed by the Country Director, Bill Whitman, then greeted by Libyan Ministry of Education official Mustafa Gusbi, the Director of English Language Education. His great contribution was writing two enlightened beginning English readers reflecting the Libyan environment and situations. His initial statements to the volunteers were mainly two admonishments:

1. You must only teach.
2. You must not drink alcohol in the school.

Mustafa Gusbi in later years

The volunteers fanned out across Libya to exotic sounding towns—in the Tripoli area, Zliten; in the Benghazi area, Ghemines, Al Marj and Ajdabia; and in the Fezzan the towns of Brak and Murzuq. As with all new visitors to Libya, it was a humbling lesson in geography. While Libya does not loom large on a map of Africa, it is, in fact, three times the size of Texas—over 700 miles wide and over 500 miles long. It was also sparsely populated—only 1.8 million Libyans spread across that vast area. 95% of it is desert.

Starting in September of 1966, things moved along smoothly for the Libya I volunteers for about four months, teaching TEFL, getting to know the villagers and townspeople, learning the culture and improving their Arabic. In El Marj, John LaViolette (Western Michigan University) taught six days a week: three English classes a day at the high school, then adult evening classes. For the latter, there was usually no electricity, so John would light a kerosene lamp. In winter the smell of the lamp was over-powering when combined with the students who were not taking baths. His typical lunch? Hummus and bread. On other days a can of tuna fish with rice or pasta.

From the time Alan Frank arrived in Zliten, he wisely kept his Jewish religion a well-guarded secret. When asked about it, he simply had to lie.

Alan Frank, Libya I

Sharing many meals, he got along well with his fellow Libyan teachers, playing endless games of Risk and Italian Monopoly. On his return from Cairo on winter break, Alan brought them an Arabic version of Monopoly.

Alan Frank's friend Mahfoud Manshuf studying Koranic clay tablet

Alan taught introductory English to 3rd, 4th and 5th level classes during the day, and at night adults seeking to finish their secondary school degrees. His ability to teach was hampered by lack of teachable materials, forcing him to rely on outdated Egyptian and Iraqi books. In self-defense, Alan used a Peace-Corps-issued ditto machine to generate appropriate customized lessons. When he passed out the freshly made dittos, the unique inky smell convinced his students that he had been drinking.

A momentous day for little Zliten was the day when white-bearded, bespectacled, 77-year-old King Idris led his royal procession through streets decorated with flags and palm fronds. Although everyone, especially the teachers, was excited to see their king, most Libyans revered Egyptian president Gamal Abdul Nasser even more. (Libya II's John Lynch reports that whenever Nasser delivered a speech on the radio, the streets in his town of Derna were deserted: everyone was inside listening to Nasser.) For his part, Idris really hadn't wanted to be King of Libya. He didn't even like Libya.

Since 1922 he'd lived 29 years of his life in Cairo. His personal entourage consisted of Palestinians and Italians—but no Libyans.

Martin Sampson was assigned the isolated, distant village of Brak in the Fezzan. Dirt streets, one-story houses. And the only food grown there was lettuce, tomatoes and barley. All other food had to be trucked in. There was no electricity, no running water. Martin lived in a house with bachelor Berber Libyan teachers from well beyond the Fezzan whose morale was severely challenged by such isolation. Two of them were former students of Rosemary Ames. They hailed from Nalut 500 miles away. For them, this was Siberia. Martin soon learned of the "fine line between wanting solitude (to prepare for the next day's classes, etc.) and being discourteous. It was dicey territory."

Also in the Fezzan, by his own choice, Marcus Wood was stationed in Murzuq, 70 miles southwest of Sebha, and a main stop for camel caravans still plodding from southern Africa to the Mediterranean. For a thousand years, from the 5th century B.C.E. to the 5th century A.D., Murzuq had been the capital of the Garamantian Empire, operating the trans-Saharan caravan trade between the Carthaginians (and later the Romans) and West Africa. Marcus's villagers were all of African descent, of the Tibesti tribe, and decidedly darker in complexion than your average Libyan Arab.

Murzuq

As he learned Arabic, through trial and error he discovered, as we all eventually did the hard way, that there were linguistic pitfalls in words that were similar or identical in English and Arabic, but which had entirely different meanings. In Arabic, "suckoff" means "ceiling," "neck" means "fuck," "kiss" means "pussy" and "marafuck" means "elbow." Politically, he learned Arabs, with Libyans no exception, would rarely utter the word "Israel." Usually, it was "Temporarily Occupied Palestine." (Euphemisms know no linguistic bounds.)

In terms of culture, Marcus once asked a Libyan friend, "What would happen if I fell in love with your sister?" The friend replied, "First, I would be obliged to kill her to assuage her honor. Then we'd have to decide what to do with you."

For Marcus, his two years were tough. He thought he'd have the opportunity to socialize with other volunteers, but here he was in the middle of nowhere, rarely seeing any fellow PCVs. His only tenuous contact with the outside world was BBC radio and the Arabic-language Voice of Cairo (that often singled out Peace Corps volunteers in Africa to be "CIA stooges"). Also, on the short wave, he'd pick up three-hour harangues in favor of apartheid from South Africa and Chinese propaganda in English emanating from a transmitter in Albania.

Thus it was that Marcus's headmaster Shahara convinced himself that Marcus was a CIA agent. In teacher meetings, he'd go out of his way to stare at Marcus and say, "C...I...A!" After too many months of this, in front of all the other teachers, Marcus said, "OK, Shahara, I'll tell you I'm CIA if you'll tell me what I can spy on around here. The oil fields? They're 1,000 kilometers away. That old, abandoned Ottoman fort next door? Our local one-man police station? Please, please tell me what I can spy on!" At this, all the teachers laughed heartily. Never did he hear the accusation again.

In 1967, the Libyan military deemed it a good idea for Libyan Army officers to learn English. One of the Libya I volunteers was assigned the job. It turns out one of his students was then-unknown Muammar Ghaddafi. (He cut half his classes.) At some point during this period he also was chosen for five months of elite military training in Great Britain. (Who knows how many classes he cut there?)

David Dittman (Wittenberg University) taught English at a junior high school in Tripoli. According to Dittman, these kids were highly motivated to learn English—they even came to his house after school for help—because if they passed their English exam at the end of high school they would automatically get hired by an oil company. Dave started a basketball team as a player-coach. It was a mix of two Americans and the rest Libyans. Air Force personnel from Wheelus played on some of the teams in the league. Once they played in front of 1,500 people. They even won the championship, at the end of which Dave got a cultural lesson. As his team took a victory lap around the gym, the spectators threw coins at them. Dave started to pick them up. His teammate Juma yelled "No! You don't take the money, it's just symbolic!"

Jack Doyle was teaching at a college in Tripoli. His class included the first five women who ever went to college in Libya.

**Mary Nygaard, Dave Nygaard and Jack Doyle
(with camera) at Leptis Magna**

The smoothness ended in February of 1967 with "The Great Junior High School Strike." For six weeks, Martin's students just disappeared. No one had any idea what was going on. Kingdom of Libya radio did not report on it. There were no phones. And mail service was virtually non-existent. With nothing to do, the teachers' morale was at a low ebb. The momentum Martin had developed in moving his students ahead in learning English was stopped cold. Finally, one of the food truck drivers explained that the junior high schoolers were striking in sympathy with University of Benghazi students who had gone on strike. Due to the delay, in the second school year, the students had to start English I all over again.

Martin and the other volunteers ran head on into a pedagogical clash compounded by a disciplinary culture clash. Memorization and regurgitation was the order of the day for Libyan education. Students were reprimanded if they didn't recite back accurately what they had memorized. Martin relates that our American style is if you forgot something you say, "Hey, if you don't know it all yet, we'll just cover that later." The American attitude was, "The glass is half full, on the way to being totally full. The Libyan attitude is the glass is half empty, period." A common form of reprimand was the stick. The headmaster of Martin's school would whack students' palms with a thick stick if they misbehaved or failed to learn enough. As an American, Martin wasn't about to dole out physical punishment. But in so doing, his students, being accustomed to being hit, didn't take English seriously.

The first school year ended on June 4, 1967. The very next day the Six-Day War erupted between Egypt, Syria and Jordan on one side and Israel on the other. Nasser had perpetrated a big lie on Arab-wide radio, claiming that the U.S. had flown air cover for the Israelis as they bombed Cairo. Afraid of reprisals against Americans in Libya due to U.S. support of Israel and in the face of the Nasser lie, the U.S. government saw fit to order all civilian Americans in Tripoli to seek cover at the sprawling, 20-square-mile Wheelus Air Base there.

The Peace Corps volunteers in Tripolitania that were sent to Wheelus were ordered to man phones and assume other administrative duties. Those in Cyrenaica (the eastern half of Libya) were taken to El Adem, a British Army base outside of Benghazi. Dave Dittman's headmaster closed off the 30-foot-high massive school gates to protect all his teachers. Dave heard "lots of guns going off, Libyans shooting into the air." All the American teachers were wondering, "How do we get outta here?" The headmaster was able to orchestrate a stealthy getaway to Wheelus.

As the war began, Marcus Wood was in Sebha getting paid. He witnessed a crowd of students that ran down a street. They burned down the USIA library. Back in Murzuq, he noticed a suspicious older Bedouin with a semi-automatic weapon under his robe, following him around. For some time, this aroused deep fear on Marcus's part, until he learned that the American Ambassador to Libya, David Newsom, had asked the head of

Libyan security to guarantee the safety of all the Peace Corps volunteers. Turns out the Bedouin was actually there to protect Marcus.

After having been removed to Tripoli for protection and having enjoyed a vacation in Europe, Marcus returned to Murzuq, determined to continue teaching for his second year. He learned that while he was gone, a group of people including headmaster Shahara went to his house, seeking to string him up. And he found himself shunned, even by former friends. At one point, a deranged Palestinian named Ahmed pulled a knife on him, holding it up to his throat. He claimed that his parents had been killed by U.S. bombs. Marcus somehow kept his cool, and along with Libyans there, talked him down.

In fear for his life, Marcus started sleeping with a dagger under his pillow and a baseball bat beside his bed. Over in Brak, Martin Sampson also kept a kitchen knife near his bed. Marcus felt that all he had worked towards, all the trust he had built up in the village had been wiped out by the Six-Day War. Somehow, eventually, he broke the ice with the villagers, with the help of two Libyan Fezzanis who took him under their wing. It helped that he kept the fast of Ramadan, often inviting villagers over to his house for the evening breaking of the fast.

John LaViolette's experience during this war was extraordinary. On June 5th an Egyptian neighbor raced up to him shouting that the Americans had just attacked Cairo and that he should go inside his home. In John's own words,

> Once inside, the first thing I noticed was a Libyan soldier standing outside my window with a machine gun. I got the BBC station on my radio and was shocked to hear that the Israeli Air Force had completely destroyed the Egyptian Air Force. BBC stated that neither the American nor the British Air Force has anything to do with the attack. Radio Cairo, however, stated the opposite. My first reaction was "Oh, shit!" I had half a bottle of sherry from the Benghazi Embassy and drank it all, hoping to calm my nerves.

The local police took John into custody for his own protection. After four days he returned home. He turned the radio onto the British Force's Benghazi station to get the latest news on the war. They reported the war was already over and that Israel had captured a large amount of territory, including the entire Sinai Peninsula.

Then the announcer said, "If John LaViolette is hearing this broadcast, please call this number immediately." John was so flabbergasted at hearing his name on the radio he didn't write the phone number down. He listened to the next news broadcast an hour later and wrote down the number.

The only phone in El Marj was at the post office. John hurried there and called the number. An American official answered and once he knew who he was talking to, he said, "My God, we have been looking for you for days, where have you been?" He then told John to pack his bags and get to Benghazi ASAP. A friend put him in the back seat of his car and told John to put a rug over his body. They safely got through a checkpoint and arrived in Benghazi. Due to a curfew, the streets were empty. Soldiers on every corner. John directed his driver to go to El Adem. The British guard said he knew nothing about a John LaViolette and told John to go to the Wavel Barracks outside Benghazi. Upon arrival, he knocked on the gate, and as it opened a squad of British soldiers trained their guns on him. He jumped back and yelled, "No, no, no! I'm an American!"

Luckily, one of the other Peace Corps volunteers ran up and said, "No, he's supposed to be here." The U.S. Embassy in Benghazi had been attacked by a mob and had been trashed, so there were hundreds of American civilians (including six Peace Corps volunteers) and British Embassy personnel there.

> I sat outside with the other Peace Corps volunteers. They said they'd heard rumors that I had been chased by a mob on the streets of Benghazi and been murdered. Another rumor was that I was safe but hiding in a Catholic church.

A CIA agent informed the group they were going to evacuate all the embassy personnel and the Peace Corps volunteers on C-130 cargo planes. Upon arrival at the airport, they observed 15 Algerian MiG fighters lined up on the runway with the canopies open and the pilots in their seats. An Air Force officer ran up to their bus and informed them that upon take-off the MiGs were prepared to shoot them down. Once on the plane, the pilot informed the group that he was going to do a full-powered emergency take-off, tilting the plane at almost ninety degrees and that once up to five hundred feet, he would do a wing-over and come back down to get lower than radar.

The pilot performed as promised—I was certain that we would crash and die—but instead we all got very sick. About midnight we landed at Wheelus Air Force Base in Tripoli. Before we arrived, Libyans had been throwing sticks of dynamite over the air base fences surrounding the gates. I was so nauseated from the plane ride I was taken to the hospital, where I could not stop vomiting. After some tests I was given medicine and recovered in a day.

After two weeks, the U.S. Ambassador came and read a telegram from Secretary of State Dean Rusk asking if the volunteers would go back to their villages and to see if it was safe for American oilmen to come back to Libya. Only three volunteers, including John, agreed to go back to their villages. When John got to his house, he discovered that everything had been removed. He reported this to the police. They said they'd confiscated his belongings for safekeeping.

For the next few days, I walked around town talking to everyone I could. All were friendly and there were no problems or hint of animosity toward America or myself. They now understood that the USA did not assist Israel in the attack. I went back to Benghazi and reported that all was OK, that the oil workers could resume their work.

At that point, John and the remaining volunteers decided to go to Greece for their promised two-month vacation. John stayed quite a while in Greece. He then stayed a week in Istanbul, then to Venice, Rome and back to Libya to resume classes. At the end of his second year, the Libyan Education Department offered John a job as inspector of English for all Eastern Libya, living in Benghazi and with his own car.

"I thought about it, but had become very homesick, tired and hungry and I told them, 'No'. I was anxious to get home."

One day, Alan was walking in Tripoli with Peace Corps volunteers

John Giordano and Steve Canfield (Grinnell College). The trio was accosted by two drunk Palestinians. They demanded that the Americans pledge their loyalty to Nasser. Alan recounted, "Apparently, my pledge was not ardent enough, and one of them called me a Jew and attacked me by smashing his forehead into mine. Luckily, a Palestinian teacher from my school was walking by. He pulled the attacker away and apologized."

Not so luckily, in the middle of a besiegement of the U.S. Embassy in Tripoli, two Libyan Jews were fatally beaten.

At this point, despite the earlier reports from John LaViolette and others, no one knew if they would stay for a second school year in Libya. The Peace Corps staff suggested that everyone go back to their villages to test the waters and see if they were still welcome. They were, and this saved the second year for them all.

During that second year, Dave Dittman took on a Libyan girlfriend whom he would drive around in a car. At a meeting, the Peace Corps country director Bill Whitman took Dave aside.

"Dave, I think it's time for you to get out of town," he said. Whitman reassigned him to the town of Zawia, some 30 miles to the west of Tripoli where he had previously been posted.

At the end Libya I, Bill Whitman received a strong endorsement. In a letter from Ambassador Newsom to Jack Vaughn, the head of the Peace Corps in Washington, Newsom said that the Minister of Education termed the Libya I program "a success." The minister went on to say that the volunteers were "good teachers and good people." And that there was a "very great difference in the English competence of those taught by the volunteers and those taught by others in the Libyan schools."

While all these activities and adventures transpired between 1966 and 1968, the next cohort-to-be of Libyan Peace Corps volunteers struggled for two years before even joining.

Pinball Years

Having a pacifist bent, outraged at the immorality of the war, deeply interested in foreign languages and culture, firmly believing in universal governmental service and infused with the idealism of youth, I had strong leanings toward the Peace Corps. Like so many of my generation, I had been inspired by John F. Kennedy's enthralling 2 AM speech on October 14, 1960, at the University of Michigan, attended by 10,000, announcing the Peace Corps. Later, Kennedy spoke at the Cow Palace in San Francisco on November 2, 1960, declaring, "We have seen enough of warmongers. Let our great role in history be that of peace makers...We cannot discontinue training our young men as soldiers of war, but we also want them to be ambassadors of peace." Heady words, on the heels of so many generations imbued with the glories of war. (In fact just two months later, on January 17, 1961, in his final speech, President Eisenhower himself— ironically the most important general in U.S. history—issued a stinging rebuke to the country's warlike tendencies warning about the dangers of the "military-industrial complex.") At rallies during the campaign, students were literally "howling" in support of a Peace Corps.

As far as I know, only two of the Libya I, Libya II and Libya III volunteers ever saw JFK in person. They are Bob Pearson, (Area Director for Libya II) and myself. Bob was training for Peace Corps Afghanistan at Georgetown University, when his contingent, among others, was invited to the State Department in July 1962. President Kennedy addressed them all, and because Afghanistan comes first in the alphabet of nations, Bob sat in a front row seat just 20 feet from the president. He recalls vividly that Kennedy "did impress" and was "a great hero to most of us."

I was ten feet away from Kennedy about a year earlier, on Sunday, January 1, 1961. I had been visiting my grandparents in Palm Beach

Florida, during Christmas vacation. As the family drove by, my father pointed out that mass was just ending at the St. Edward Roman Catholic Church. He encouraged me to hop out and stand on the side of the church entrance where quite a crowd was waiting. Sure enough, president-elect John F. Kennedy walked right by. He carried a resplendent, charismatic smile, and sported a deep, glowing tan. We all burst into spontaneous applause and cheers.

While Kennedy made it all happen, he was not the first to propose a Peace Corps. Back in 1904 the American philosopher William James, speaking at the 13th Universal Peace Conference in Boston, suggested a "peace corps." Much later, in 1957, Senator Hubert Humphrey introduced legislation to establish a "Peace Corps." It did not pass. In 1951, Harris Wofford founded The Student World Federalists, proposing a "peace force" of volunteers for development projects in communities abroad. (He later became instrumental in the creation of the Peace Corps.) And in 1958, African-American Reverend James Robinson launched Operations Crossroads Africa (OCA) that sent young people to Africa to provide practical aid, exactly as the Peace Corps would do. Kennedy acknowledged this inspiration, as reflected in his welcome to Robinson and OCA volunteers in 1962 at the White House

1962 White House: President Kennedy, Reverend James Robinson and Hubert Humphrey

The official implementation of the Peace Corps was March 1, 1961. (Note that just two months later, on May 25, 1961, President Kennedy announced the plan to send a man to the moon.) Kennedy assigned his brother-in-law, R. Sargent Shriver as the first Peace Corps director. The advertising slogan was a twistful inspiration: "The toughest job you'll ever love."

Some were not impressed. Dwight D. Eisenhower called the Peace Corps "a juvenile experiment." Barry Goldwater called it "a post-graduate course in beatnikism." And the DAR passed a resolution, voting 2,600 to 1, that the Peace Corps would make "socialists" of American youth. Highly influential columnist Robert Ruark called the organization "Kennedy's Kiddie Korps." And lovable old Richard Nixon called it a "haven for draft dodgers." (So much for the nay-sayers!)

So, roused by President Kennedy's example, I did not realize that for the next two years all us Peace-Corps-volunteers-to-be (at least we males) were to be put through the proverbial wringer. Going into my junior year at Princeton, in the fall of 1966, I had no idea of the vicissitudes and in-certitudes that would plague me through the end of my senior year. I was to be caught in a vise between peace and war. All of this over and above a demanding academic schedule from a demanding school. This would all occur in parallel to Libya I's 1966—1968 term of service.

In October 1966 I took in a Peace Corps recruiting film, then applied for a special pre-Peace Corps 1967 summer program in Thailand. But, as French major, I opted for the Princeton Summer-Work-Abroad program to be a teller at the Banque Nationale de Paris in Nice, France. What a coincidence it was to have a singer in our Andover rock band, The Torqués, named Bob Marshall, (who penned and sang a mock-rock song, "Nobody," that preceded Sha-na-na by five years) walk up to my teller window at the bank. I hadn't seen him for three years.

Things went along busily until February 15, 1968, where I noted in my diary, "Got accepted at Columbia Business School, I'm really happy about it." Since that was my #1 choice, on February 16 I "sent regrets to the other six business schools." My joy, however, was short lived, for the very next day, February 17, the U.S. government eliminated graduate school deferments. I was beyond crestfallen.

During these two years from 1966 to 1968 I took tests from the Army

Reserve, NROTC, OCS, The Selective Service College Qualification Test, the business school test, the law school test and a psychology test from the Peace Corps. I worked in seven physicals, two interviews, and made multiple trips to such exotic places as Philadelphia and Ft. Dix, New Jersey. (As if I had nothing else to do!)

In my diary I wrote, "The future is taking up all of my present."

Just before graduation in 1968, I was accepted by the Peace Corps. On June 11, the day of my graduation, instead of celebrating after the ceremony, I had to take 3 ½ hours of tests at the Army Reserve. The same tests I had taken three times before!

How ironic it was that the unjust and immoral Vietnam War—like an evil twin—evolved at the very same time as the emergence of the humanitarian and idealistic Peace Corps. We boomers careened from pillar to post. John Maclean, recently graduated from the University of Hawaii and soon to be a colleague at Peace Corps training, summed up what millions of other draft-agers endured: "I felt like I was in a pinball machine."

Evil Spirits

The months leading up to my Peace Corps training were wrenching. Besides the ongoing carnage, rioting and grief over the Vietnam War, within two months of our arrival at Peace Training both Martin Luther King, Jr. and Robert F. Kennedy were assassinated. Our generation's psyches were benumbed with bewilderment, tinged with profound sadness. And as cannon fodder males, we were whipsawed by governmental forces. Feelings ran high. Trainee Rufus Cadigan (Lawrence University) wrote, "I was scared. I felt lonely and I was plenty angry. I faced being drafted into the army to go fight in a war in Vietnam. Or electing to go to Canada as a draft evader. I was a passionate dove and an ardent protestor against The War on my campus. I thought the Peace Corps would be a possibility, but I didn't think I was eligible because I would be required to serve in the Army."

Sunday, July 14, 1968 was the last day at my 295 Mercer Road home in Princeton, New Jersey. The longest period I'd ever been away from home? Three months. The Peace Corps would be a full two years—a new, exciting milestone in my life. My parents drove me to Newark Airport where I boarded a Boeing 720 jet to Chicago. On the connecting flight to Salt Lake City I sat down next to a fellow trainee, an affable red-head named Mike Culkin, newly graduated from the University of Scranton. It was cool we'd both brought guitars.

After setting down at Salt Lake City Airport we took a bus to Clearfield, Utah, 30 miles to the north. The Peace Corps had chosen Clearfield for our training because it approximated the Libyan climate—hot and dry. The temperature on our arrival day was, fittingly, 95°. Every remaining day in July exceeded 91 degrees, including one of 100°. 108 American men from 29 states converged on Clearfield on this day. The core group, 70 of us, 65% of the total, and my group, had just graduated college in June of 1968. As befitted our Boomer generation, we were a rebellious, restless, boisterous, irreverent, mischievous, anti-authoritarian, skeptical, prankish, testosterone-and-raging-hormone-fueled, adventurous, self-reliant, resourceful, team-oriented, rambunctious bunch. The Clearfield staff, older, stiff and academic, would turn out to be sorely ill-equipped to handle this new generational zeitgeist.

Not amongst us from the class of 1968 were others who would go on to make history. One was starting out at Harvard Business School, one was starting a career in real estate, one had just won a Rhodes Scholarship and was on his way to Oxford. It was only 49 years later, with the benefit of hindsight, that fellow PCV Peter Hawkes told me that all three baby boomer presidents to date were in the class of 1968. Pressing the coincidence further, he pointed out that three of our group were in the same classes of those same presidents. Dave Munro was at Yale with George W. Bush but didn't know him. (Trainee Jim Luikart did know Bush at Yale but was class of '67.) Bill Cagle was in the same class at Georgetown as Bill Clinton but only met him decades later. Peter Hawkes himself was in the same class at Fordham as Donald Trump, but didn't know him either. (Little known fact: Trump spent two years at Fordham before transferring to Wharton.) I added a third level of coincidence by telling Peter that fellow trainee Bob Marshall (Harvard) and I not only knew George Bush well as classmates at Andover, but that Bob, George and I were in the same rock and roll band, the Torqués. I played lead guitar, Bob was a singer and George was a screamer. (This was in 1964 during the Beatles invasion, with all the girls screaming their heads off. Our band added classmates who would scream during our performances while rushing the stage, to imply that we were better than we actually were.) Of note, all three of these presidents were born in 1946, the most presidents born in the same year in U.S. history.

Clearly, the Vietnam War was a major factor for many of us being there. One unpleasant surprise—no women trainees. I'd been in all-male schools since 4th grade and was hoping this would finally be my day. (I call it the curse of the "P's": Princeton Country Day, Phillips Academy, Princeton, and now Peace Corps.) The Peace Corps decided to train the women—18 who were single and 43 who were there with their husbands/fiancés—in a separate location from the men, deep down in Bisbee, Arizona, on the Mexican border, 900 miles away! (The Peace Corps decided to isolate the male trainees to help them appreciate that they were unlikely to have much contact with the opposite sex in Libya. Thanks a lot!)

In Clearfield, we descended upon what we understood had been an abandoned naval base. The terrain was scrubland punctuated by scattered trees, sagebrush and weeds. Via trial and error, we figured out we belonged in a large, white, two-story, 150-foot-long, cinderblock barracks. (On the site were a few other large burned-out and gutted buildings.) The walls were a dull green. As no one had provided us any direction, I meandered to the second floor and plunked my bags down on a random bed to stake out my territory. Rather than the usual military long rows of aligned beds, they were arranged in groups of four. Each array had a mix of double-bunk beds and non-bunk beds with neatly tucked-in sheets and gray blankets. We each had a seven-foot-high olive-green locker and a small wooden vanity for toiletries. In effect, each group of four was a set of roommates.

As I wandered around introducing myself, I was pleased to bump into two fellow Princetonians. One was Cameron Hume, from my class of 1968, who had brought a clarinet, the other was Jack Seifert, class of 1967, the largest player on the football team, weighing in at 235 pounds. He was a roommate of a dear friend from our rock band, The Nightwatch. (In fact, Jack had named the band.) He had studied some Arabic at Princeton. I met Stoney Bird who had studied classical Arabic at Yale, then modern literary Arabic at the Institute of Foreign Studies in Monterey, California. That gave them both a leg up on language learning. Affable Yalie Jim Luikart declared on the spot that he would become secretary of state. And I met Tom Furth, a wise-cracking, mischievous New Yorker and Hunter College graduate whose spark and irreverence would make him popular with us all. Born in New York of Jewish refugees from Germany, he spoke primarily German for the first four years of his life and was still fluent.

We were hardly a model of diversity, although to be fair, this was 1968. 105 of us were white, two were Jewish and one, Bob Suzuki, (University of Illinois) was Japanese-American. Nary an African-American amongst us. (In Bisbee the same profile, all Christian white men and women, with just one Jewish couple. Of all the three Libya contingents, there was only one African-American, Peter Mayberry in Libya I. In the 1960s the Peace Corps was overwhelmingly white—African-Americans averaged 3% vs. 13% in the general population.) None of us had chosen to go to Libya. We were assigned to a place we had barely heard of.

Randolph W. Hobler

34

**The 74 bright-eyed male Peace Corps trainees
in Clearfield, Utah who went to Libya**

We joked among ourselves at the absurdity of a naval base 760 miles from the nearest ocean. Subsequently, I learned that it was actually called the Clearfield Naval Supply Depot, a transship facility established in 1943 to stock and forward weaponry, naval parts, and ordnance to the Pacific theater in World War II at a safe remove from any Japanese air attack. And I learned the facility had been vast: 48 warehouses totaling 5.6 million square feet, plus a Marine barracks.

Massive Clearfield Naval Supply Depot—1943

By the time we arrived, the handful of buildings remaining were owned by the Thiokol Chemical Company's Job Corps site. (Another co-incidence: in 1942, my father once dated Peggy Longstreth, the daughter of the President of Thiokol). Many years later scandal enveloped Thiokol when it was found responsible for the failure of their O-ring joints that caused the explosion of the Space Shuttle Challenger in January of 1986. The Job Corps was sponsored by the U.S. Department of Labor to train young men, most of them African-American, for various occupations. They housed 1,300 trainees there.

Clearfield, Utah Naval Supply Depot—1968

Gary van Graafeiland (Union College) wandered into one abandoned building and noticed an enormous floor-to-ceiling spiderweb, occupied in the center by a black widow spider. Needless to say, he beat a hasty retreat. Arriving at the cafeteria, I was stunned to spot Bob Marshall (as was he to see me) after our coincidental run-in just a year earlier in Nice. I knew him as an avid bird-watcher, a solid tennis and basketball player, an eloquent writer (sports editor at *The Harvard Crimson*), an adept punner, a mischievous player of mind games and, by-the-by, a fainter if he didn't lie down when he got a shot or vaccination.

Richard Massey (Stanford) described the offerings at the cafeteria: "The food here is terrible. The hall is stifling. We only get milk in the morning. I can't even get water. I have to drink Coke, Sprite or orange drink. I think all my teeth will fall out before I leave."

Another surprise was the 31 Libyan men joining us in the barracks. This was the first time the Peace Corps had ever included host country nationals with volunteers. Washington, D.C.-based Peace Corps Libya Desk staffer Dave Benson had hosted them on their way west. When he arranged a dinner for them, they complained, "There is no food!" What they meant was there was no food they liked. Then they declared, "There is no bread!" So

Dave ran out to a French bakery to take care of that. One Libyan came to Clearfield through New York City. A housemaid at his hotel found a gun under his mattress, which was promptly confiscated (the gun, not the mattress).

The notion was that Libyans would teach us Arabic and we would teach them English. An efficient idea in principle, but not in practice. The Libyans were rather deer-in-the-headlights, as they had never been outside of Libya—many of them never outside the Sahara. They had names like Abdelgader, Abdullah, Saleh, Hosein, Abubaker, Belgassim, Ali, Omar, Issa ("Jesus"), Farag, Tahir, Nuri, Joma and, of course, Mohammed. (Like the religious name "John" in 13th century England, the majority of Arab men are named Mohammed. In fact, Mohammed is the most common first name in the world. While there are variations of practice, the general rule is that the first name is your personal name, your middle name is name of your father, and your last name is the name of your grandfather. Years later, I opened a Riyadh, Saudi Arabia phone directory and found nine pages of people with the name Mohammed Mohammed Mohammed, each with a different phone number.) These Libyan guys were outgoing, friendly and fun. Dan Peters wrote, "Most of the nights the Libyans sing and dance. We join in with a lot of hand clapping." Despite being, on average, five years older than us (ranging in age from 19 to 38), the Libyans bonded quickly with us. Kevin Hunt (Sacred Heart University) was a bunkmate of a Libyan teacher whom he came to like a great deal.

The stimulation of this huge, meaningful step in my life, of meeting so many new people, of seeing three people I already knew, and the thrill of anticipating God-knows-what for summer training and beyond was captured in what I wrote for the only time in 31 years of writing my diary, "whatadaywhatadaywhataday!"

My first baby steps were to learn to count to seven in Arabic. I learned that one of the three "h" sounds in Arabic is the word for "one" (*wahd*). It's a sound we don't have in English but we can replicate: The sound of that quick puff of breath we exhale on our glasses to fog them up before wiping them clean. It was hard to get used to such sound carrying the status of a phoneme.

We went to bed that night with no idea of what we were supposed to do. No schedules. No agendas. No introduction to staff. No orientation. No nothing. An early hint of Clearfield Follies.

The next day, in an organic, spontaneous meeting we volunteers self-organized. This was second nature to us, having grown up with umpteen pickup games of baseball, basketball and football over the years. "Who's going to take care of the garbage?" Someone raised his hand, "I got it." "Who wants to organize the laundry?" Another hand up. "What about cleaning the floors?" Another hand. "There are no screens on these windows, who'll pick that up?" Done. "Who'll figure out how to handle sending and receiving mail?" Done. "Who's gonna move the lockers indoors?" Done. "Who'll figure out bus schedules?" I raised my hand and several days later found schedule information which I organized, typed up and mimeographed for all the bus schedules to/from Clearfield, Ogden and Salt Lake City and passed them out to everyone. In retrospect, all of this should have been taken care of by the administration.

We took a number of lengthy psychological tests on that second, oppressively hot day, including the over-500 question MMPI (Minnesota Multi-Phasic Personality Inventory). Here are some of the True-or-False questions, with their numbers:

2. I have a good appetite

6. I like to read newspaper articles on crime

10. There seems to be a lump in my throat most of the time

11. A person should try to understand his dreams and be guided by or take warning from them

14. I have diarrhea once a month or more

15. Once in a while I think of things too bad to talk about

16. I am sure I get raw deal from life

19. My sex life is satisfactory

The 31 Libyan teacher-instructors at Clearfield, Utah, 1968

21. At times I have fits of laughing and crying that I cannot control

22. I am troubled by attacks of nausea and vomiting

24. I would like to be a singer

26. Evil spirits possess me at times

28. I am bothered by acid stomach several times a week

30. I have nightmares every few nights

Strange questions and tricky to answer. Many constituted open invitations not to answer them truthfully. For example, even if one actually thought oneself possessed by evil spirits (Question 26) would one admit to it? Besides this psychological inventory, according to John Becker (San Luis Rey College) we had to compose short biographies of ourselves "to see if we were nuts or not." The staff was armed to the teeth with psychologists ("Field Assessment Officers"—doesn't that sound so much better?) One of these, Benne Williams, was the point man to coordinate with our draft boards. Becker had applied to be a conscientious objector and needed permission to leave the United States. Williams assured him that this would be no problem.

One output of the MMPI, as related by Neil McCabe (University of Scranton) was to place each of us on a 100-point Masculinity—Femininity Scale. In debriefing Neil, one of the psychologists told Neil he was a 50. Neil didn't know if that meant he was only half a man or totally average, so he just shut up. Ted Kelley (University of South Carolina) describes the psychologist who interviewed him as a "weird dude." Ted could tell he was really trying to piss him off. For example, "He insulted all the Libyans. He said me, 'You're not worth shit.'" Ted managed to stay calm and said, "At least one person I know thinks I'll make a great volunteer."

That evening they broke us up into discussion groups (D-Groups) of ten men each. Under observation from behind a one-way mirror and being videotaped, we were presented with hypothetical problems and incidents to resolve or comment on as a group. My first impression was this was fun.

The next day a more scheduled routine kicked in as we took TEFL and Arabic classes. The goal of the Arabic training was to get us to FSI (U.S. State Department's Foreign Service Institute) Level 2. It's a five-level scale, with 5 being "Native or Bilingual Proficiency" and 2 being "Ability to satisfy routine social demands." Unbeknownst to us at the time, the Libyans wanted to teach us fussy, ornamental classical Arabic. Luckily, they were over-ruled and told to teach us Libyan street Arabic, which every shop owner and villager would understand. Then, in the evening, more D-groups. The Peace Corps had us on a six-day Arab week, with Fridays, the Moslem sabbath, off. To acclimatize us to such chronological rhythms. I learned to write some Arabic letters. And I continued to acquaint myself with more of the guys, both American and Libyan.

In terms of travel experience, over half of us had traveled outside the United States, many to a dozen or more countries. Europe was a common destination, plus India, Japan, Russia, Ghana, the Middle East and even one guy to Libya itself. As for me, I'd been to 17 countries: Canada, Mexico, France, Iceland, Ireland, Italy, Belgium, Switzerland, Luxembourg, Germany, Monaco, The Netherlands, Austria, Liechtenstein, the UK, Granada and Venezuela. And others to more than that. This concentration of men enamored of foreign travel was no co-incidence, as that is one of the two main attractions of the Peace Corps. The other being that of service to others. While sitting around getting to know one another, Bob Marshall (who had traveled throughout Europe and spent a summer in Japan) asked Clarence Young, a North Carolinian with a thick drawl and a recent Mars Hill University grad, "Hey, are you from Brooklyn?" And he replied, "Whaay nobody ever asked me thaat before!"

I made friends with Martin Mueller (Brown), very bright and possessing a spontaneous sense of humor. 50 years later, another coincidence.

Martin Mueller and a stenciled camel caravan

Marty's father, Rudy, had been a Lieutenant Colonel in the U.S. Air Force. He flew P-38s in WWII. He flew B-52s during the Cuban Missile crisis. He would periodically get new assignments. When Marty got accepted into the Peace Corps, he excitedly called home, only to find out that his father had just been assigned to Wheelus Air Base in Libya. "You can imagine my shock," Marty recounts, "when I called my parents to tell them the news and they gasped that my dad had also just been assigned to the same country!"

In the Thiokol gym, sitting in bleachers, we had our first general meeting of staff and volunteers, led by the project director, Al Wight. A stubby, goateed man eerily reminiscent of a garden gnome, he sported a gold neck chain, elevator shoes and a bad toupée. He told us, "The intent of the program will be to conduct as much of the training as possible as a laboratory." This sounded half promising, half worrisome. Like laboratory rats? More encouragingly he added, "We expect you to work." He promised us that we would be speaking Arabic all of the time, not just in the classroom.

Peter Hawkes recalls one staffer at this meeting who inspired fear and dread when he warned that if you were driving around in the Fezzan and the car broke down, with no other cars nearby, you could easily die in the heat.

In-country Libya Director Bill Whitman, a slightly rotund, Harvard-educated RAF-trained former English professor, then spoke. He wore an African safari outfit—khaki jacket, shorts and lots of pockets. Among other things, he explained that for the first time in Peace Corps history, the host country would issue motorcycles to all of us—Italian dirt bikes called Moto Guzzis—so we could teach in two villages distant from one another each day. Thus, an important part of our training would be to learn how to ride a motorcycle. We had about 30 Suzuki motor bikes on site and when we could, we took turns trying them out. Since motorcycle repair shops were well-nigh non-existent in Libya, Whitman promised we would be taught to take apart and put back together a Moto Guzzi, lest we be left stranded in the desert.

Some 50 years later, I learned from Mark Lepori (Wheaton College) that he and some cohorts would periodically charge into one of the abandoned dusty, musty and fusty barracks buildings, set up ramps with boards and zoom around on their Suzukis in the dark, with only headlamps to guide the way. He remembers them gunning their engines, the noise, the dust, the smell of oil as they careened around inside their rickety race track. Like some kind of indoor Mad Max adventure.

For the Bisbee trainees, many new, challenging experiences lurked, not the least of which were the come-uppances the single females were to face.

Gulches and Gullies

The 112 Peace Corps trainees arriving in Bisbee on July 15, 1968 hailed from 23 states. In addition to the single women and married or engaged couples were six lucky single men training to be inspectors. Also converging on Bisbee were 27 male Libyan teachers and three Libyan female teachers. One of the Libyan women was Fatma Haadi El Turki Gusbi, wife of the Libyan Director of English Language Teaching, Mustafa Gusbi, who spent many weeks in Bisbee that summer. Robert Kohls, from the Westinghouse Corporation, was the project director. Many of the couples got married in the months before the Bisbee program began, because the program was only open to couples who were married, or had to be married before their flight to Libya. Harold and Mary Ellen McElhinny (Santa Clara University and UC Berkeley, respectively) were married a scant two weeks before training began.

Chuck and Jane Beach (Hamilton and Vassar) were inspired to join the Peace Corps for several reasons. These included helping others, learning a foreign language, living in a developing country, representing America and offsetting the "Ugly American" image of Americans overseas. (The enormously popular and influential 1958 book *The Ugly American*, by Eugene Burdick and William Lederer, went through 55 printings in just two years; Senator John F. Kennedy sent a copy to every U.S. senator in 1959.) Trudy Swartzentruber, who had graduated from Eastern Mennonite University, sought escape from her strict Amish/Mennonite background. Jeanne Maurey (Rollins College) was "searching for my freedom, my responsibility, my gift to humanity, understanding and friendship."

John Ziolkowski (Bowling Green State University) was enticed to join the Peace Corps by a brochure he received in the mail, entitled "The Peace

Corps Goes to Paradise" with pictures of white sandy Micronesian beaches and shimmering blue water. "Gee," he thought, "paradise would be fine."

Peace Corps bait-and-switch promotion from the 1960s

At Cathy Kaiser's graduation from the Foreign Service School at Georgetown in 1964, the guest speaker was the first Peace Corps director, President Kennedy's brother-in-law Sargent Shriver. However, just as he began to talk a heavy thunderstorm intervened and he had to beat a hasty retreat from the podium—a bit of historical foretaste for Cathy.

On the heels of teaching Libyan culture for Libya I, Libyan Dr. Othman Shemisa was recruited for the same in Bisbee. His experience flying to Bisbee from Tucson on Apache Airlines was a strange reversal of the smug condescension some Americans exhibit when traveling in third-world countries. Instead of a standard counter at the Tucson airport, Apache Airlines had set up a rickety wooden table. Atop the table was a cardboard box with "Apache Airlines" written in magic marker. He checked his bags and boarded the plane. Coming in for a landing at Bisbee, the pilot reported that the runway lights were not working. And the radio wasn't working. When Shemisa went to claim his suitcase, he was told, "Oh, we don't take suitcases on the plane." He asked, "Then where's my suitcase?" Reply? "We send the baggage by bus. You can come back here tomorrow to pick up your suitcase."

Like Clearfield, Bisbee, only seven miles north of the Mexican border in Cochise County, in the rugged Mule Mountains, has a semi-arid, semi-desert climate. Bisbee volunteers recall that the landscape was very much Libyan. The trainees were greeted with a toasty temperature of 95°. Cicadas filled the local poplar trees and buzzed their evening melodies.

Bisbee was named, for those intensely interested in the origins of things, for 1880s-era Judge DeWitt Bisbee, a financial backer of Phelps Dodge's Copper Queen Mine. (Before being dubbed "Bisbee" it was known as "Mule Gulch." Other gulches included Hendricks' Gulch, Uncle Sam Gulch and Silver Bear Gulch.) By the time the mine closed in 1985, it had yielded four billion tons of copper, 152,000 tons of lead, 186,000 tons of zinc, five million pounds of silver and 180,000 pounds of gold. Back in the day, Bisbee had been the wealthiest city between New Orleans and San Francisco, even boasting its own stock market.

Historically at its peak its red-light district in 1908 boasted 35 brothels, 50 saloons and gambling halls. The ladies of the night had been quaintly referred to as "shady ladies," "hurdy gurdy girls" and "soiled doves." Their colorful names included Trixy Fawcell, Sibyl LaVerne and Crazy Horse Lil.

The Bisbee Red Light District, circa 1906, featuring a "soiled dove."

Courtesy of the Bisbee Mining and Historical Museum, Art Kent Collection

Some married couples lodged in Brewery Gulch, where thunderstorms swamped the streets just about every afternoon, causing a surge of over two feet of water down the street and carving out gullies in its wake. Other married trainees were boarded in the Philadelphia Hotel and the Silver King Hotel. None of these hotels were air-conditioned.

Lorraine Slawiak (Erie County Technical Institute) recalls that all 17 single women were assigned to a dorm-style layout in Miner's Hotel, in Brewery Gulch, characterized by Andrea Murphy (Boston College) as "a real dive." No longer a boom town, no doubt one attraction for Peace Corps management was that in Bisbee, hotels were cheap. Maggie Brossoit (St. Cloud College) remembers Bisbee as being in decline, "down and out" with many abandoned buildings.

The Miner's Hotel: opulent quarters for the single women trainees

To maintain privacy, the single women improvised by hanging sheets between their beds. Jeanne Maurey recalls they were living out of suitcases, as there were no closets. And there were only three johns. "This place is like a boot camp with everyone trying to get into the bathroom at 6:30 in the morning to be in class by 8:00."

One female volunteer recalls that across the street from the Miner's Hotel was a tall pole with a red light on it. This was turned on every night because it was a brothel and much frequented by the Libyan teachers.

The five single male inspectors (Tom Weinz, Jay Shetterly, Jerry Priori, Larry Maguire and Ed O'Shea) and the engaged single males were housed in the attic of the local YWCA. The inspectors' jobs in Libya were to observe and evaluate the Libyans teaching English. The inspectors-to-be generally had more experience or greater qualifications than the other volunteers. For example, Jay Shetterly (Harvard plus one year of Harvard Law) had previously taught in India on a Fulbright (learning Hindi along the way).

Initially the Bisbee volunteers ate their meals at the Copper Queen Hotel dining hall. The Americans and the Libyans hated the food. For the Libyans, it was bland-cafeteria-style fare. They were used to hot spices. Their favorite meat was lamb and they complained there was none of it. The hotel head cook got really angry at them. "How dare these Libyans tell me how to cook!" Some Libyans just went and cooked their own food. Ibrahim Bakush, who was a favorite among the Americans and a bit of a clown, was so fed up (so to speak) he survived on a diet consisting solely of hard-boiled eggs for the rest of the summer. The final straw for the Americans was when cockroaches showed up in their soup. A mass revolt ensued. The trainees were immediately given meal tickets to eat at local Bisbee restaurants.

The Copper Queen Hotel: lodging for married Bisbee trainees

Speaking of insects, Jeanne Maurey wrote to her parents in July that "the girls around me are running around in hysterics because we just killed a scorpion that came sneaking out from someone's bed." She also reported a smattering of centipedes and rattlesnakes in Bisbee. Inspectors Tom Weinz (Concordia Teachers College in Nebraska) and Larry Maguire, who were supposed to be a tad more mature than the other trainees, liked to go out and catch tarantulas. They would put a tarantula inside a jar made of smoky glass so one couldn't see inside. They enjoyed approaching female volunteers, extending the jar and saying, "Have you seen this?" and as they opened the jar, enjoying the females' shock and surprise. Inspector Jay Shetterly loved collecting insects as a kid. He would venture into the desert outside Bisbee and collect tarantulas as well.

The Bisbee contingent also had strong relationships with their Libyan teachers despite the fact that only four of them spoke English. They noted that each Libyan had a different temperament. Some were open, some were moody. Younis Mughrabi was a poet. The head Libyan, Mohamed

Mahjoub, always wore dark glasses. (No doubt he fancied himself the Roy Orbison of Libya.)

The women had to pay especial attention to Libyan culture. Jeanne Maurey wrote,

> The PCVs from Libya I have painted a pretty harrowing picture for the single girls. Dresses will be long, women will not be allowed to go outside unescorted, men will always be approaching us and goosing us, we must wear scarves (especially blondes) at all times. We cannot drink, smoke or eat in public Libyan restaurants, we cannot date military men, we cannot go to the market alone, we cannot acknowledge any man on the street, even if he is a teacher in our school. When walking down the street, you must look straight ahead or at the ground and when a man comes toward you, you must quickly move aside just before he passes or else you will be pinched, jostled or grabbed. Pleasant, isn't it? The Peace Corps doctor recommended that all the single women take free birth control pills issued by the Peace Corps because that will protect them from pregnancy in the case of rape.

Maggie Brossoit remembers being told that the women PCVs would gain weight in Libya due to the constraints of not being able to go on runs, not walk to the market, not walk much in public.

Initially, Bisbee trainees endured seven hours of intensive Arabic training per day. Later this was reduced to four hours a day, to free up time for TEFL and cross-cultural training.

After only two days of orientation and almost no TEFL training, the Bisbee trainees were sent across the border on a bus daily to nearby Naco, Mexico to practice teach for four hours at a time. Way premature! The town was decrepit. The roads were dirt. The rooms had no windows. Bats inhabited the bathrooms. John and Andrea Murphy were shocked at the poverty. But they remember smiling kids and friendly teachers.

Naco, Mexican boy students

Naco, Mexico girl students with their certificates

Bob Conway (Williams College) found the program in Naco to be a "disaster." The classes had an unwieldy 30—40 students. And the charismatic style of teaching he learned in TEFL training not only didn't work, it caused chaos in the classroom. Don and Lani Leydig (both from Stanford) found the kids to be "not interested." In fact, it went beyond "not interested." Don found them to be the most unruly class he had ever seen. The kids jumped out of the windows and ran away.

In Cathy Kaiser's schoolroom most of the window panes were missing. There were swallows' nests in each corner of the room, inhabited by "little bitty baby birds." Various floorboards were missing, making it difficult to keep eye contact with students while moving about in such a way as not to break an ankle.

At the end of their sessions, on September 16th (Mexican Independence Day) the Mexicans hosted a parade and a feast for the volunteers to thank them for their help. A mariachi band was in the parade. The Bisbee trainees marched in the parade. There were fireworks, including bamboo wind fans that spun off high into the air. There were horses. There were greased pigs. The Libyans joined in, galloping up and down the street on the horses.

Mohamed Mahjoub: Mexican Independence Day, Naco, Mexico

Along the way, Bob Glover (Ohio State University) cajoled non-drinker John Peterson (Nyack College) to do tequila shots with lime chasers. Having no idea about how many were appropriate, John downed 13.

Later, he went back to the room where his wife Rebecca (also from Nyack College) was crocheting an Afghan blanket for her mother. He promptly threw up all over it. After the Naco feast almost every American got quite sick—Montezuma's revenge in Montezuma's backyard. Back at the hotel Pepto Bismol was liberally passed around. The lines at the bathroom were long. "The walls of our hotel were so thin," recalls Nanette Holben, "that you could hear the moaning, groaning and flushing all night long."

Back in Clearfield, due to locker room nudity, the Libyans shot a cultural shot across the bow.

TEFL, Toilets and Towels

In Clearfield, we settled into a daily routine of Arabic classes, TEFL classes and D-groups. On the heels of our initial MMPI tests, we were each interviewed by one of the Field Assessment Officers.

Free time was filled with bumper pool, bull sessions, tennis, basketball, touch football, swimming at the Job Corps pool, ping pong, naps, singing songs, hanging around listening to the radio, reading, playing penny-ante poker, introducing ourselves around, trips to the General Store, forays into Clearfield proper—some three miles away—to toss back a beer or two at a bar and singing (with me on guitar). I particularly remember harmonizing with Bob Marshall on a #2 Billboard hit by The Cyrkle, "Red Rubber Ball," a highly infectious, upbeat song that holds up wonderfully to this day. (I'd heard them live in Shea Stadium in 1966, the warm-up act for the Beatles.) One day, ear to the radio, Bob perked up and declared, "This is my favorite song!" Everyone thought this rather lucky for Bob, what a nice moment for him. A few days later, hearing another song, he redeclared, "This is my favorite song!" This became a running joke, as, by the end of training, Bob had declared some 47 songs to be his favorite.

We also found time for creative decoration of our premises. When we learned that the most remote and isolated town in Libya was Ghat, on the border of Algeria some 800 miles from Tripoli, one geographically-intensive trainee created a sign: "Ghat Yacht Club, 5 km."

Ubiquitous camp followers

One thing that did impress us in Clearfield was the TEFL methodology (which the Peace Corps did not develop, but did teach). English teaching theorists figured out that all children, in all countries, learn the structures of language identically. The first insight was the order of learning. The first thing children learn? Nouns. Parents will point to something and say, "Hand!" At some point the child will pick that up and repeat it. They then move to prepositions, so "The hand is on the table." "The spoon is in the hand." The classroom process moves on to add in other verbs, adjectives, etc. Once you have equipped students with the above sentences, you introduce a new noun, like "plate." Then you put a plate on the table and you say "Where is the plate?" They magically utter an English sentence they have never uttered before, "The plate is on the table." (This same methodology can be used to teach any new language. I did precisely that later in teaching French in the Teacher Corps.)

The second insight was to make sure that children only hear the words in the language being taught. So, in TEFL, you purposely do not say to a Libyan child in Arabic "This is a hand (*yed*). The way we say 'hand' (*yed*) in English is 'hand.' " It takes extra, cumbersome, unnecessary effort to think of what a word is in your language and then convert it to English. So you drill their brains directly with English.

The third insight was that instead of the teacher talking 80% of the time, the TEFL teacher only speaks 50% of the time. It's constant, rapid, call-response as the teacher points to objects:

Teacher: "Hand!"
Students: "Hand!"
Teacher: "Book!"
Students: "Book!"
Teacher: "Pencil!"
Students: "Pencil!"

Along the way, the Libyans had a bone to pick about our western behavior. The barracks had group showers. In his diary, Richard Massey wrote, "The Libyans wear pajamas to the showers, only taking them off when behind the curtain—strange!" Having had at least 10 years of experience with locker rooms, we Americans would nonchalantly walk naked around showers with towels draped over our shoulders. The staff, to their discredit, did not know that for Arabs nudity is tabooed from infancy. (Don't ask me how the Moroccan track and field teams handle showers.) The Libyans marched into director Wight's office en masse to complain. The net result was that partitions were erected in the showers; we volunteers were instructed to wrap towels around us as we moved to/from the showers; and sheets were draped around the Libyans' beds so no one could see them unclothed.

Another sign of staff cluelessness came to the fore quite early when the Libyans complained about the toilets. With the exception of hotels and private Western homes, the rule of the day in Libya was Turkish toilets, i.e., a hole in the floor with two foot spaces astride the hole. This involved squatting, not sitting on an elevated throne. (Snarky American travelers refer to them as "squat-o-matics.") This had been the Libyans' practice all their lives and they weren't about to stop now. The project staff were caught unawares. They were not about to rip up floors and re-engineer all the plumbing in the barracks. They finally came up with another jerry-rigged solution that satisfied the Libyans. They built a plywood platform around a few of the toilets up to the level of the seat. The Libyans could then clamber up and place their feet on the plywood, squat with the seat level of the toilet serving as the hole. We also had to supply them with a can of water as they used their left hand and water instead of toilet paper to "tidy up". This is source of the left-hand taboo in Arab countries.

In addition, no one on staff told us that it was an insult to Arabs to expose the sole of one's foot to them. Some of the trainees in Arabic class would absently put their feet up in class. We learned the hard way that the Libyans were quite upset about this cultural faux-pas.

I churned out a regular stream of letters ("snail mail" for the Millennials amongst you). I had brought along my manual Smith-Corona typewriter. Having learned to touch-type, I could type at 80 words-per-minute. During the summer I sent 30 letters (one every two-three days) and received 44, from 13 different people.

A curious side story: we had camp followers. A bevy of 12-year-old African-American kids hung out with us—in the barracks, outside, preening on motorcycles. To this day I have no inkling where they were from.

Enthusiastic camp followers

A pattern, or rather a lack of pattern, with respect to our Arabic classes soon kicked in. Some days we'd have five Arabic classes. Some days four, some days three. Then the administration abruptly changed up the schedule. After that, one day we had six hours of Arabic. Then one day none of the Libyan Arabic instructors showed up at all, so zero hours of Arabic. This did not go unnoticed. As young, idealistic, energetic volunteers we had expected a rigorous, consistent, professional routine that would challenge us and optimize our Arabic fluency in the short time we had. Most of us had learned a foreign language in school before Clearfield and were accustomed to a systematic, demanding approach to the pedagogy. One trainee described the Libyans as school teachers straight out of the desert and maddeningly incompetent.

The street-Arabic training was not from any textbooks. It was generated on-the-fly, haphazardly, with random dialogue hastily written on mimeographed sheets with no notion of building vocabulary in any systematic way.

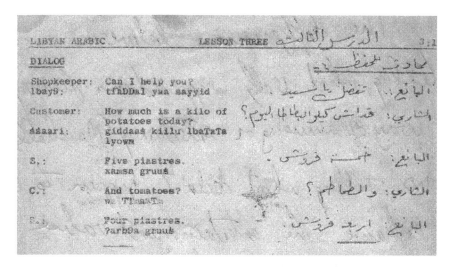

Mimeographed Libyan Arabic lessons

In Clearfield, we soon found ourselves enmeshed in "bitch meetings."

Despicable Deselections

So, we Clearfielders reached the end of July, just two weeks into the program, when 12 trainees, including Chuck Bonamer and Rich Stephens, were "deselected." Roused abruptly early in the morning they were secreted away by van to the airport. No chance to say goodbye to anyone. (In Alan Weiss's book about Peace Corps Nigeria, *High Risk/High Gain,* he writes, "The Peace Corps…did their best to whisk these undesirables off the premises immediately, before they could poison the minds of the other trainees with their experiences.") For years we assumed that they had been deselected because of evaluations in their D-Groups.

We had assumed the Peace Corps' thorough vetting of applicants had definitively established our qualifications to be volunteers in a foreign country, and that the training was simply one stage on the way to our in-country assignments. We'd filled in applications with detailed questionnaires and six personal references. We'd taken a six-hour exam, including sections on biology, ecology and parasitology. And unbeknownst to us at the time, we were checked out by the FBI. Which, at the time was headed by the notorious J. Edgar Hoover. I only learned about this in 2017 from RPCV Tom Furth. For years, the Furth family had rented a cottage in the summer in Hunter, New York from a Mrs. Mudge, whom Tom had given as a reference. By sheer coincidence, the Furths were in the cottage the summer of 1968 when an official-looking man in a dark suit knocked on the door and asked if this were Mrs. Mudge's cottage. Tom's father said, "No, she's in that cottage over there." Afterwards, Mrs. Mudge told Tom this was an FBI agent checking out his reference. I also learned that, if you were gay, you would be deselected. Who our gay colleagues were was not evident to me until 50 years later.

In the D-groups we had to periodically evaluate one another with total frankness on a one-to-ten scale. Richard Massey observed, "Most people were upset to have to do this since no one wants to put someone else as a 10." Factors to rate people on included "talkativeness, influence, listening, understanding and warmth." On August 19, Dan Peters wrote, "Tonight there was a big chaotic discussion about this. Most of the people were trying to out the Peace Corps Director on the spot, arguing about the purpose and value of rating." Charlie Cross (Duke) recalls, "We didn't want to rate everyone. We were told this was for our own good. Wight promised that the ratings would be kept within the groups. But then they publicly posted how everyone was rated." The results, based on subjective, superficial evaluations by peers (not professional psychologists), were factored into deciding if someone should be deselected. Bob Marshall saved one wrap-up of evaluations and noted that many were based on subjective emotions like jealousy and personal chemistry.

Jack Seifert's feelings were hurt when he got a note from a participant criticizing him for being a "suck-up to the staff." Even if this were true (which it wasn't) what relevance did this have to do with coping with life in Libya? At this point, only two weeks into training, we felt an ever-present level of tension to the Sword of Damocles hanging over our heads, so we gamed the system by not ratting on one another. We all felt our time could have been much better spent on Arabic, TEFL, Libyan culture and motorcycle training.

This growing dissatisfaction with Al Wight came to the fore at one of what initially were called general meetings led by Al Wight, but which we now termed "bitch meetings." We knew from his directory bio that he was working on his Ph.D. in psychology at the University of Utah. We knew we were being observed in the D-groups. Jeff Taylor, an outspoken Brown grad from Illinois, connected the dots and spoke up, accusing Wight of using us as material for his Ph.D. dissertation rather than focusing on our Libya training needs. In preparation for this book I obtained, via the Internet, a copy of Wight's Ph.D. dissertation in order to see how exactly he was evaluating us. It was entitled "A Study of Rater and Ratee Characteristics." However, it wasn't us he was studying. The guinea pigs were the largely 142 African-American Job Corps trainees next door to us on the Thiokol site. Among many other activities, they had to fill in a

185-question survey, (which smacks of the unethical practice known as "research by the pound"). From this Wight dumped endless charts and gobs of gobbledygook. The very last question illustrates the weirdness:

185. In filling out this questionnaire, I have:

A. Been very careless. I am not at all sure my answers

are correct.

B. Been somewhat careless. Some of my answers may

not be entirely correct.

C. Neither been careless, not very careful, but I am not

sure all of my answers are correct.

D. Been quite careful, but I am not sure all of my answers are correct.

E. Been as careful as I could. To the best of my knowledge,

all answers are correct.

I have now realized I'd stumbled upon the truth. Something that clearly explained why Wight had dropped so many administrative balls. Wight had been burning candles at both ends. When he was supposed to be devoting 100% of his time in Clearfield to the Libya Project Directorship, he was moonlighting as he researched and wrote his Ph.D. dissertation.

For Royse Crall in Bisbee, a controversial overnight exercise in self-examination resulted in a stink.

Bisbee Bumblings, Escapades

It was in 1968 that D-groups, or sensitivity training, suddenly came into vogue. But the Bisbee and Clearfield programs misused them as deselection tools. Bisbeean Malcolm Travelstead (Duke University) described D-groups as "dreaded," "...where we all were supposed to 'be open and honest' about our feelings." They were the subject of jokes. One spunky female volunteer refused to attend after the first session, declaring the staff was not competent to conduct them. "They tried to deselect me later and I said, 'Go ahead. You'll be deselecting your best female volunteer.' "

Don and Lani Leydig remember their D-group facilitator, a psychologist named Bob Newsome. He was on the warpath to find people to deselect. Turns out he had a degree from Culver Stockton College in psychology and *zoology*. (Can we say "culling the herd?") The Leydigs found the forced heart-to-heart dialogue cringingly uncomfortable.

Dysfunctionally, the D-groups turned into a hotbed of competition between couples. Because they were used as a deselection tool, as Bob Conway describes it, each couple thought, "We have to show we're better than other couples so we don't get deselected."

In Bisbee, unlike in Clearfield, they conducted '60s fad-like est (Erhard Seminars Training) sessions. People would sit on the floor in dimly lit rooms and be instructed to "imagine you are a tree." Cathy Della Penta (Harpur College) could not understand how on earth imagining oneself as a tree would help her in Libya. A number of Bisbeeans boycotted these est sessions. Kohls & Company had not anticipated the number of free-thinking, cynical trainees they'd be dealing with.

In yet another exercise in Bisbee at culling, trainees were dropped off at isolated spots in the desert, provided a pup tent and the barest of essentials to "survive" for 24 hours alone. They were exhorted to "think about whether you *really* want to go to Libya." John Murphy (Harvard) felt the exercise was a "silly waste of time." A number of Bisbeeans refused to participate at all. Rebecca Peterson found the experience bizarre. Cathy Kaiser remembers being given a bag with some food and three matches. She had to scrounge to find kindling. She then relaxed and gazed up at the stars while she played on a recorder. But in the middle of the night her tent blew over on top of her. A skunk ambled into Royse Crall's tent and sat on her chest.

A further condemnation of D-groups and the psychological testing derives from the earliest history of the Peace Corps. The very first Peace Corps contingent ever, to be posted to Ghana in 1961, trained in Berkeley, California. In an assessment after the training, Peace Corps HQ inspectors reported "...peer group ratings were definitely inadvisable." Can we say "lack of institutional memory?" In the end, Joseph Blatchford, the Peace Corps Director who came on board during our tenure, eliminated psychological evaluation during training for all Peace Corps programs.

After a time on this former naval base, cabin fever set in at Clearfield, triggering a series of escapes.

One Saturday in July, a bunch of us bused down to the Lagoon Amusement Park in Farmington, Utah, 16 miles south of Clearfield. Rather than Bob Hope entertaining the troops, we had to settle for the rock group Big Brother and the Holding Company performing, featuring Janis Joplin. Ted Kelley vividly remembers the group sported the biggest amps he had ever seen. Standing near the stage, he could feel the metal in his teeth vibrate.

Janis Joplin at the Lagoon, July 20, 1968

Jack Seifert has fond memories of hearing Blind Faith and Jimi Hendrix at the Lagoon. Craig Owens (Wichita State University) whose lifelong passion was guitar, heard Jefferson Airplane. John Maclean once escaped to Salt Lake City and caught a Donovan concert.

One form of escape for an outgoing blond guy from Alabama, Bill Cagle, and few of his trainee friends was smoking weed in the bushes at the base of the barracks. Once on a stayover at a Salt Lake City hotel, Tom Furth and two other trainees smoked some weed, stuffing towels at the bottom of the door to prevent the odors from escaping into the hallway.

Bob Marshall and I visited a college friend of my father's, Roswell Miller and his Auntie Mame-like wife Bunny. His major claim to fame was being a grandson of Andrew Carnegie. However, the only philanthropic largesse we received was a few drinks and being introduced to two young lovelies, Kiffy Brown (a UUU—University of Utah Undergrad) and Jane Harrison (an SUU—Stanford University Undergrad). We escorted them to the Lagoon where we saw Paul Revere and the Raiders.

Frank Nicosia, a Penn State grad with a masters in history from Georgetown, needed to get away, so on a Tuesday (Tuesday!) he rented a truck and drove Craig Owens, Dan Peters, John Maclean, Bob O'Keefe and a Libyan to Jackson Hole, Wyoming—250 miles away. In the beautiful Grand Teton Mountains they came upon a dozen attractive waitresses sitting around a campfire and fraternized the night away.

Tom Furth, Jack Seifert, Rufus Cadigan, Victor Gramigna (University of Scranton) and Mark Lepori rented a car and drove 293 miles to Yellowstone Park. Tom had worked at a car dealership and knew how to disconnect the odometer so as to minimize their rental charge.

One afternoon, one of the guys said, "Hey, wouldn't it be nice to go to the movies in Salt Lake City?" Tom Furth piped up, "Well, I know just the way to do that." Risking deselection, he stole the keys to one of the program's buses. He loaded ten volunteers and two Libyans on board, and without a bus license, and having never driven a bus before, drove the 30 miles to Salt Lake City where they caught the movie sensation of the summer, *2001: A Space Odyssey.* Upon their return that evening, he stealthily replaced the keys. Never got caught.

Dennis Carlson, Peter Hawkes, Bill Cagle, Greg Strick (Notre Dame) and others would periodically drive Suzukis out to the nearby salt flats, zooming along at full speed.

Bill Cagle and fellow trainee out on the Salt Flats. Note: no helmets.

Randy Melquist, a friendly University of Puget Sound grad, met a red-haired nurse in Salt Lake City and started seeing her. She was a single mom separated from her husband, but didn't want the kids to see Randy, so when they were around, she regularly hid him in the laundry room.

One weekend Stoney Bird flew to San Francisco for a weekend to be with Julie Dunn, who later became his first wife.

One Friday, Randy Melquist, Rich DiGeorgio (Holy Cross) an engaging, outgoing guy whom everyone took a liking to, and I took a bus to Salt Lake City then took a room at the Hotel Utah. After dinner, we gravitated to the Crow's Nest bar. I met a pert, charming brunette named Nancy Waddoups. I danced with Nancy all night, getting to bed at 3 AM. We ended up dating when we could, till the end of training.

John Farranto grabbed a room at a low-end motel, and while basking in the sun by the pool, caught way too many rays, turning purple and suffered severe burns. He was rushed off to the local medical center.

Rufus Cadigan and another trainee bused into Salt Lake City one night and accidentally attended a drag show.

Hitch-hiking back from an appointment with an optometrist in nearby Ogden, Utah, Peter Hawkes was picked up by a shapely, beautiful blonde, who, like Nancy, had a red convertible. She told Peter she was a student of religions—Buddhism, Islam, Taoism, etc. But she added that one religion was superior to them all.

"Which one is that?" Peter asked.

"Mormonism."

The rest of the ride back to Clearfield, she tried to convert Peter. Peter was much more interested in having her drop him off at the dining building, where all the guys could take in the eye candy. However, no one was there. Peter was at pains to get the woman's phone number and invited her to the Janis Joplin concert that night. Later, other volunteers encouraged Peter to join them on the Clearfield program bus headed for Salt Lake City.

"Oh, no you guys go ahead, I've got a date coming back to pick me up."

After several hours of anxious waiting, the blonde was a no show. Peter called her phone number. Her mother answered the phone.

"Who are you? What do you want? Are you a Mormon?"

"Can I speak to her?"

"No." She hung up. And Peter was hung up alone in the barracks that night.

Then there was my mini-escape to Sandusky, Ohio. Dear friend and keyboardist from The Nightwatch, Kit Hinsley was getting hitched and wanted me to usher. I got permission to fly the coop for the weekend to Sandusky, Ohio and back

On September 30, Dave Munro, a clean-cut Yalie sporting Harry Potter glasses, Tom Furth and Ted Kelley trooped down to Salt Lake City Airport to protest against arriving vice president Hubert Humphrey before his speech. Hubert Horatio Humphrey had been harried, harassed and hassled on the campaign trail due to his support of the Vietnam War. On the way in, Humphrey came up to the fence where Tom shouted out, "Stop the bombing!" Humphrey replied, "Just listen to what I'm going to say tonight."

George Carter (Colorado State) made fast friends with David Kermani, an Iranian-American of means who was into Persian carpets. They escaped one weekend to Salt Lake City and were able to stay in a fancy suite because David picked up the tab. David later decided to quit Clearfield training because Libya had no opera house.

And while this next example wasn't a physical escape, it was certainly an emotional one. Peter Hawkes saw a trainee throw a rock through one of the windows of an abandoned barracks building, making a satisfying crash of glass. Peter and others then periodically followed suit, finding that smashing windows helped relieve the stress from the D-groups and learning a difficult foreign language.

At the end of July, many trainees enjoyed a more official letting off of steam at an afternoon picnic, care of the program team at Clearfield.

**Dan Peters, David Klein, Jack Hoffman, Ritchey
Newton, James Lawler, unidentified**

No doubt thanks to the salubrious effect of the many wives in Bisbee, Bisbeeans' escapes were tamer than Clearfielders'. They visited Fort Huachuca (a U.S. Army base), the Sonora Desert Museum, Old Tucson (including re-enactments of robberies, stage-coach driving) and Nogales, Mexico where they witnessed a bullfight, visited a tortilla factory. Dianne Goode and other female trainees hitchhiked to Tucson to take in a rock concert. Kohls was horrified and said what they did was "very dangerous." Almost daily, John Peterson and Bob Glover and some Libyans went spelunking in Bisbee's abandoned underground copper mines. There were two thousand miles of old mining tunnels beneath the town. Some of the shafts go down 1,500 feet. The mines featured picturesque names like "The Cochise Pit," "Juniper Flats Mine" and "Whitetail Deer Shaft."

■

Life is, of course, full of sometimes remarkable surprises, and I was soon in for one come August.

The Guns of August

August 1 was an instance where hard criticism flipped to a back-handed compliment. Language Director Donna Carr summoned me to her office. She told me I had scored #1 on the first Arabic language test we had just taken. Before I had a chance to puff my chest up with pride, she asked, "Have you studied Arabic before?"

I said, "No."

"Then how can you have scored so well on this test? This is hard to believe."

"Well, I've never studied Arabic."

"Did you cheat?"

"No, of course not."

She furrowed her brow. "Are you certain you did not cheat?"

Almost speechless, my mind was scrambling to defend myself. After all, she was a Ph.D. and I a mere B.A.

"Well, in grade school I learned Latin and French. I continued with French through high school. I majored in French in college and minored in Spanish, so I already know three languages."

"So?"

Jeesh, that wasn't good enough? OK, she wants more.

"So, once you've known one language, you know the drill. Figure out the grammar. Learn the parts of speech. Memorize the pronouns. Memorize vocab. Identify new phonemes and master them. To optimize time, when you're out for a walk, practice counting. In the shower, rehearse the alphabet."

That grudgingly satisfied her.

Speaking of phonemes, Arabic includes nine sounds not in English, that makes it one of the more challenging languages. There's a heavy "t." A heavy "d." A heavy "th." A heavy "s." The aspirated "h" I mentioned before. A trilled "r" like in Spanish. But also a French "r." The harsh clearing-of-throat as in "ach" in German. There's the glottal stop, which is a phoneme (the sound Americans make for the two t's in "Manhattan." Or, if you will, how the Scottish pronounce the double-t in "bottle," or the word "Scottish" for that matter.) The glottal stop is doubly tricky, because it sometimes lands at the end of a word. And finally, there's the "ayn," a highly unusual sound in Arabic and some related languages which is an unvoiced constriction of the throat that is extremely hard for native English speakers to hear, much less pronounce.

Another difficulty factor with Arabic is the lack of related words (cognates) in English or Romance languages. We only have a handful of Arabic words in English, including algebra, algorithm, sugar and admiral (from *amir el bahr*—"prince of the sea"). With many other languages, you can often guess a word is similar to English. For example, the English "problem" is "problème" in French; "problema" in Italian, Spanish and Portuguese; "problem" in German, Polish and Russian. However, in Arabic, it's "mushkila." Thus, in Arabic there's an enormous burden of brute vocab memorization. Ironically, the part of Arabic that looks the most strange and difficult—its script—is the easiest. There are only 29 letters in the alphabet, each corresponding to a specific sound. (In English, we have 26 letters and 46 sounds.) Learning 29 things is a walk in the park compared to thousands of words of vocabulary.

On August 5, on a TV in the cafeteria, we started watching the Republican National Convention in Miami, Florida. By the 8th, Richard Nixon was their presidential candidate with Spiro Agnew as his vice-presidential candidate.

On August 9, we learned we would be practice teaching English for a number of weeks at Navajo elementary schools in Arizona. We would be grouped three Americans to one Libyan living in a hogan near each school.

Soon, in an all-hands meeting, Al Wight asked for 30 volunteers to drive the Suzuki motorcycles to Arizona, 500 miles away. Initially, half raised their hands. However, after the meeting many had second thoughts. Bob Suzuki (whose name rings ironically) suggested this was a terrible idea. Rich DiGeorgio also chimed in forcefully with multiple rationales. Almost all of us were total tyros when it came to motorcycles. And the exposure alone of 30 young men driving 500 miles, (round trip for 30 men, a total of 30,000 miles) was a major danger. Then the chance of serious or deadly accident was multiplied further—we wore no helmets. Furthermore, motorcycle instructor Bob Ellis chimed in that the Suzukis were in too poor a state of disrepair to travel 500 miles. Plus, he pointed out, the cycles were being broken in, and wouldn't go over 30 mph. So that meant 16 hours of cycling. He also pointed out there were strong winds in the Arizona desert. And that if it rained, there was the peril of slick roads. As a group, we agreed this was breathtakingly irresponsible.

By the next day, there were seven wound-up core leaders, led by Rich DiGeorgio, who, in the spirit of self-organization we had already shown in taking care of the barracks, led another bitch meeting with Al Wight. Wight doubled down to defend his plan, but faced angry jeering. Rich DiGeorgio, for one, was particularly eloquent in criticizing Wight's idea. He, Ted Kelley and others presented a written petition to Wight, flatly refusing to drive the cycles to Arizona and demanding that the motorcycles be trucked down to Arizona. While that morning transportation specialist Quentin Harris had argued that it would cost $1,500 to ship the cycles, the practical-minded gang of seven counter-suggested they simply rent three cars with U-Hauls. So much for that objection. Many upset volunteers spoke up to say they would write their congressmen about this. Wight blew up at Rich. But in the face of the uproar which Wight must have realized was justified, he finally caved. But this turned out not to be the end of the story.

A few days later, some of us were chewing the fat with some Libyans in the barracks. I noticed a glint in Mohammed's locker.

"Mohammed, what's that in your locker?"

He looked startled, closed the partially-opened door and said "Oh, nothing."

"C'mon, Mohammed, there's something in there."

"No, no, it's nothing."

"Mohammed, you're going to have to open that door."

He sheepishly backed off, and as he opened the locker, he said, "It's a gun."

"Why did you buy a gun?"

"It wasn't just me, we all bought guns."

"You all did?"

"We heard we were going down to the Navajo Indians' place."

I thought, "Omigod, western movies! They're terrified of war-painted, war-chant-whooping, hatchet-wielding, scalp-brandishing savages!" 31 Libyans with guns let loose upon 31 Navajo villages? The *New York Times* headline flashed into my head:

Late Edition
Today, mostly cloudy, morning rain, afternoon showers, cooler, still humid, high 74. Tonight, brief showers, low 66. Tomorrow, variably cloudy, high 76. Weather map, Page 85.

"All the News That's Fit to Print"

The New York Times

VOL. CLXVI .... No. 57,668   © 1968 The New York Times Company   NEW YORK, TUESDAY, SEPTEMBER 3, 1968   TEN CENTS

WAR ERUPTS IN ARIZONA BETWEEN LIBYANS AND NAVAJOS THANKS TO THE PEACE CORPS

Of course, I forthwith reported this to the administration. Despite their efforts to convince the Libyans to surrender their guns, the Libyans stubbornly stuck to their guns, as it were. Al Wight & Co. were flummoxed. In desperation, they called Peace Corps Washington. The very next day a worldly-wise old Washington hand arrived. He summoned all the Libyans to a Come-to-Allah meeting. Knowing that Arabs respect power above all else, he came right to the point: "Either you all immediately turn in these guns or tomorrow we're putting you all on a plane straight back to Libya."

They turned in their guns.

Later this summer, Bisbeeans had to cope with a string of flying hypodermic needles.

Smelly, Long-Haired Kids and Wayward Syringes

In mid-August, the Bisbee Libyans put on a "Senussi Army Day" show (after King Idris of Libya of the Senussi tribe). Instead of just performing for the trainees, the Libyans used a high school auditorium and invited the entire populace of Bisbee to come. Per Judy Putnam: "One fellow danced a Tuareg dance, dressed in a stark black cape and white turban wrapped around his head and over his face, to the accompaniment of a drum. Then a Gazelle Dance was danced by a fellow in a white long-john-type suit, painted gray and brown. Whenever he got near the drum, it would explode like a shot and he was frightened away. It was very emotional and beautiful."

Libyans perform for citizens of Bisbee

Dr. Eugene Coulson was to be our on-site doctor in Libya. He had served in World War II and hailed from New Mexico. His duty post for the summer was Bisbee.

Dr. Eugene Colson, in-country physician, Tripoli, Libya

He did have a maverick streak. One of his responsibilities was administering inoculations. After each shot, instead of walking across the room to drop the used syringes into a designated plastic garbage can, he would cavalierly fling them across the room. Sometimes they landed in the can, sometimes the needles would thwang and stick into the side of the can. Once, his aim went astray, embedding a needle into the thigh of a female volunteer.

In the absence of any formal training on their motorcycles, some Bisbee men took Moto Guzzis *ad hoc* out to the dirt airstrip at Bisbee Airport. Finally, instead of hiring someone, program management tapped trainee Tom Weinz to handle motorcycle instruction. Tom set aside a weekend to take two buses of the men and their cycles to a remote site to train. Along the way, they stopped at a small gas station. The trainees trundled into the store to buy drinks and snacks. After the training, Tom happened to stop at the same store. While there, he overheard the clerk complaining to a customer about the "long-haired and smelly kids who were here yesterday. What a travesty that they are representing our country!"

In another outing, after dinner the Libyans danced to the pounding of drums in the Libyan step-and-hop style in a circle around a large fire. They even made up a song in Arabic about Bisbee, singing *"Ya Bisbee, masalama, inshallah shuff senna thanya."* ("Oh, Bisbee, goodbye, if Allah wills it we will see you in the next year.")

In a final talk from the Libyans to the American trainees, one Libyan academic, according to Jay Corrin, "laid out for us his own ideas about women and why they needed to be covered and largely kept indoors. Much to our collective surprise, he explained that they required such veiling because they were driven by devil forces to sexually seduce males." Later, Jay reports that hard-boiled-egg-eater Ibrahim Bakush regaled a smaller group with his views on women. He said "that he had to restrain himself throughout our training because he could easily seduce all of our wives who were eagerly awaiting his charms."

Harold McElhinny has his wife to thank for ending up in Libya at all. Turns out the Field Assessment Officers had rated everyone on a 1–10 scale, with 10 being the worst. His wife Ellen rated a "1" and Harold was rated an "8." Their FAO explained that had it not been for Ellen's terrific rating, they would not have gone to Libya. In retrospect, Harold admits he wasn't mature, did not take things seriously and exhibited a reckless sarcastic streak. In fact, Harold's nickname was *Al Agrab* (the scorpion) because everyone thought his sense of humor dangerous.

Speaking of the McElhinnys, they were dismayed by ugly Americans at home. A local country club had invited many of the volunteers and Libyans to come over for a swim. Once they showed up, the locals could not but be aware of the Libyans' dark skin and they were politely asked to leave. Up in Ogden, Utah, near Clearfield, Mike Lee (Seton Hall) remembers that he and Craig Owens were asked by two Libyans to help them get a haircut. Mike and Craig took them to a barbershop. The barber took one look at the Libyans and said, "I don't do that kind of work." While Mike and Craig were embarrassed at this racist display the Libyans were oblivious and were forced to let their hair keep growing.

Back in Clearfield, the deselection follies continued apace.

Nicknames and Protests

The most delightfully engaging and funny trainee was a full-of-moxie, sharp-as-a-tack Michigan grad, Bob Albertson. Perhaps in reaction to Al Wight's increasing intransigence, Bob scurried off to the nearest Western Union office and sent a prank telegram to the director, pretending to be a muckety-muck from Peace Corps Washington.

By a month into training, the quirks of the program staff were evident. Some wag amongst us came up with the hyper-clever concept of nicknaming staff members, not just with funny apt names, but with movie titles to fit their characters. So, the Ph.D. candidate, do-nothing Al Wight was dubbed "Dr. Dolittle." Robert Larson, a language specialist reporting to Wight became "The Sorcerer's Apprentice." Bus driver Willie Esquibal, who was fond of a tipple or two (or three), was "The Days of Wine and Roses." The widely reviled LaMar Lindsay? "How to Succeed in Business without Really Trying." Language director Donna Carr, who often sported pink outfits, became "The Pink Panther." And a micro teaching specialist Patti Miner's bizarre personality inspired no less than three nicknames. The first was "Peppermint Patti." The second one, reflecting her antsiness, was "Cat on a Hot Tin Roof." The third captured the actually more intense nature of her personality, her frantic, wide-eyed-on-amphetamines mien: "Speed Queen." This carried an additional kick with "Speed Queen" a brand washing machine that conjured up images of agitated, roiling water.

One day, Speed Queen was lecturing us on the relationships between various phonemes in the English language. She chalked a matrix on the blackboard and filled in the spaces. I noticed what I thought was an anomaly in one of the cells of the chart and duly raised my hand.

"Miss Miner, (this was before the coinage of 'Ms.') I don't see how that entry in the lower left corner fits with the rest of the chart."

She replied, "No, no, that entry is perfectly OK."

"But it doesn't seem to consistently relate to the adjoining entries ..."

One volunteer chimed up, "Miss Miner, you know, I think Randy's right."

"No, he's not right, this is correct."

Another volunteer: "Wait a minute, I think Randy's right, too!"

She tried to dismiss this, but everyone started to pile on. There arose a spontaneous chant by everyone in the room. "Randy's right! Randy's right!"

This flustered her to no end. She yelled "Quiet!" waving both arms in a thrusting dramatic arc and uttering a shrill shriek, "Charts are never wrong!"

In contradistinction to the program's widespread inadequacies, there were a few bright spots. One of those was the transformational appearance in late August of someone we immediately dubbed "Super Teach," a Dartmouth professor named John Rassias. Rassias, a Zorba-the-Greek-out-there personality, had developed the Rassias Method of teaching foreign languages. It was deployed across many Peace Corps programs. His method? Immersive and theatrical. It included rapid-fire back and forth drills between teacher and students. One principle was the teacher as performer. If you are performing, that entertains the class, thus maintaining high interest, thus more learning. Rather than dry-lecturing us, he demonstrated it with us as students, a mesmerizing, inspiring performance. PCV John Becker recalls his urging us to be spontaneous. He said, "If your ass itches, scratch it!" He proceeded to drop his trousers, scratch his ass, then hike his trousers back up. Becker relates that the shocked expressions on the faces of the many Mormon men and women staff were memorable.

I later applied Rassias's methods to great effect in Libya.

John Rassias, force of nature

Credit: Dartmouth College/Joseph Mehling '69

Also in late August, Mustafa Gusbi introduced the textbooks we were going to teach with that he himself had written, his "Gusbi Readers." He was an enlightened advocate of customizing language learning to the local culture. For us, it was refreshing to see Nuri and Salma rather than Dick and Jane. Instead of a Leave-it-to-Beaver American suburb setting, it was desertified Libya. Instead of Spot the dog and Puff the cat—a camel and a donkey. Instead of American culture, food, customs and situations, it was Libyan. He advised us, that in-class opportunities would crop up that we should be alert to and incorporate into a lesson. In fact, one such memorable opportunity did pop up for me in Libya.

English textbook customized for Libya

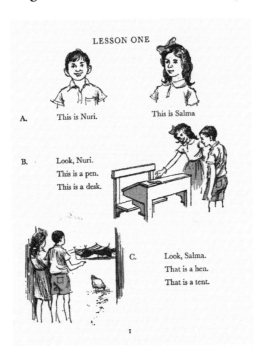

LESSON NINE

A. AMINA: Hello, Ali.
ALI: Hello, Amina.
AMINA: Ali, are those your camels? Are they your camels?
ALI: No, they aren't my camels. They aren't my camels,
       Amina. Are these your goats?
AMINA: No, they aren't my goats, Ali. Are they your goats?
ALI: Yes, Amina. Yes, they are my goats. Is that your
       bag, Amina? Is that your bag?
AMINA: Yes, it's my bag. Is that your hat, Ali?
ALI: Yes, it's my hat.

B. Is this your book?   Are these your books?
   Is this your pencil?   Are these your pencils?
   Is this your cow?   Are these your cows?
   Is this your hen?   Are these your hens?
   Is this your tent?   Are these your tents?

                 No, it isn't.
                 No, they aren't.

12

Several felicitous shows served to reinforce Libyan-American relations. On July 26th, the Libyans delighted us with a short, hilarious play replete with singing. The plot centered on an American teacher in Libya who wore short pants and a hat. Dan Peters wrote at the time, "I laughed so hard my sides still hurt." On Libyan Army Day, in mid-August, the Libyans put on a show depicting how the Libyans drove the Italians from their land. This was fleshed out with a film, Libyan tea, singing and folk dancing. On another occasion, the Libyans recited two hours of 13th-century Arabic poetry from memory for a mesmerized American audience.

Complementing this, someone amongst us suggested we put on our own show, so we threw together what amounted to a variety show. We called it "Sargent Shriver's Lonely Hearts' Club Band." Among other songs we performed was "There is Nothing Like a Dame." I played guitar. The show went over very well. On another talent night Mark Lepori, Stoney Bird and Frank Dauterich played recorders while John Lundin did the vocal for a 15th-century piece by Renaissance composer Guillaume Dufay. (Stoney's father had told him for years that he was a "historian for the

State Department," but in fact he was an analyst for the CIA. When his family moved to Ghana his father told him he was a Pillsbury flour salesman. Only when he turned 18 was Stoney told who his father's employer really was.)

Along the way we did learn some Libyan history. In 1911, the Italians occupied Libya. From 1930 to 1934, the tyrannical Marshal Rodolfo Graziani arrived on the scene, slaughtering the Senussi Bedouin tribes, earning him the sobriquet of "The Butcher of Fezzan." He force-migrated 100,000 Libyans into 15 concentration camps where they lived in harsh and squalid conditions. Some died by hanging, some by shooting (executions averaged 30 a day). According to Pulitzer-winning Libyan Hisham Matar, "Official Italian census records show that the population of Cyrenaica in those years plummeted from 225,000 to 142,000. Graziani also ordered the machine-gunning from airplanes of entire herds of livestock. He ordered all wells to be cemented up. He deployed poison gas against the populace. The Italian army reduced the number of sheep and goats from 270,00 to 67,000. So many died of starvation. (And by the way, *Graziani* comes from the word "grace" in Italian.)

From the beginning of Italian rule, Omar Mukhtar emerged as an armed resistance fighter, and for almost 20 years conducted ambushes on Italian troops. He wasn't captured until 1931, when, at the age of 70, he was hanged in the presence of 20,000 Bedouins in Sulug, just south of Benghazi. (In 1980 Anthony Quinn brilliantly portrayed Mukhtar in the movie *Lion of the Desert*. His central antagonist was Graziani.)

Since our orientation in 1968, I've learned that in March 1937 the Prime Minister of Italy, Benito Mussolini made a state visit to Libya, where he declared himself "The Protector of Islam."

Benito Mussolini, March 20, 1937. Tripoli, Libya. Bearing the Sword of Islam

He also attended the opening ceremony for "The Marble Arch," a triumphalist monument erected that day on the exact border between Cyrenaica and Tripolitania. You will notice in the detailed photograph below that there is a statue of a naked man, semi-supine and twisted in agony. Actually, there's another almost identical statue on the other side of the arch. And therein lies a tale. As legend has it, in the year 350 B.C.E. or thereabouts, the Carthaginians (in Tripolitania) and the Greeks (in Cyrenaica) disagreed about where the border was between their two regions. The solution was not a modern American one like flipping a coin or rock-paper-scissors. Their idea was to have two sets of runners; one set (the Brothers Philaeni) would run eastward at the same time as a set of Greek runners would run westward from Cyrene. Wherever they met, voilà! (or however you say that in ancient Carthaginian) that's the border.

However, the Philaenis met the Greeks suspiciously far to the east. The Greeks cried foul. But this required yet another solution. In order to appease the cheating accusations, the Carthaginians had to agree to the only possible solution—burying the Philaenis alive. Hence the twisted agony.

The Marble Arch

This was quite the tourist spot until Muammar Ghaddafi, citing it as an example of Italian imperialism, dynamited the arch in 1973. Jeanne Maurey took a dramatic shot of the detail at the top of the arch showing one of the brothers Philaeni.

Detail atop the Marble Arch

To fulfill Bill Whitman's promise to train us on taking apart and putting together a Moto Guzzi, (a high priority of his), Al Wight hired Bob

Ellis. Ellis, however, had two other jobs, so the only time he could show up was briefly at suppertime. Many times he did not show up at all. And he professed to know little about the Moto Guzzi. (Talk about extreme vetting!) I and many others made repeated complaints about the inadequacy of the Moto Guzzi training. We made the constructive suggestion that they find a real expert on Moto Guzzis, have him come about four times, mount the motorcycle on a table and walk us through the procedure step by step. We were totally ignored. Except for one not terribly helpful session with bus driver Quentin Harris. Gathering us all around, Quentin popped open the hood of a Land Rover and pointed, saying, "This here's a carburetor. These here are spark plugs. The gas goes through this here carburetor and into these here pistons where these here spark plugs explode this here gas."

A few weeks before the end of training, Bob Marshall, clearly a smart and outgoing guy, was called in to a meeting with Al Wight. Al informed Bob that he had a bad attitude, and that this bad attitude would be a problem for him overseas. Bob protested that he hadn't said anything negative. Al Wight's response? "I can tell you have a bad attitude by the way you look at me." (Well, that settles that!) Bob escaped any further needling. Needless to say, once in country, Bob's stint in Libya was notably successful.

Director Wight singled out the highly capable and amiable Greg Strick. Interviewed him twice. The first was an innocuous "getting to know you" session. In the second one, "He told me point blank, 'Greg, why don't you just leave? You're not going to make it.' " Greg guessed that Wight was either trying to challenge him or make him more committed. He was shaken internally by the attack, but externally he maintained calm. "It made me more committed. I said to myself, 'I've got to do it.' What I said was 'I'll be fine. I'll be successful.' " (And he was, to the nth degree. Just read the Epilogues at the end of this book.)

By late August, it had sunk in that I had way too much time playing guitar, writing letters, playing bumper pool, reading (over the summer I read *Improving Your Memory*, an Ian Fleming book, *The Arrangement*, a 700-page Nietzsche book, many issues of *Sports Illustrated*, *The National Observer*, and several *Playboys*). Richard Massey: "We have an hour after lunch when just about everybody sacks out." In my diary: "Fairly worthless day. I'd better do something soon or will die of unconstructiveness."

Another disappointment was Al Wight's aloofness. He never ate one meal at the cafeteria with us (by my calculation he had 186 opportunities to do so). And he never visited us in the barracks—except once on the very last day of training. This would have been a terrific way to informally learn about trainees' concerns, to build up positive relationships.

Also at the end of August we took in the chaotic Democratic National Convention taking place in Chicago. 10,000 anti-war protestors rioted. CBS-TV reporter Dan Rather was roughed up on the convention floor. And Lyndon Johnson's vice president Hubert Humphrey was nominated for the presidency, giving a speech that strongly supported Lyndon Johnson's Vietnam War. Joe Connor remembers everyone yelling and cursing at the TV.

In the department of giving credit where credit is due, during the program we did learn a kind of Peace Corps creed (borrowed and adapted over the centuries from Lao-Tse, the Italians and thrown into the mix, the Navajos) that has stuck with me ever since: "Give a man a fish and he can eat for a day. Teach a man how to fish and he can eat for a lifetime."

Clearly, as will be seen, in Clearfield, we were not immune from immunizations!

Shots in the Arm
and the Ass

Certainly, one thing the Peace Corps gets an attaboy for (assuming organizations are considered male, as opposed to ships, e.g., which are designated female) was protecting us from disease. Starting in late August, we got a series of vaccinations including yellow fever, smallpox, Sabin polio, plague, typhus, rabies, tetanus-diphtheria, and typhoid. (This last left my arm very sore for days.) We took a tuberculin test. A nurse took our blood. Unfortunately, this was the 1960s when needles were thicker than today, plus the bumbling nurse had a hard time finding our veins. In my case she poked me painfully about four times before she found one. At the tail end of the summer (so to speak) we got two gamma globulin shots in the rear, a week apart, to strengthen our immune system against hepatitis. In the gluteus maximus, because the cc's required and the size of the needle required were so big. After each, I had a painful lump in my buttocks the size of a golf ball that took a week to subside.

September 1, 1968. Time to trek down to the Navajo Nation Reservation to practice teach. Thanks to our volunteer revolt, we would not be riding Suzukis to the reservation. These were loaded onto pickup trucks, as was our luggage. One truck was driven by Jack Seifert. Once he got to the huge reservation area, he picked up two hitch-hiking Navajo teenagers, who rode in the back of the truck with the luggage. At one point they got off, thanking Jack. When Jack arrived at the orientation school, he discovered that luggage for three PCVs was missing. He figured out that the hitch-hikers had tossed the bags off the back of the truck a little before disembarking, then doubled back to collect their loot.

We were loaded onto two school buses. One yellow and one blue. The Libyans took assorted rides south, including hitch-hiking. Neil McCabe, a jovial, rambunctious, hail-fellow-well-met, late of the University of Scranton, mounted a poster on the yellow bus dashboard that read "La Puta Marching Band." (*Puta* is prostitute in Spanish.) Having got wind of this, Al Wight gave Neil a dressing down before we departed. One bus driver was Quentin Harris, the other was Willie Esquibal of "Days of Wine and Roses" fame. According to John Farranto, Willie drove recklessly up and down narrow mountain roads. This provoked two opposite reactions from the trainees on board—terror and laughter.

Spirits were high. It was exciting to get away from the rut. Exciting to see an Indian reservation. Exciting to practice TEFL. Stoney Bird remembers we dubbed the trip "The Magical Mystery Tour."

The Blue Bus, labeled after the Beatles' "Magical Mystery Tour."

In my yellow bus, to pass the time, Neil McCabe started a rhythmic chant repeating the Arabic word for "she," that we all joined in on, like a college football crowd: "*Heeya, heeya, heeya, heeya.*" It carried a triple meaning in all. Its cadence was identical to a stereotypical Indian chant and its expression a cry of hormonal release from our monastic existence. Whenever we got bored, we'd lustily reprise the chant.

In the meantime, the blue school bus broke down and all the volunteers on board were forced to hitch-hike to the reservation.

For those of us in the yellow school bus, the plan was to spend the night in Moab, Utah, 260 miles south of Clearfield, on the edge of Arches National Park, renowned for its many dramatic arch formations.

From Top to Bottom: Kevin Hunt, Mike Lee and Frank Reese. Arches National Park, Utah

In the late afternoon, we wandered into a mini-canyon-like campground populated with rock formations. Lanky, adventurous, dark-haired Stoney Bird nonchalantly decided to climb to the top of a fifty-foot high egg-shaped pinnacle of rock. How impressed we were with his bravado! He struck a proud pose. He reveled in our adoration for about one minute. Then he realized the only safe way down was by rappelling and he had no rope. People desperately threw out ideas. We all took off our belts and tied them together as a lifeline. This didn't work. Someone rushed off to find a park ranger who threw him some rope to rappel down. Phew!

After ambling down to Moab for beer and dinner, we wended our way back to the campground. Dan Peters wrote "We camped in an amphitheatre formed by giant red boulders." It was now dark. Somehow there were flashlights with beams bouncing off the rock walls. Voices bouncing off the walls, an eerie echo effect. Then a remarkable, sustained piece of spontaneous magic. Inspired, Glen Curry piped up "Hey let's have a convention!" We immediately zoned into it. After all, we had volunteers from many states. We had just been exposed to two political conventions. We had swilled a fair amount of beer. As if choosing for a pickup baseball game, we self-organized on the spot. But instead of two teams, there were about 20 caucuses. Glen self-appointed himself chairman.

"OK, everyone from New Jersey, over here!"

"Everyone from Ohio over here!"

"Illinois here!"

John Maclean, among others, ran around trying to line up delegates. Soon, 20 clumps of convention delegates formed. Each delegation decided who would speak for them. Someone took the role of chairman. Maybe it was Munro. (Nobody remembers, even Munro, because it was 50 years ago.)

"The convention will come to order. Roll call!" It duly proceeded in alphabetical order:

"The chair recognizes the state of California."

The designated speaker for California spoke in exaggerated oratorical tones.

"Mr. Chairman, California, the home of the Golden Gate Bridge, casts its 86 votes for its favorite son, Governor Ronald Reagan!"

Applause, hoots, mixed with boos.

"The chair recognizes the state of Michigan." His voice echoed against the canyon walls as if he were speaking through a microphone.

"Mr. Chairman the great Wolverine state of Michigan hereby casts its 44 votes for the next president of the United States, George Romney!"

Claps, laughs. At this point I noticed that we had an audience.

Not a television audience, but a live one. Campers. Wound up in our self-involvement, we simply hadn't noticed them. I couldn't tell if they were entertained, bewildered or just plain pissed off at us…for the noise, and for keeping them up late.

"Mr. Chairman, Minnesota, the land of 10,000 lakes, casts its 26 votes for Hubert Humphrey!"

The perceptive among you may notice we were mixing Republicans and Democrats, but we didn't care. We were on a roll. It was increasingly evident this was an improvisational tour de force. OK, we were on a roll, but how would it end? How can we top this?

"Mr. Chairman, the great state of New York, home of the Statue of Liberty, casts its 92 votes for its favorite son, Governor Nelson D. Rockefeller."

Whoops, whistles.

"The chair recognizes the state of Oregon."

"Mr. Chairman, Oregon, the Hazelnut State, proudly casts its 18 votes for Navy veteran and Senator, Mark Hatfield!"

Jim Seroogy (University of Wisconsin) remembers, "Dan Peters and I represented the Wisconsin contingent. We took turns voting on various issues and policies as our states were called. I don't remember what the policies and issues were other than nobody cared too much for Richard Nixon. But there was still lots of time for jokes, silliness, and complaining about the establishment." The Wisconsin caucus also objected that all the Southern states present could not vote because they had no Negroes in their delegations.

And so it went on with increasingly rousing rounds of applause and cheers. Then we reached a dead end. Each of our 20 states had cast votes for 20 different candidates. No one had a majority, much less a plurality. Of course, the premise of this improvisation was to go by the rules.

"We have no candidate," said the chairman. "We have to move to a second ballot." No one had the heart to go through another full round of balloting. But we had to do something. One bright star among us, who knew convention parliamentary procedure, came to the rescue.

"Mr. Chairman! I move that we make a vote by acclamation. I nominate *Willie the bus driver* for president of the United States!" A galvanizing moment. We all instinctively knew we were saved. The chant started right away and grew to a crescendo.

"Willie! Willie! Willie! Willie!"

Willie had been standing to the side watching all this. Bewildered, he was quickly escorted through the crowd to the "podium."

"Willie! Willie!"

He had no idea what to say. The chairman just grabbed his arm and held it up in triumph amidst the cheers. John Maclean remembers the night as the funniest ever. And ever so therapeutic.

By 1 AM we'd simmered down and dispersed. I somehow found someone's unlocked car, flopped inside and fell asleep. Phil Akre, late of Cannon College, climbed atop a small flat rock formation. He lay on his back, aglow with the magic of the night, staring up at the stars. No pillow, no knapsack, no blanket. He closed his eyes.

■

Leave it to Peter Hawkes to next go water-skiing on a lake full of venomous snakes.

Hellos and Hogans

The next morning, we left at 7:45 AM for the long trek to the Senostee Navajo Boarding School in New Mexico, arriving at 10:30 PM. Senostee housed about 500 Navajo students, all in the sixth grade or younger. After a day-and-a-half of bland orientation, we were assigned our schools. For me it was the Indian Reservation in Hunter's Point, in Apache County, Arizona, rooming with arguably the two most difficult trainees, John Forsythe and Ron Novakowski. In my diary, "…can't help thinking that they're testing me." We were joined by a tall, gangly, black Libyan with a huge sunny smile and the most infectious laugh, Juma Zardak. The other trainees fanned out to 25 reservations in Arizona and New Mexico.

Our accommodation at Hunter's Point Elementary School consisted of a hexagonal sandstone Native American hogan: one room, with two bunk beds, a table, some chairs and some storage shelves. The only downside? The bathroom was 200 yards away. In addition to practice teaching, we were to teach Juma English. He, in turn, would teach us Arabic.

Our hogan at Hunter's Point Elementary School

Juma Zardak in our hogan

While there, I felt so tired, I had to take naps. In my diary I ascribed it to the altitude. (Turns out Hunter's Point is 6,600 feet above sea level, 1,000 feet higher than Denver. No wonder!)

Sam Cangemi, an earnest Clarion State College grad, was assigned to a reservation school outside Farmington, New Mexico. He was shocked to learn that these K-to-8 school kids were boarding away from their families. And further shocked that they were forced to sleep three kids to a single bed.

At Dzilth-Na-O-Dith-Hle (don't ask me how to pronounce that!) Community School in New Mexico, one thing that sticks in Kevin Hunt's craw to this day was the desperation of these young kids in missing their parents, brothers and sisters.

Dennis Carlson describes many of the young children crying extensively. "One young boy sat with his legs crossed and simply rocked back and forth all day, never speaking." Dennis reports that runaways were a constant issue. In one case, three boys ran away, getting lost overnight in the freezing desert. The three had cuddled together for warmth. The boy in the middle survived, the other two died.

At dinner at his BIA principal's home Craig Owens was aghast when told the principal's goal was "...for every bit of native American culture to be removed from these children." John Farranto observed that the BIA principals were inflexible, rigid and racist. They wanted to convert the heathen and make white men out of every student.

On September 9th teaching kicked in for me. I practice taught English to Miss Newsome's second grade twice. The 30 kids were as cute as buttons. Every day I taught Juma English for an hour-and-a-half. He taught me Arabic for three hours. This immersive one-on-one was so much more an efficient and satisfying way to learn Arabic. Daily, I rode our Suzuki in circles around the hogan to get the feel of it. I must've gotten the hang of it pretty quickly, as two days later I drove it a couple of hours north to Window Rock, Arizona and Fort Defiance.

At his Navajo school, Bill Cagle was impressed that the kids could make "fry bread," a concoction made with flour, baking soda, salt and water.

In stout Neil McCabe's class, he would say "Shush" to keep the students quiet. *Shus* means "bear" in Navajo, so his kids dubbed him "Shush."

On the first day of classes at the Chuska Boarding School in Tohatchi, New Mexico, Peter Hawkes asked a Navajo boy where the classroom was. The boy stuck out his tongue at Peter then moved it to the right. When Peter finally managed to find the classroom, he complained to the teacher how rude the little boy was. "Oh, no. He wasn't being rude at all. That's how Navajos give direction."

The morning of his first class of first graders at Aneta Boarding School, Ted Kelley was surprised when one of the kids went into an epileptic fit. He was then super impressed to see that the other students knew just what to do. They fetched a wet paper towel and placed it between the child's teeth.

At the Tohatchi reservation, the lake was aswarm with water moccasins. A local lad who had been foolish enough to go water-skiing had been promptly bitten by several of the venomous snakes. Despite this fore-knowledge, Peter Hawkes took a swim in the lake. 48 years later, I asked Peter why he would do such a thing.

"I was 21," he said.

In the Toadelena, New Mexico reservation, John Maclean was stationed near a crazy old, white-haired, long-white-bearded sheep herder and his wife. He invited John and others up on a hill, built a fire and roasted corn which they ate and downed with watered-down wine. He said he had been a sheep herder for the Navajos for his entire life.

On his first class day, Greg Strick was unnerved to be in front of 18 Navajo third graders. The female teacher introduced him, "This is Mr. Strick." Greg said how happy he was to meet them. Then a couple of kids got up and approached him. Then others followed suit. He found himself surrounded by a dozen kids. They touched his hands. They touched his pant leg. Greg found this to be a weird tactile encounter. After a bit, the kids melted back to their seats. Then the teacher explained, "They're just trying to get to know you."

At one point, Greg visited the Hubbell Trading Post in Ganado, Arizona. There he bought a turquoise and silver ring there. Decades later interested in having it appraised, two jewelry experts declared it was "Bisbee Turquoise." (A surprising coincidence for him so many years after Peace Corps training.) A particularly valuable stone, it was a by-product of the copper mining in Bisbee. The spidery brown veins in it derive from the copper. Bisbee turquoise, also known as Bisbee Blue, is amongst the finest turquoise found anywhere in the world. Greg still wears the ring today, along with his wedding band.

One weekend, I guess being antsy, Charlie Cross decided to flee the coop and hitchhiked 250 miles to Lake Powell on the Utah-Arizona border, then hitchhiked all the way back.

Also itching to travel, Bob Marshall and Mike Lee decided that one Saturday they would hitchhike to Santa Fe, some 210 miles away. They managed to get to Santa Fe and spend the day. But on the way back, they were dropped off in a tiny town called Bernalillo, some 190 miles from the reservation. After several hours and no rides, it was getting dark and they were getting worried. Suddenly, a mini-caravan of gaily painted school buses, vans and campers alit at their location. It turns out this was America's longest running mobile, LSD-infused, extended family hippie commune known as The Hog Farm Family. The next year they gained fame by digging fire pits and cutting trails at the 1969 Woodstock Festival. The Hog Farm Family persists to this day.

The Hog Farm Family in '60s regalia

When the time came to return to Clearfield, the group scheduled for Willie's bus had been promised that they would stop and see the Grand Canyon on the way back. Richard Massey wrote: "Most of us wanted to stay over and see the Grand Canyon in the morning, but our leaders said our sleeping bags couldn't take it and decided to leave. We didn't even get off the bus!"

Being an impatient soul (perhaps my greatest failing), rather than slog a two-day trip back to Clearfield on a bus, I made reservations to fly back on Frontier Airlines so I could have two extra days with Nancy.

Unfortunately, the propeller-driven DC-3 flight was hardly non-stop. We landed and took off at Farmington, Cortez, Grand Junction and Moab. Five take- offs and landings in few hours rendered me nauseous. With great relief and anticipation, I finally arrived at Nancy's. We talked well into the night and hit the hay at 2 AM.

The next day, we drove to the Brighton Lodge in Brighton, Utah, some 30 miles to the southeast of Salt Lake City, up in ski country, where I coincidentally ran into the parents—Perry and Louise Sellon—of a freshman roommate at Princeton. We then motored to the Utah State Fair. The Byrds played. Orville the Clown sat on this metal chair. His schtick was four sticks of dynamite under the chair that he would light. After the explosion, he toppled straight off to the side. (Clearly, an early candidate for CTE.) Then, a guy I'd never heard of—Evel Knievel—zoomed his motorcycle over 10 cars.

The next day we heard a concert of the Mormon Tabernacle Choir. We hung out. Nancy made tacos. A week later, supper at the Hofbrau Haus. We crashed a Mormon wedding reception but left after 10 minutes since no alcohol was served, so we patronized several Clearfield bars. Then Nancy dropped me off at the barracks. Our last date. We never saw each other again.

In Clearfield, we had five days left before home leave, before proceeding to JFK for flights to Libya. I traveled to Salt Lake City to buy clothing—including an Air Force flight suit I intended to use while riding my motorcycle (I have it to this day). At the department store restaurant the waitress asked me what I wanted, I said, "Oh, I'll just have a BLT and a Coke." She said, "What's a BLT?" Surprised, I enunciated each key consonant, "Why, it's a <u>B</u>acon-<u>L</u>ettuce-and-<u>T</u>omato sandwich." And she said, "Whhhy, thaaat's a good idea!"

While waiting at the bus station in Salt Lake City for a half-hour with some volunteers and Libyans, some Mormons quite aggressively tried to convert the Libyans to Mormonism. I kept telling them they were Moslem and that this was a hopeless case, but they persisted.

Three days before leaving, in front of Bill Whitman, Al Wight accused us of not learning how to ride the one Moto Guzzi we had. I and a handful of others finally rode it for only ten minutes each on the day before we left. And of course, we were not shown once how to disassemble and re-assemble this motorcycle. Bob Gausman remembers that we were all summoned to a general meeting about in-country assignments. Training managers pointed out that 90% of us would be living on or near the coast where the major Libyan population centers were. 10% of us would be going deep into the hinterlands. We were given the old Peace-Corps-idealistic-challenge pep talk. "We're looking for the toughest of the tough. The bravest of the brave. We need ten men to be assigned deep in the desert. Who wants to go?" Ten of us, including Bob, eagerly raised their hands. He ended up going to God-forsaken Samnu, deep in the Fezzan and 500 miles south of Tripoli.

Our Peace-Corps-issued trunks arrived. At this late date, three more trainees were deselected, including, to our general surprise, Rich DiGeorgio. Like, hunh? Rich was very popular. He shined in D-groups. He worked hard at memorizing Arabic vocabulary lists at night. It made no sense.

Unless you take into account Rich's leadership in the group insurrection about the motorcycles. On their way to the airport as the three deselectees were pre-emptively whisked away from the Clearfield site, they learned that of the 14 hours the Final Selection Board spent on all the trainees, fully two of them were spent talking about Rich DiGeorgio. That seemed extreme. However, I and others had heard that Al Wight argued strongly against Rich. It was pretty clear to us why. Wight had been majorly humiliated in front of all the volunteers and the staff.

The actual issue was the *safety* of 30 volunteers given the very real dangers described before. Where was the sense of values with Al Wight, fulminating about Rich when it was Wight *himself* who caused the trouble.

Wight should have *thanked* Rich DiGeorgio for his principled stand. What if even one of the thirty volunteers had been killed driving 1,000 miles without a helmet? Or just one with serious injuries? And how many congressmen would have swooped down on this dereliction of duty in a nano-second? How would the families of any killed volunteers have felt— for the rest of their lives?

I spoke to Rich DiGeorgio 50 years later. He said this deselection hit him hard. He felt this was the first time in his life he had failed at anything. He had always worked hard and never failed to reach his goals, whether in life, school or athletics. For 50 years he has felt this pain. However, how would he have felt if he hadn't stood up to injustice, arrogance and bad judgement? What if just *one* volunteer had died and he hadn't acted?

I would argue that in the larger scheme of things, Rich was *not* a failure. He did the right thing. All of us, I know, are *proud* of what Rich did in the interest of safety. And he should be, too.

I would argue further that having read over 40 Peace Corps memoirs, I can attest to scores of examples of Peace Corps volunteers who took the bull by the horns, acted against the powers-that-be in their host countries, and exercised leadership to galvanize community development projects in their villages. This kind of leadership is precisely what Rich DiGeorgio was exercising.

The night before we left, we had a special dinner—the *only one* Al Wight attended—with songs, diplomas for the Libyans and an official Peace Corps swearing-in ceremony, the wording of which, interestingly, is the same as that for the Marines, the CIA and the Foreign Service. A lot of fun. Bob Marshall and I stayed up till 1 AM singing as I strummed along on guitar.

On departure day, October 4, 1968, I said goodbye to the Libyans I was close to. Packed. Cleared out of Clearfield forever. Of the 108 original trainees we were now down to 74 (through deselections and volunteered droppings-out). Strangely, Tom Furth drove half of us to Salt Lake City Airport in one of the buses. I don't know who was supposed to drive the bus back. Maybe it's still sitting there 50 years later in the Salt Lake City airport.

I flew to JFK via Denver. Sister Debbie met me at the airport. At home, my sister Bassett suggested I look up a Rollins College schoolmate, also headed to Libya in the Peace Corps, Jeanne Maurey, who had trained at Bisbee. At the library, found a comprehensive and fascinating *National Geographic* about Libya. (Where was that at training?) I called an Arabic professor at Princeton and asked what he would recommend for an Arabic grammar book and bought it at the Princeton University Store.

Given the lack of tools we'd been provided, it's amazing how we managed to persevere once we settled into Libya.

Hastened Hitchings

On the day before shipping out to Libya, I typed up a six-page critique of our training and sent it to Robert Steiner, head of the North African Desk at the Peace Corps in Washington. I pointed out that program director Al Wight had promised that Arabic would be spoken at one meal, and English at the next. No Arabic homework was meted out. He called for cross-cultural case studies. Never done. He called for training in geography, economics, religion, folklore, architecture, art, music, dances, handicrafts, agriculture, transportation, dress, ethnic groups. Never done. He praised role play as an ideal, practical teaching tool. Never done. At meetings, we would make up to twenty suggestions. He never once wrote one of these down.

He pooh-poohed war stories from RPCVs as "undigested experiences" of "limited value." *Au contraire*, M. Wight, we found these rare presentations fascinating and invaluable. Of many suggestions from RPCVs from Libya I like that of Alan Frank, many were of practical advice, e.g., before putting your shoes on in the morning, shake them out, because scorpions love to snuggle up inside shoes during the night. The core idea of D-groups he espoused was that participants would learn to work in groups. However, in Libya, we would be operating as individual teachers, not part of groups at all.

I concluded in my report:

> The mismanagement of our program reduced our morale, our sense of direction and purpose, our confidence our idealism, and worked almost at conscious cross-purposes to the objectives of the Peace Corps. I strongly recommend

that Mr. Al Wight not be invited to any further Peace
Corps programs in a managerial or supervisory capacity.

In parallel to my interim activities, on October 7 Neil McCabe
went to hear a Hubert Humphrey speech in his hometown of Scranton,
Pennsylvania. Apparently he didn't make much of an impression on Neil
because he ended up voting for the Peace and Freedom Party ticket of
Dick Gregory (comedian) and Mark Lane (JFK assassination conspiracy
theorist).

John and Andrea Murphy and Don and Lani Leydig left Bisbee training a few days early to go to Boston—to get married. At Bisbee airport,
they were supposed to get a flight on the aforementioned ace airline,
Apache. Apache was to fly them to Tucson, where they had a connecting
flight to Boston. The Apache Airlines plane, instead of landing, simply
circled the field twice, then left! With their bags, the two couples hopped
onto a Peace Corps truck driven by Tom Weinz to high-tail it to Tucson,
some 95 miles away. Then the truck had a blowout. There was no spare.
The Murphys and Leydigs hopped out of that truck and hitchhiked in the
back of a pickup truck, urging the driver to hotfoot it. They barely made
their flight.

There was a fly in the ointment for Bob and Anne Conway. Despite
their having done well in Arabic and getting along famously with people,
they were told by a hard-ass Field Assessment Officer at the end of training
in Bisbee that they were being kicked out of the program. Being children
of the '60s, instead of flying home, they flew directly to the Peace Corps
office in Washington, D.C. to protest. They spoke to an accommodating
staffer who said he'd look into it. He got back to them and said that
someone had anonymously accused them of smoking dope. The Conways
found this to be a rather flimsy excuse to deselect them. They lobbied day
after day to get reinstated. It was touch and go as the flight to Libya was
only days away. They were finally cleared and managed to get to JFK at
literally the last minute.

Somehow the Bisbee program administrators had forgotten to give
the last set of gamma globulin shots to the volunteers. So, before boarding
their plane at the TWA transit lounge, all the men had to pull down their

pants and all the women had to pull down their slacks or raise their skirts to get their shots in the rear.

Only in 2018 did I discover, thanks to Kevin Hunt, that 17 male trainees, including him, were told that they had not been cleared to go to Libya by their draft boards, but they must nonetheless show up at the airport fully prepared to both go to Libya or to be severely disappointed at not getting a deferment. Talk about trepidation! At the very last minute, they all got "presidential deferments." (No wonder there was so much drinking on the plane!)

On October 11, 1968 with great anticipation, I rode out of the East Side Bus Terminal to JFK Airport. I sought out and met Jeanne Maurey who turned out to be a pretty, petite, spunky blonde. (Beyond spunky, I didn't know till researching this book that she had won the Senior Prize for Best Sportswoman at Rollins. Turns out she had never met a sport she didn't like and did them all—basketball, volleyball, softball, archery, gymnastics, etc.) We boarded a chartered TWA 707. (Another flight, a chartered KLM plane, flew other Bisbee trainees from JFK to Amsterdam, Rome and then Tripoli.) According to one Bisbee woman, right after take-off, the pilot circled the Statue of Liberty so we could see it from both sides of the plane.

On the flight I got to sit next to Jeanne, with Mike Lee on her other side. While I was crestfallen that she was going to be posted to Benghazi, a full 700 miles away from my village, we and the jet covered a lot of ground. Jeanne's recollection of the flight was far more colorful than mine, "I had a ball meeting 90 single men, singing, exchanging notes on training programs, drinking wine and scotch and forgetting all about our destination." I must have made a tremendous impression on Jeanne as in a letter to her parents she wrote, "I ended up between two guys on the plane."

It is only in hindsight some 50 years later that I realize how blind I was—or just too busy thinking about my Libya future—to what a large circle of new friends I had embraced in mere months. This included 108 trainees, 31 Libyans, several staff members, a handful of teachers and 30 students at the Hunter's Point Navajo school, Kiffy Brown, Jane Harrison, and my girlfriend Nancy Waddoups. Of course, among them there were those I hung out with more and whose friendship I now so treasure. At the time, lost on me. Callow youth!

Also, in hindsight, here we were thinking we were about to hop on a jet plane to travel well over 4,000 miles to a foreign country. What we were really doing was traveling to the past. It turned out we fell into three categories of such travel. Those of us stationed in cities were only slightly in the past. Those of us in towns more so. Those of us in remote villages with no electricity and no running water, were literally embedded in ancient times.

How to conduct a bus tour without talking? Read on!

Pepsis, Poker and Pimples

Saturday, October 12, 1968. Approaching the Tripoli airport, Tom Furth, sensitized to Libyans' attitudes towards Jews (and warned by the Peace Corps of the serious danger he would face were his background to be revealed) stared at a field in the required landing card asking for "Religion," He wrote in "Protestant." As we touched down, three "Hoorays!" filled the cabin. "Three" tied into the origin of the Libyan capital's name. Tripoli comes from the Greek "tri" for "three" and "polis" for "city." The three cities the Greeks were referring to were actually spread out over 165 miles. Two of the cities, Sabratha and Leptis Magna, are to this day major, well preserved Roman ruins replete with arches, columns, buildings, amphitheaters, columns, etc. In fact, Leptis is the most intact Roman ruin in the world. And it's 1.5 square miles in size. The third city, where the current Tripoli is, was Oea, which in 1968 was the name of a popular local beer. The Libyans Arabicized "Tripoli" into "Trablus" (since there is no "p" in Arabic). Our first hint of history was spotted at the airport, where John Murphy observed a hangar still riddled with bullet holes from World War II. As we rode our buses into town, I gazed out the window. I saw a camel, many horses, and prickly pears lining the roads. I learned later that prickly pears are a favorite snack of camels, whose lips, tongues and mouths are so thick they are oblivious to spines.

Harold McElhinny noticed that the road from the airport to Tripoli, lined with eucalyptus trees, was gaily decorated, with rugs on display and crowds energetically waving Libyan flags. He told the volunteers on the bus that this was a planned Welcome Wagon greeting for the Peace Corps. The volunteers enthusiastically waved back. It was only later we learned that King Idris had just proceeded us along the same parade route.

More touches of history as we noticed that much of the architecture in Tripoli was yellow Italianate buildings with arcades above the sidewalks, which some describe as "Mussolini Modern."

Quintessential Italianate façades in Tripoli.

To my dismay, there was no chance to linger with Jeanne as all the Benghazi people shipped out that very day. I took a room at the Capitol Hotel with lanky, square-jawed Michigan grad Ern Snook. Conked out for four hours. Supper? Pepsis and chicken. Later we learned there was nary a Coke to be had in Libya due to an Arab-world-wide embargo because they sell Coke in Israel. They pronounce the drink "bebsi" of course. (The way to teach an Arabic speaker to properly pronounce a "p" [which is a plosive, meaning air is propelled outward] is to hold a lighted match in front of him and make him say a "b" but in such a way as to blow out the match.) Diary: "Don't believe I'm here…No culture shock yet at all."

Before flying off to Benghazi, Cathy Kaiser and other Benghazi-bound single-women PCVs were told, "We're going to give you a bus tour of Tripoli." What a delightful prospect! They hopped on the bus. A Libyan tour guide stood up front. He proceeded to say absolutely *nothing* for the whole length of the tour. It turns out that Libyan men are not allowed to speak to one woman, much less a busload of them. A mini-lesson for us to anticipate the unanticipated.

At 7 AM the next day I was awakened by a combination of early morning light, the clamor of street noise and a shower which went on all by itself. I ventured out to change money at a bank. I noticed that the Libyans don't form lines. They just swarm. You have to just keep pressing forward and hope the flow eventually gets you near a teller. (I learned years later while in Saudi Arabia the trick to getting to the front of the herd. Since 80% of Arabs are named Mohammed, you just wave your hand and shout "Mohammed" at the teller. 80% of the time he'll think you must be a friend, and he'll wave you up front.)

We all met with country director Bill Whitman for a few hours in the morning, then were treated to a reception at Ambassador David Newsom's house, hosted by gracious and pretty Jean Newsom.

When volunteer Peter Hawkes explored Tripoli, he noticed an outdoor coffee stand. To order the coffee, he wanted to say *"Nibbi haliib ib gahwah"* ("I want milk with coffee"). But what came out of his mouth was *"Nibbi habiib ib gahwah,"* which means "I want love with coffee." The man selling the coffee reached over and covered Peter's hand with his. "I quickly withdrew my hand but learned an important lesson: good pronunciation can be critical."

The next day I went to the Peace Corps office for motorcycle training, but it never happened. To avoid total loss, I studied some Arabic word lists while there. I went out to buy aerogrammes (thin-paper, pre-paid stationery that folds neatly into an envelope) and toilet paper. Since we already knew Arab toilets had no toilet paper, I was careful to stuff a wad of it in my right rear pants pocket. This saved my butt, literally, many times over the next 12 months. I toured the old city, more colorful and exotic than Tripoli proper by far.

King Idris I's palace—Tripoli

Libyan lady doll-maker in Tripoli

Tripoli: sifters and darbukas

Tripoli street scene

Tripoli: shoe shop

The next morning, I studied some verb lists, read *Newsweek*, then hopped on a bus with Dan Peters, Mike Lee, Gary Dallman, Stu Magee (Franklin and Marshall College) and Ed Collier for the two-hour-plus drive to Garian, a mid-sized city of about 40,000 in the mountains where we would stage before venturing out to our villages.

Tripoli bus station

Formerly, Garian had been a troglodyte town. The residents lived in caves that were carved out of solid earth below ground level. Now, they lived in houses but used the old cave homes as cooler summer homes. I was immediately struck by the friendliness of everyone there.

Garian, Libya at sunset

I enjoyed speaking French with the Tunisian and Algerian staff at the Hotel Jebel ("mountain") which boasted no hot water. To pass the time that evening, I whipped out my guitar and sang songs with Peters, Lee and Magee. We didn't know how long it would be before we went to our villages. Unbeknownst to us at the time, the school year had started a month earlier and you would have thought the Ministry of Education would want to whisk us out as quickly as possible to our villages. This was our first inkling that in Arab countries time can be more expandable that we're used to in the West.

Over the next eight days, I shopped for various items: a kerosene stove, kerosene, a radio, a washtub, a blanket, a frying pan, a can opener, Tide, a broom, a plate, some glasses, a cup, a spoon, a mirror and a bed. Learned how to play two Libyan card games, Scuba and Scunbeel. (In a letter to his parents, Dan Peters wrote, "in Scunbeel, the jack is higher than the queen. We had a discussion on whether this reflects the Moslem attitude that women are inferior.") Also played poker and hearts with the guys. Managed to vote in the U.S. presidential election via absentee ballot. Played my trumpet. Studied Arabic. We soon learned that Garian had no restaurants, so for meals we improvised. One meal consisted of bread, mackerel, bananas, cheese, pear juice and "Bebsi." One supper I was exposed for the first time to the hot pepper (cayenne) so common to Libyan food. It burned my tongue. In Garian I was plagued with diarrhea. Took a long walk to the south of Garian with Dan Peters. Read *A Comedy of Errors*. Read some *Seize the Day* by Saul Bellow. A number of charming small talks with shopkeepers. Marveled at people riding around on donkeys and a man who clambered about on all fours. I marveled also at the displays of fruits and vegetables outside the shops. In the U.S. I was used to goods that were canned, packaged, jarred or frozen. Here, nothing of the sort. Everything was fresh and piled into burlap sacks, open for inspection. I availed myself of two delicious fruits I had never eaten—dates and pomegranates. I didn't know at the time how important dates were to the local economy. Not just as a foodstuff, but dates were a key staple lugged in bulk by camels as sustenance for caravan travel.

The last four days were rainy, foggy and cold. Due to lack of hot water and wearing the same clothes for over a week, I broke out in itchy pimples on my feet, my back, my arms, my shoulders.

Despite having spent a full eight days in Garian, talking to locals, taking long walks here and there, not a soul mentioned to us that just outside the city limits was an incredible, huge and unique work of art. Had I known (instead of learning about it 50 years later), I and the others would certainly have made a bee-line there. It was known as "The Lady of Garian."

The remarkable story goes back to World War II. In July 1942, an Arabic-speaking American volunteer ambulance driver of Egyptian and Lebanese heritage, gifted artist and muralist serving in Field Marshal Montgomery's 8th Army, sustained a severe shrapnel wound to the head. His name was Clifford Saber. After six months of recuperation, he doggedly insisted on getting back into action, participating in the liberation of Tripoli on January 23, 1943. (By the by, Winston Churchill found the time to visit soon thereafter.)

**Winston Churchill and Field Marshal Montgomery,
reviewing troops in Libya, February 3, 1943**

Photo by Struan MacGibbon

The brigade was ordered to post to Garian. A letter of Saber's conveys
their relationship with the Libyans:

It's always a great mystery in the 8th Army where the
natives come from, where they are going, and how they
manage to survive in the barren waste. It seems that as
soon as a convoy pauses, no matter what part of the desert it is traveling through it will be seized by several wogs
[pejorative term used by Westerners to describe Chinese,
Arabs, etc. It stands for 'Wily Oriental Gentleman'] carrying eggs of questionable age and producing squawking
chickens from the folds of their cloaks. They are only too
eager to barter for precious tea. In the most violent sandstorms, they amble up to the cars, begging cigarettes and
trading eggs. We met two brothers who were typical of
the Tripolitanian Arab: honest, hospitable and friendly. I
soon learned that those poor Arabs who refused to fight
for the Italians were shot, hanged or bayoneted.

Upon arrival in Garian, they housed themselves in an abandoned Italian barracks. Saber came upon a huge, empty recreation hall. As Saber recounts it, "Its bare white walls were a temptation to doodle, especially for me. Being a muralist and having time on my hands, I decided to do some large-scale doodling." He goes on:

> I had previously done pinup-girl murals on board ship, under the bunks and on cabin doors (these in good taste). On the coast near Sirte were some intact Italian houses. In one of these, I had done some murals which caused quite a commotion among the women-starved men. The one opposite the door depicted three luscious nudes, one reclining, one facing the door, and one whose back was turned. For the recreation room at Garian, I decided upon a super-duper nude encompassing the entire wall, 30 x 15 feet.

The result was a fanciful combination of a voluptuous nude woman whose body contours formed the Libyan Coast, and scores of mini-illustrations of parachuting soldiers, boots, airplanes, tanks, and soldiers drinking water, soldiers sitting atop a mosque's minaret, soldiers rowing a boat. A true *pièce de résistance.*

"Lady of Garian" master mural

Herewith some details that you can't suss out from the overall photograph above:

"Lady of Garian" detail

"Lady of Garian" medium detail of mural

The piece was completed on March 3, 1943. After the war it became, of course, a major tourist destination. Sometime around 1996, during

Ghaddafi's reign, this priceless artwork was destroyed, no doubt for puritanical reasons. Ghaddafi himself eliminated two other priceless monuments. In 1980 he destroyed a statue of the Emperor Septimius Severus that had been pilfered from Leptis Magna. And in 2000, he bulldozed the tomb of Omar Mukhtar.

On October 24, a sunny, warm day, we scarfed down scrambled eggs and potatoes for breakfast. Then associate director Martin Sampson helped Dan Peters and me stow our belongings aboard his International pickup. We headed off to our villages. We were part of a staggered roll-out of Peace Corps volunteers fanning out all over Libya. Many single males were assigned to live alone in remote villages. Jack Seifert was assigned to Ghat in southwesternmost Libya, 830 miles south of the Mediterranean. Mike Culkin was headed to a Saharan oasis in Al Taj in Cyrenaica (the vast eastern province of Libya), 615 miles south of Benghazi. Some men were doubled up with one or two other PCVs. Some with Libyans. The single women from Bisbee were to be stationed in the two large cities— Tripoli and Benghazi—or in fair-sized cities like Derna, in groups of two or three. The married couples from Bisbee were scattered throughout the country, including deep in the Fezzan in the remote city of Sebha. As you can see from the map at the beginning of this book, the distribution of we volunteers was not evenly spread out. It was driven by coastal areas and oases, i.e. wherever there was water. The rest of the country consisted of vast swaths of nothing.

A memorable event transpired in the spring of 1968, when Bob Pearson and Bill Whitman, the country director, were scouting schools in the Fezzan. They arrived at one village at dusk. Not finding the principal in his office, they were told he was behind the school. Behind said school, in a field, silhouetted by the orange setting sun, the entire male population of the village, 200 strong, chanted in Arabic. Not wanting to intrude, Bob and Bill stood back to watch. It turns out the village males were all chanting the entire Koran by heart. Bob and Bill watched, transfixed, for an hour.

Bob Pearson tells the Kafka-esque backstory of how the villages in Cyrenaica were chosen for the volunteers. In September of 1968, he had met with the Minister of Education in Derna to learn which schools would be part of the program. When Bob asked "Why not?" she explained that no one had visited the schools to get permission because they had no vehicles. So, Bob, English inspector Bill Perkis and Sudanese Ali Suleiman had to traipse all over Cyrenaica in a commandeered International Harvester Scout for weeks to arrange for 50 locations of assigned schools. They personally met with the *mudir* (headmaster) of each school, asking if he would welcome an American teacher to teach English in his fifth grade.

The famous "Mae West" mosque in Benghazi

**Benghazi: outside Jeanne Maurey's temporary room
at the single women's hotel—The National**

A fair-sized contingent of single women and couples descended upon Benghazi. Once they arrived in Benghazi, Cathy Kaiser and her friends needed to taxi to their assigned post in Derna, a coastal town some 180 miles to the east. The way taxis work in Libya is you get into a Peugeot. But you can't go yet. You have to wait until the taxi is filled, *then* you go. Packed with two other women (Mary Buelt and Trudy Swartzentruber) and four men (including Mark Lepori and John Lynch) the taxi finally took off. With no rest stops or gas stations one has to stop periodically to relieve oneself. The substitute, for both men and women, was ruins. The taxi driver would stop at a Greek ruin, Roman ruin, Italian ruin along the way. The women had to "find a nice cozy wall out of sight to take care of things."

None of these PCVs had been given any directions to find the Ministry of Education in Derna. So, upon their arrival, this Libyan, Mohammed Mejnoon, rushes up to greet them, saying "Welcome! Welcome to Derna! I'll take care of everything." The PCVs were relieved, feeling they were in good hands. (They had apparently not yet learned that *mejnoon* is "crazy" in Arabic. That would've been their first clue.) Mohammed explained that there were only two hotels in town and one was filled with a visiting soccer team. He guided them up to the other, a fleabag hotel that had been built for German officers in World War II and said "I'll pick you up in the morning." Since their bags were coming separately, the group had no change of clothes and had to sleep in dirty shirts. At 5 AM they were shaken awake by the megaphone blast of morning prayer from the minaret of the mosque next door to the hotel: "Allaho El Akbar! Allaho El Akbar!"

Mme. Fatia Ashura was the dynamic, fearsome, highly respected Egyptian who was Minister of Education for Cyrenaica. She was married to a prince and nephew of King Idris, soon to be dubbed by PCs as "The Gas Station Prince." Through the grapevine, she had heard where these newbie PCVs were.

It was then time for her to officially dispatch these new Peace Corps volunteers to their villages. But when it came to normal-sized John Lynch, who had been promised to the villages of El Gaigab and Laluda, she re-assigned them to the large and imposing Mark Lepori. John protested, "Hey, those are supposed to be my villages!" She replied, "You can't go to those villages, they will eat you alive!"

She initially assigned Cathy, Mary and Trudy to an apartment already occupied by an Egyptian woman named Selwa and a Palestinian named Sohaila. The American women's total quarters consisted of a screened-inporch with three Army cots. Mme. Fatia (whom the men PCV's had dubbed "Madame Fats" due to her girth) moved them out after a couple of weeks into an apartment with beautiful tile floors and huge rooms.

To get to his village of Al Gurta Ashati deep in the Fezzan, Kevin Hunt was driven through magnificent, aerodynamically sculpted sand dunes via Land Rover. Despite the beauty of the scene, he was quite frightened as they raced up and over the dunes. He ended up rooming with four Libyans.

Ern Snook was assigned to two villages in The Fezzan, Ubari and Dissa. He had 36 students in Ubari but only four in Dissa. However, in Dissa they had set up a ping-pong table where proficient players Ern, a Pakistani electrician and a Palestinian teacher ended up playing fierce games including slams and trash talk, with amazed cheering from the students. "We paused one game so that the locals could light a fire around a scorpion in the courtyard and watch it sting itself to death."

Ern Snook's fifth grade classroom in Ubari

Picturesque approach to Ern Snook's second village of Dissa

Stoney Bird and other PCVs had to hole up in Sebha for weeks awaiting their Moto Guzzis. No sooner had Stoney's group arrived than Madame Soo, the wife of a Taiwanese doctor, invited them over for dinner and bridge. Going forward, every Saturday night the Soos invited Stoney and two or three tables' worth of visitors to play bridge. Eventually Stoney was able to get out to his oasis village, Ar-Rugeiba, 24 miles southwest of Sebha.

As for Dan and me, from Garian on our way to our postings, the first stop, after an hour, was my village, Al Gala, ("castle" in Berber) in the Nefusa Mountains, 85 miles due south of Tripoli. The next stop was Dan's village, El Khozeur, on a mesa at the foot of the mountains some ten miles away.

Tiny village of El Khozeur

And, in the next chapter, who knew that there was a unique form of Libyan tribesmen who wore veils!

Buongiornos!

One might expect that my emotions, upon finally reaching my appointed village would have been overwhelmingly transported, transformative, transcendental. All my training and anticipation had led up to this very moment. But, "The diary does not lie." I simply wrote, "Good to be here." I plunked my stuff down into an apartment attached to the local high school.

My hillside apartment adjoining the high school in Al Gala

A light-yellow structure on the top of a deeply canyoned village with a kitchen, very large main room, and two large other rooms. No plumbing, no electricity. I walked down the very steep hill about a half-mile into the village. (In recent cartographical research I was able to determine that from the lowest elevation in the village to my place it was 662 feet, or more than the length of two football fields. Way steep!) I noticed electricity poles and wires strung out all over the village, later learning that at some indeterminate time they would turn on the juice. (I never got any.)

As I entered the center of the village, I noted that all the houses were one-story light-yellow adobe-like structures. A klatch of screaming ragamuffins wearing shib-shibs (flip-flops) kicking up dust like so many Pig-Pens immediately surrounded me.

"Buongiorno! Buongiorno!"

At first I thought this strange, then realized the only pale-skinned people these villagers had ever seen were the Italians whose occupation of Libya ended in 1945, a mere 23 years before I arrived. For them, this was the circus come to town. Thanks to our training, and super-teach (John Rassias from Clearfield) in particular, on impulse I decided to turn this into a teachable moment.

"No!" I said, "Hello, how are you?" They were taken aback.

"Hello, how are you?" I repeated.

"Hello, how are you?" they shouted, trilling the "r." In my forays into the village I was invariably accosted by these urchins. I coached them until they totally forgot "Buongiorno" and assailed me instead with "Hello, how are you!"

In Aujila, an oasis town in the Sahara, 252 miles to the south of Benghazi in the Eastern Province of Cyrenaica, Bob Marshall encountered the same kind of mini-me mini-mob chasing after him in the streets. "It really bugs me to be followed by kids when I go anywhere." He did relate there was an old man in town that always greeted him with "Buongiorno, Maestro!" Just getting to Aujila had been an ordeal. On his way the Ministry of Education's Land Rover broke down six times, averaging two hours for each breakdown, a total of 12 hours of just being stuck. Upon arrival, he noted in his diary: "It is a carless hamlet, with narrow sand pathways weaving between the sheer clay walls of old houses. Palm trees are everywhere." Struck by the unusual bumpy architecture of what he termed the "Friday Mosque" in the village, Bob to stopped at length to sketch it for posterity.

Bob Marshall's sketch of the Friday Mosque in Aujila

Dan Peters was a tad shocked when he showed up in the isolated village of El Khozeur. "No electricity, no running water, no cars in the village, no shops, no cafés and a mailman only once a week if I am lucky."

Greg Strick's assigned village was Sidi Mahius about 100 miles northeast of Benghazi. A van dropped him off on a plateau six miles away. He had lugged his suitcase most of the way when a beat-up old Hillman car approached. It was his headmaster. He'd been driving into Benghazi, but instead drove him the rest of the way to his village.

In Qasr Bin Gashir near Tripoli, one of John Maclean's schoolrooms has to have been the smallest in all of Libya—8 feet wide and 14 feet long.

Bob Suzuki was posted way east in Tobruk, near the Egyptian border, in an area that had been occupied by Germans during the war. Various walls in the town still displayed instructions in German from The Führer.

It took Bob Gausman 18 hours on a bus to get to Samnu, deep in the Fezzan. Every few hours, the bus would stop. All the men would go off on one side of the bus to pee, and all the women would go to the other side to squat. Samnu was on the old trade route from black Africa, and thus many darker-skinned Libyans living there.

Richard Massey was posted to the village of Farzougha near Benghazi.

Children of the *mudir* (principal) of Farzougha School

For some reason Neil McCabe and Roger Scott were the last ones placed. They were posted to Gara Bulli, an hour to the east of Tripoli, an area with many truck farms. Instead of Moto Guzzis they were issued an International Harvester truck. It couldn't go more than ten feet without getting mired in the sand. So they were vehicle-less for a spell, walking or hitching rides, usually on a tractor, to and from their schools each day. Finally, Neil and Roger were issued Moto Guzzis.

Maggie and Mark Brossoit were posted to Tripoli, living kitty-corner from King Idris's palace. She and Mark were assigned to teach at the Men's Teacher Training College, as were Lani Leydig and her husband, Donald. Their commute? A three-mile walk, followed by a bus ride. The students were in their early twenties, and when the two women marched into the college courtyard the first time, the balconies were ringed with students who stared. And stared. (They later got used to having these women teachers around.) Conditions were so crowded there were three students jammed into desks meant for two. One of their fellow teachers was a Palestinian who had no electricity. To prepare his lessons, he was forced to go out in the street and squat under a streetlamp to work.

Jim and Joyce Swanson were posted to the medium-sized town Tarhuna, about 60 miles southeast of Tripoli. It was considered to be a garden spot, because it sported a number of almond trees. While they had running water, they had no electricity but they had a neighbor who threw an extension cord over the wall so they could partake. I would guess that Jim, who taught at a teacher training school, had the largest class in Libya, 60 students strong.

John and Andrea Murphy were posted to Suani-ben-Adem about 15 miles south of Tripoli. John taught two all-boy classes, one at the Suani school and the other in the village of Mia Min five miles to the south. In this latter school, the ages of the 5th grade kids ranged from 9 to 20 years old. (The older boys had flunked 5th grade up to 11 times!) Andrea taught two classes in Suani, one all boys, the other 20 boys and six girls. An indication of the acceptance of women in education could be found in the junior high school. At that school, there were 250 students, only three of whom were girls.

John Murphy's classroom in Mia Min

King Idris owned a compound on the outskirts of Suani. Three royal guards there asked John to teach them English. He obliged, teaching them at the junior high just 50 yards from John and Andrea's home. After each lesson, instead of letting John walk back to his nearby house, the guards insisted on taking him all the way back to the compound courtyard, then driving him home the 50 yards in the king's Mercedes-Benz coupe.

Bob and Anne Conway were posted to Brak in the Fezzan where Martin Sampson had served in Libya I. The villagers very much admired "Teacher Martin" as, among other things, he had fasted for Ramadan. His best friend, Omar Ahmed soon became the Conways' best friend. Bob taught at two nearby villages, Agar and Tamzawa. He found the small classes and the children's positive disposition "a dream." And the kids adored Bob and vice-versa. "I want to emphasize that, among all the intense experiences, the response of the kids was far and away the most rewarding. What a leap of faith for them to accept us so quickly and so fully, then to work so hard and learn so much so eagerly." Joe Connor was posted to Aljmail, where all the kids wanted to know if he personally knew Mohammed Ali.

The McElhinnys were assigned to Zawia on the coast to the west of Tripoli. Their home was right next to a mosque. At first, they thought this a nice picturesque touch. Until 5 AM every morning, when, even before chanting *Allaho Al-Akbar* over the speaker system, the muezzin would clear this throat, hacking away at the mike on at full blast for several minutes before launching into his summons to prayer.

Being further away from the mosque, Diane Forasté remembers, "Five times a day, we heard the call to prayer from the local minaret. We grew to love that sound, as well as the Arabic music we heard from our neighbors' places."

As for me, I asked about and managed to meet the principal of the Al Gala school, Belgassim Aribi.

My sketch of Belgassim Aribi

Belgassim Aribi in the flesh

I also met a delicately featured, thin, bright teacher my age named Milaad Ahmed Khalifa. I shopped a bit. This didn't take long as there were only two small one-room shops and one butcher. Milaad treated me to supper in his small, one-room shack with a corrugated iron roof and a dirt floor. He used one pot to cook everything. He had obviously never cleaned the outside as it had about a quarter inch of baked-in black soot all over it. We got along right off the bat.

Milaad makes tea

Back *chez moi* my automatic instinct was to flick on a light switch. Not! Gotta learn how to fire up the ol' Coleman lantern! I had earlier poured kerosene into the silvery base of the lamp. But kerosene lamps need alcohol to jump-start a steady flame. So, you first need to pump pressure into the base with a five-inch long embedded pump handle. Inside the glass housing above there's a "mantle," a suspended spherical, white, netted piece of silk that is, in effect, a fancy wick. You pour some starter alcohol on the mantle, light it with a match, then the kerosene wicks up and provides a continuous fuel for the flame. It's a nice bright light for short distances and the lamp emits a soft hissing sound. A lot more steps than flicking a light switch. It did have a handle on top so you could carry it around. (I've since learned that the mantle was permeated with thorium oxide. Radioactive! They've since replaced it with non-radioactive yttrium.)

The very next day, a Friday and the weekly day off, I decided to grow my first mustache. I have no idea what symbolism this had for me. Milaad and I hitchhiked to a nearby town named Yifran, getting several rides in the back of Volkswagen pickup trucks. Hand signals for hitchhiking vary from country to country. Milaad demonstrated the Libyan style to me. You dangle your right hand by your side and move it back and forth.

(Hitchhiking was much more prevalent and easier in Libya than the U.S. at the time, no doubt driven by the requisites of poverty.)

Yifran's population was about 8,000, vs. Al Gala's perhaps 500. I bought a lamp, a meat grinder, a rug, a can-opener, a funnel and various doodads. Upon my return, I had to get water. On this topic anyway, the Peace Corps had prepared us well. At their behest, I had purchased two plastic jerry cans that held several gallons. And some burlap. And some rope. Next door in the courtyard of the high school was an underground cistern that collected the rain run-off from the school roof. It was quite large, about sixty feet long and 15 feet wide. Totally covered, except for a hinged trap door at one end with a bucket on a rope. I'd drop the bucket into the water, haul it up, pour water into my jerry can via a funnel. And repeat till the can was full.

I hauled the jerry can back to my apartment. Of course, such water is hardly fit for human consumption, so I used the kerosene stove to boil water, then poured the water into the other jerry can. I swathed this jerry can with burlap and secured it with rope. Then, I soaked the burlap with unboiled water. This triggers evaporation, which cools the water. The result was safe and tasted fine. When water is so scarce, you soon develop a deep appreciation for every drop of it. While the average annual rainfall in the U.S. is 30 inches, in Libya overall it's six inches. In the Libyan Sahara desert it's two inches. And in Jim Seroogy's village of Ajedabiya it's virtually zero!

In Derna, Mark Lepori used another recommended method to purify the water and it worked for him. He'd fetch water from his well, then just add iodine to kill the bacteria.

Speaking of evaporation, in another example of Clearfield staff not providing us with useful tips, John Maclean learned a trick to cope with the heat they never told us about. Wet a sheet, position chairs at either end of your bed, stretch the sheet as a canopy between the chairs. Lay in the bed. Then, the evaporation of the water cools you off.

Another adjustment, which fortunately the Peace Corps had instructed us about, was dealing with toilets. Mine was a Turkish toilet (hole in the floor, two designated areas to place your feet and squat). We were to pour unboiled water to flush, but the soiled toilet paper had to be burned as it would not flush down. So, beside the toilet was a pack of matches and a tin can to burn the paper in. After dark in Sabratha, John Forasté would surreptitiously take a metal bucket of used toilet paper out to "a small pit outside our house and start a fire. One time I was visited halfway through this ritual by friendly neighbors. They didn't seem to notice the toilet paper, nor my great embarrassment, only the warmth any fire brings to a conversation."

In Surman, Sue and Bob Glover had a Turkish toilet in their home. Handy Bob built a toilet seat out of an old desk so they could sit down without squatting. Bob also built a bathtub out of corrugated aluminum. He ensconced a propane stove under it so they could enjoy hot baths. Sue then figured out the bathtub could do double duty as a place to wash clothes. Ever-resourceful Bob also figured out how to mount a screen on the windows. Once the word got out, everyone in town wanted Bob to build them screens.

Don and Lani Leydig, like most of us, also had a propane stove. But the pipe from the propane container did not directly connect, no matter how they tried, to the stove. There was a short gap. So, to light the stove, Don would light a match and turn his head away until the gap exploded as it made the connection.

I ventured into my village and sat down on the dirt floor of Abdu-Salaam's ("Servant of Peace") shop. For the first time, I witnessed the Libyan tea-making ceremony with its multiple steps, including adding sugar, the pouring back and forth of the tea from one blue teapot to another. The tea-maker adroitly pours it from a distance of two feet through the air—very impressive.

Elaborate Libyan tea ceremony

In fact, Libyan men love to make a competition out of it this, to see who can pour the tea from the greatest height. This serves to aerate the tea to enhance the flavor. The tea, nice and bubbly, is served in shot glasses, often with peanuts or almonds added to make things special. (Jim Putnam in Aljmail recalls them shelling the peanuts, roasting them, putting them onto brass trays, then onto a scale, then rolling their hands on the peanuts to take off the skins. The peanuts would then get nicely crisp and brown.) They offered me a glass. Delicious! Upon finishing my glass, I started to get up. Someone put a hand on my shoulder pushing me back down into sitting position. They poured me another glass. I inferred from this that the custom is to have two glasses of tea. After my second glass, I started to get up again, and again, a hand pushed me down. OK, we'll see where this goes. After the third glass, I got up to go and no one stopped me. So, the rule is you must drink at least three glasses of tea. (I had assumed this was a custom throughout Libya, but later found out from Bob Marshall that in Aujila the standard was two, with an option to add mint.)

With respect to the Libyan's elaborate tea ceremony, I was finally able to replicate the pouring of the tea from teapot to teapot in a two-foot long stream and served it often.

On June 19, 1969, Ed White (who had studied Arabic at Princeton and Harvard) took over the country directorship in Libya from Bill Whitman. He was on his way to visit a village. A car passed them, then slowed up, then let them pass the car. Then the same car passed them again, slowed up and let them pass. Mystified, Ed pulled over. The Libyans in the other car stopped. The Libyans said, "Why didn't you stop?" Ed said, "Stop for what?" The Libyans said, "We wanted to give you tea. You can't take a long drive without tea!"

The next day, on the heels of preparing my first lesson plan, Saturday, October 26, 1968 I taught my first, honest-to-goodness class of 35 boys in fifth grade. (For individual photos of all my students, see the Appendix.) The classroom was threadbare, with open windows (no glass, no screens). A battered, worn wooden door. From the get-go, I realized I was conducting things too slowly and needed to pick up the pace.

I taught the same class another time later in the morning and observed that they learned very fast. Belgassim, the principal of the Al Gala school, invited me to lunch. It was the first time I had ever had couscous, and for sure it would not be the last. Loved it.

I noticed that my fellow teachers and villagers referred to me as "Mr. Randy." Quaint! Since then, I've learned this was standard fare all over Libya, "Mr. John," "Mr. Roy," etc. Cathy Kaiser was called "Miss Cathy." Jeanne Maurey was "Miss Jeannie." But there were some exceptions. Rebecca Peterson let her fellow Libyan teachers know she was referred to as "Becky." But they said they couldn't call her that. She asked why not and they replied that "becky" literally means "cry" in Arabic. "Why would your family give you a sorrowful name," they asked. So they called her "Rifgah," which means "companion." Trudy Swartzentruber's first name, for some reason, was difficult for her students (let them try the last name!) so they ended up calling her "Miss Tree." Mary Ellen McElhinny was called "Yebla Mary," a term of respect for a teacher. And in Tripoli, since she neither smoked nor drank, Kathy Lamoureux's landlord called her "Hajja Kathy" (meaning one who had gone on the Hajj).

Meanwhile, over in the village of Athrun in Cyrenaica, Dave Munro, on his first day tried to cook a small pot of stew on a wobbly, small, three-legged Primus kerosene stove on the floor. The stove keeled over, spilling the contents. Dave scraped it off the floor and gamely placed it back in the pot. The local police chief, Abdul Al-Jalil Omar (known more familiarly as "Hajj") had observed this and took pity on Dave. He said "Forget it and just come to my house for supper." This was not a one-off event—for the whole year Dave ate every single evening at Hajj's! Hajj had served with the British in World War II. He was in the habit of ostentatiously parading about Athrun in his sergeant's uniform, sporting a jaunty beret, while he swung his swagger stick about. He also was the proud owner of a WWII-era BSA motorcycle. He taught Dave how to ride his Moto Guzzi and was "invaluable at keeping my infernal machine well maintained."

Dave taught TEFL to six fifth-graders in Athrun (five boys and one unveiled girl) and to a class of nine (six boys and three unveiled girls) in the neighboring village of Ras Al-Hilal, driving his Moto Guzzi between the two schools. As Dave describes it, "I had a beautiful half-hour drive along the Mediterranean coastline every morning, dotted with numerous coves where chiseled white cliffs overlooked the blue-green sea and past a few ancient ruins, framed sentinel-like at the water's edge."

He made the acquaintance of an eccentric, dotty "relic of bygone colonial glory, Miss Olive Brittan, MBE. Miss Brittan was the King's Bee Keeper, responsible for a sprawling bee farm." She'd been a volunteer British Army ambulance driver in Palestine during World War II. After giving Dave a short tour around her farm, Miss Brittan asked Dave what exactly he was doing in the Peace Corps. When he responded, she declared, "Well, you should be teaching them hygiene, not English!"

"She then caught my arm and said, 'Whatever you do, don't eat any Libyan food. You might be poisoned.' " Dave moved to leave, but she squeezed his arm still further, while sweeping her other arm out in the general direction of the sea. "I have to be watchful," she said. "I know they're coming to destroy everything. Me and the farm—all of it!" Dave asked "Who? Who's coming?" "The goats, you fool, the goats!" With that, Dave bid her a final adieu. Bob Marshall's first reflections when he started teaching? "Teaching gives me a real kick, and I hope the students are as responsive and appreciative after the novelty wears off."

Jack Seifert was driven out from Sebha, the capital of the Fezzan region deep in the Sahara, in a Land Rover, on rough desert track road towards his village. The 350-mile trip took 16 hours. But the worst part was the hard bouncing. Jack felt beaten to a pulp. His body was bruised and his feet beaten up. Later on, in sheer self-defense, he figured out how to ride more comfortably. This meant to sit up as if you're on a galloping horse and not lean on anything in the car.

He arrived in Libya's most unusual town, Ghat. It's a collection of three ethnically separate villages, a few hundred yards from one another. One group were Arabs, but with an admixture of sub-Saharan blood, so they were darker than the average Libyan. The second village was populated with Hausa and Fulani blacks from northern Nigeria. The third group were Tuaregs, famous for being fierce fighters. They are so fierce, so well known as combatants of the first order, so consumed in their war-like attitude, that they don't do any work—except being warriors. The Tuareg men wear veils (for protection from wind-blown sand and to ward off evil spirits, of course) while the women do not. They eat their food by passing the food under their veils and even wear their veils at night. The women are also, as Jack recounts, "...free to love as they wish in their own society." The Tuaregs are known as "The Blue People of the Sahara," because the indigo fabric they wear stains their skin blue.

Tuareg veiled man

Their homes were caravanserai—mud-brick, square roadside inns for caravan travelers trekking from northern Nigeria to the Mediterranean. These buildings have large inner courtyards, and a wide, single portal large enough for fully-packed camels to enter. In the summer, the Tuaregs would cook, eat and sleep on their roofs. All three sets of villagers spoke Arabic, with the Hausans also speaking Hausa and the Tauregs also speaking Tuareg Berber.

A decade later I heard a story about the ferocity of Tuaregs who were often hired in Africa to be security guards. A western businessman who lived in Nigeria told me that after suffering a pair of burglaries, he hired a Tuareg to guard his house. Coming back from a business trip, he was shocked to see a beheaded man in his front yard. He asked the Taureg what the hell was going on. "This man tried to rob your house, so I killed him and left him here as a lesson to stop anyone else from trying to rob your house."

The afternoon of October 26, I strung up a clothes line. I also strung up bare copper electrical wire on the roof as an antenna and connected it to my battery-powered radio. Result? Tremendous reception. (Luckily, as a kid, I had futzed about with my father's short-wave radio and knew how to string antennas.) This roof wiring, however, would soon cast suspicion upon me. I practiced playing trumpet. I tried to make tea—unsuccessfully. On Sunday, I walked to my second village, Um El Jersan, to teach the fifth grade at the school there. (My motorcycle had not yet arrived.) Sitting on the stoop of the school was a wizened old man, Abdullah ("Servant of God"), who brightened when seeing my face. He started flapping his arms to his shoulders spouting, *"Freddo! Freddo!"* ("cold" in Italian). Some weeks later I was startled to learn he was only in his late 40s. (In 1968, the average life expectancy in Libya was 53.)

"Freddo" from Um El Jersan

Despite being in a smaller village, the Um El Jersan school was quite large, with two light yellow buildings with five classrooms each across a courtyard from one another.

**My 5th grade class at Um El Jersan flanked
by two 22-year-old students**

In my classroom there were 24 males and one sweet girl, Aisha ("happily living"). (Charlie Cross had one school with 48 boys and one girl.)

Aisha

The desks were in two pairs with an aisle between them, with the youngest students in the front, their heights and ages increasing till the back row. This was because the fail rate in Libya at the time was 40% and anyone who failed was put back a year. At the very back were two very quiet, very tall young black men of about 22 years of age who had flunked fifth grade seven times. While the Um El Jersan students were slower than the Al Gala kids, they were a damn sight better behaved.

Another dose of hospitality arrived as El Haadi ("the calm one"), the tall elegant, spiritual principal of the Um school, invited me and 20 teachers for lunch at his place. He had a charismatic aura about him that I had never seen in another human. It was particularly remarkable in the middle of nowhere.

Hajj El Haadi, principal of the Um El Jersan school

The food was delicious. The meal lasted till 5 PM. I was stuffed. That evening I created lesson plans for the next day, read some Shakespeare, trumpeted, guitarred, and fell asleep reading Genesis. (I had resolved to read the Bible all the way through.)

The next day, I taught a boisterous Al Gala class and a disciplined Um class. "They really whip them into shape over there in military fashion," I noted in my diary. I walked a mile towards Yifran and observed a man and his father tilling fields with their camel. I'd never seen a camel hauling a plow. Quite a sight to see as the camel got up quite a head of steam loping with its long legs. Also, camels having minds of their own, once at the end of the field the camel kept going, overshooting the field by about 50 yards despite ferocious rein-yanking and shouting by the elder farmer. Once headed back in the opposite direction, the camel galloped down the furrows and once again overshot the other end of the field by fifty yards. This overshooting spectacle continued for about a half hour, at which point the two men took a break and invited me to share lunch. Over the next two days I took an Arabic lesson from Milaad, finished reading *A Midsummer Night's Dream*, did laundry, trumpeted, guitarred, Bibled, started to chart out what radio stations I could get and what their frequencies were—hundreds to decide from—tried unsuccessfully to make couscous, typed a letter to Nancy Waddoups, fetched water, practiced writing English the way Mustafa Gusbi prescribes we do it in class and agreed to teach the teachers at Um El Jersan English at one Libyan pound a throw.

On Halloween 1968, I did nothing in particular to celebrate. Of course, there were no ragamuffins coming to the door prattling "Trick or treat!" in Arabic. But the McElhinnys took Halloween quite seriously. Harold took the trouble to buy a huge pumpkin. It was so big he couldn't carry it and had to hire a Libyan with a donkey cart to get it home. Ellen made a jack o' lantern out of the pumpkin, placed it in a dark room and lit the traditional candle inside. She invited some of her Libyan women-friends over for a party. At one point she invited her friends into the dark room. They started screaming, "The evil eye! The evil eye!" and raced out.

On what was to become an almost weekly ritual, Dan Peters showed up at my apartment on Thursday night (the eve of our day off), having walked the 10-odd miles from his village. He carried an empty backpack, as his tiny, remote village of El Khozeur offered no canned goods, no meat, no vegetables, not even bread, forcing him to stock up in Al Gala. My initial impression of Dan was that we would have little in common. Sporting thick glasses and an even thicker mustache, he struck me as a rough-hewn, overly serious farm boy from Menasha, Wisconsin. However, right off the bat we had a ton to talk about, comparing our initial experiences and sipping Libyan tea till sundown.

He was living with five Libyans, a happy-go-lucky, loopy wiseacre named Issa Ali, Khazam Khalifa, Ahmed Kayal, Abdullatif Shoush and

Ali Ambea. Normally, part of the greeting exchange in Libyan Arabic was "How are you?" with the response "I'm fine." Issa used to delight in replying to "How are you?" with "Better 'n' you!" Their water supply consisted of three large metal milk-can-like canisters of unboiled water. One canister had green worms flailing about inside. One had yellow worms. The third, red worms. Dan said the only choice was what color worms you wanted to contend with. This was my first clue as to the *in-extremis* nature of Dan's living conditions.

Issa, Khazam and Dan Peters in Al Khozeur

Our dinner menu that night consisted of tuna, fried potatoes, apples, bread and honey, washed down with a local bottled orange soda called Mirinda. (John Forasté relates that one of the female PCVs in Libya made Mirinda her staple. Upon returning to the States, she sustained 35 cavities.)

The next day Dan and I shelled out the equivalent of $1.50 to hitch a ride to Yifran where I purchased a small, two-burner propane stove and a canister of propane to upgrade my kitchen. Dan bought supplies, including meat. Back in Al Gala we were invited to have delicious couscous and fruit for lunch. Then Dan trudged back 10 miles over the roadless moonscape to El Khozeur to start another school week.

As for my routines, teaching was six days a week from 10 AM to 2 PM. First at Al Gala (where the kids were consistently unruly—the Peace Corps hadn't taught us a single method for dealing with that) then walking to Um El Jersan to teach the angels there. Every day, Abdullah would greet me, flapping his arms saying *"Freddo!"* For their part, the Libyan teachers would cook lunch, venture out into the countryside to sit and talk, then cook and eat supper and talk till 9:30 PM. Then they'd hang around and talk some more till midnight or 1 AM before hitting the hay. I didn't appreciate it at the time, but this was a schedule that afforded me a lot of free time. My Protestant ethic unconsciously kicked into gear as I kept myself busy teaching English to the Um teachers, reading, trumpeting, guitarring, writing letters, writing lesson plans, and studying Arabic. There were exceptions to the busy-ness. I enjoyed having frequent suppers with teachers, Belgassim, villagers; hanging out in Abdu-Salaam's shop drinking tea and talking; hanging out with Milaad. And after a bit, instead of a quick turn of a spigot for instant water or a flick of a finger for instant light, the extra steps of processing water and ginning up the lamp became second nature.

As often as I could, I'd take a sponge bath. I'd pour room-temperature water into a plastic tub, strip down, lather up, rinse off, towel off. In Ghemines, Peter Crall punched holes in the bottom of a large can for himself and Royse, hung it from the ceiling as an improvised shower. "The temperature once reached 130 F and after you showered you didn't need a towel because you dried off so fast."

Many of us soon found out about a taboo that was actually complimentary.

Noticings, Pre-Love Letters, Moto Guzzis

I had no idea what to expect for November weather. It started off hot for three weeks, including some incredibly windy days. It only rained a little on two days. But temperatures plunged at the end of November to 32 degrees at night and cold during the day. (Cathy Kaiser says it got so cold in Derna that her hand cream froze.) I was sleeping on a rickety aluminum tube bed with a mattress, inside a sleeping bag. At 32 degrees, this was a mite uncomfortable. Luckily, Martin Sampson drove by near the end of November with a kerosene heater.

My living room, replete with lantern, kerosene heater and burlap-wrapped jerry can for water

Much to my relief, it worked quite well. He also dropped off the standard cardboard mini-bookcase of 250 books that was given to all Peace Corps volunteers. When my Libyan friends saw all these books they were alarmed. They could not understand why anyone would want to read so many books. One of the standard-issue books was *The Fanny Farmer Cookbook*, included because so many volunteers right out of college had no idea how to prepare meals. All lanky Quaker Paul Rhodes had to cook on was a small hot plate. So, he eagerly opened the cookbook to a recipe he liked. The first instruction was "Pre-heat oven to 350 degrees." As for my kitchen, it was at least equipped with a propane tank.

My kitchen: note cloth wrapping to better seal the cous-coussier

According to John Ziolkowski the onset of cold weather combined with Libyan taxi drivers' frugality led to a sharp increase in a certain kind of accident. At night the heat dissipates from the ground and the sand, but is retained by the asphalt on roads. This attracts camels to walk on the roads. At the same time, to save on their car batteries, on moonlit nights Libyan cab drivers would drive with only parking lights on only or with no lights at all. The result was many serious accidents as taxis slammed into camels. One late night Tom Furth was hitchhiking going from mountainous Garian to Azzizia in a car with the lights off. With all the switchback turns, cliffs and lack of guardrails, Tom found the trip one of continuous terror. Sue Glover recounts, "The road to Garian was the most dangerous, curvy dirt road ever in our experience. Buses would back up in order to make the curves."

Dan Peters wrote home from El Khozeur, "I am picking up Arabic steadily. I am learning twenty new words a day these last two weeks. I tried hard at plowing behind a camel. Sure wouldn't want to make a career of that! I have been eating almost nothing but macaroni here. Some things are beginning to bug me. Last night I wanted to sleep but they were singing for hours in Berber. Because we are all friends my roommates think that all my possessions are open for their use and inspection. They also use my radio and yesterday forgot to turn it completely off."

Some of my students had blond hair and blue eyes, and many were lightly complected, which led the teachers to explain to me that I was living in a Berber village. The locals were Berber, and totally at home in both Arabic and Berber.

Solliman: light-skinned Berber student in Al Gala

When the Arabs invaded Libya in 644—646 A.D., there was, of course, resistance from the Berbers, but the Arab forces enjoyed overwhelming force. Many Berbers escaped from the lowlands into the mountains. And here I was in the Nefusa Mountains. I made it a point to learn some Berber phrases like *itch ocho* ("eat the food") and *enni feriul* ("ride the donkey"). Over in Aujila, 750 miles to the east, Bob Marshall discovered his village was also Berber and he also learned some of that Berber dialect, called, not surprisingly, Aujilan. It is estimated that Berbers constitute 13% of the Libyan population.

One day between classes, as usual, the teachers and I sat down outside on the dirt to talk while the janitor, more euphemistically labeled a "school custodian," Aribi Elourbaan, made tea. Aribi was a rotund, jolly fellow with chubby cheeks pockmarked by smallpox. I told everyone that my hobby was to learn how to count to 10 in various languages and that I would like to learn the same in Berber. So, I whipped out a little notebook and a pen and queried them in Arabic.

"How do you say 'one' in Berber?"

One teacher said, "*eegin.*"

I duly wrote this down.

"How do you say 'two' in Berber?"

Another said, "*sin.*"

I wrote this down.

"How do you say 'three' "?

No sound. I looked up, my pen poised.

"How do you say 'three' "?

"Well, we don't have a word for 'three.' "

"OK, then, what's the word for 'four' "?

"Uh, we don't have a word for 'four.' "

"Five then?"

"No."

"Six?"

Shaking heads.

"34?"

More shaking.

"156?"

"No."

"1,467?"

No.

"Well, then, how do you say any number that is more than two?"
"We just say... 'a lot.' "

With effort, I stifled a bursting laugh as I imagined a Berber math teacher drilling his students on their multiplication tables.

Teacher: "Abdul Rahman, how much is 9 times 9?"

Abdul Rahman (stroking his chin as he pondered carefully on this). "A lot?"

Teacher: "Yes!"

When I recounted this to John Maclean many years later, he asked, "Well, what is the ultimate thing a Berber math teacher would ask?" I said, "I dunno." He said, "He would ask the kids 'How much is a lot times a lot?' The kids would be stumped, and the teacher would say, " 'A lot more!' "

A bit of irony here. Whereas almost every culture counts to ten on their hands (although with different ways of opening or closing fingers, e.g. in Japan and Korea), the Libyans can count to 28 on their hands. They just count the segments between their joints on the fingers.

Peace Corps Libya management had put in place a rather clever practice. They decreed that we should be paid *less* than the lowest paid person in our villages. Typically, that would be the janitors. The reason for this was that if the subject ever came up, none of the Libyans could accuse us volunteers of having come to Libya for the money. The subject did, indeed, come up and helped inspire confidence in me by the villagers. And, since nothing is ever simple, for some volunteers this practice had a bit of a boomerang effect. Since the Egyptian and Palestinian teachers were paid significantly more than us this caused Libyans have lower respect for the Peace Corps teachers. (You can't win'em all!)

That afternoon, between classes at Um El Jersan, a grizzled old man named Ahmed approached me. He said he had fought with honor in World War II in 1943 for the Field Marshal Montgomery's 8th Army in Libya against the Germans. (Since then I've learned that the British recruited five battalions of Libyan men, called "The Libyan Arab Force," to help battle the Germans. They were instrumental in defeating the Axis powers in Libya.) Delving into his wallet, he pulled out an old, browned, folded piece of paper, worn through at the creases. As he delicately opened it up, he told me the British Army had promised him he'd be awarded three medals for his heroism in battle, and here we were 25 years later with no medals. The document, in English, was on official British Army stationery and included Ahmed's full name and confirmed the award of the medals.

"Can you help me?" he asked.

The challenge was immediately obvious. Over two decades had passed. What were the chances they still had this obscure Libyan's records? With no access to phones or telegraph, the only option was mail. I had no idea where to even send a letter of inquiry. And mail in this third world country was slow and unreliable. I couldn't, therefore, send along his official letter for fear of losing it. And Xerox machines were in relatively short supply in this village.

"I'll see what I can do," I said.

That evening I began the search process by composing a letter in which I copied down all the official information, requested the medals on Ahmed's behalf, and, for lack of anything better, addressed it to "British Army Headquarters, London, UK." With fingers crossed, I mailed it the next day at the Al Gala Post Office. This was not a particularly busy place, just a small, light yellow one-room building, staffed by no less than seven people. (One quarter of a person would've done.) They would hang outside all day, squatting, gossiping, drinking tea. One of these was a friendly young black man named Sassi. When I would pause to talk to this group, the other six would point excitedly at Sassi and shout *"Zenooji! Zenooji!"* ("Black! Black!") as if I couldn't tell.

I did notice patterns over time with respect to the villagers' clothing. Everyone dressed exactly alike. The core item was called a *holie* and consisted of a single wide swath of light, white cloth about eight feet long. Two corners were linked with thick string that slung over one shoulder, then the rest of the cloth was swaddled around their bodies, going down to their toes at the bottom and swirled around their heads at the top. These incredibly functional holies, being light and white, of course, protected against the heat. At the head they could wrap the cloth tightly to cover the face when there were sandstorms. And, in the absence of outhouses, you could just squat to do your business (usually at a discreet distance) with the ample holie acting as a virtual bathroom stall. In the winter, to protect against the cold, they would wear the same style but with thicker, brown cloth.

The way Libyans achieved some small measure of individualism was by wrapping these folds of cloth in a great variety of configurations about their upper body. They got so good at it, that they could nimbly flash their arms about for two seconds and have a new look. All of this without a single button or zipper. Beneath the holie, Libyans sport a vest, which can often be quite elaborate in its stitching, needlework and color, called a *farmla*. And under that a shirt.

On the head, every single villager wore a shortened red fez-like skull cap, whose generic name in the Arab world is a *taqiyah*, but which they called a *caboose*. This carries religious significance as Mohammed was known to always cover his head. In my village, they would even keep this caboose on all night in bed. In the wintertime, they switched to black cabooses.

On their feet, they sported flip-flops which they called *shib-shibs*. (There were a number of such Arabic doubled, charming words, including *fil-fil* [pepper], couscous, *swa-swa* [same], *mish-mish* [apricots] and *shweya-shweya* [little by little]). The level of conformity shocks the system of any Westerner. It would be as if you were walking down the street in New York City and every single man in the street was wearing a white shirt, a black suit, a red tie and black wing-tips.

Teacher Belgassim and Sassi with typical garb

Teacher Belgassim and his fourth grade

Mohammed and my friend Tahir with his prized VW

As for the women, they were covered head-to-toe (only the feet and one eye showing—always the left eye) in light flowing robes, called *burkas* or *barracans*, sometimes in plain white like the men, but often more colorful, exhibiting alternating stripes of turquoise, purple, deep blue and bright pink hues, enhanced with gold embroidery. They displayed gold chains with tiny golden horns to ward off evil. Golden hearts and keys symbolized happiness and prosperity. Their shoes were typically crimson or chrome-yellow. The one eye deprived them of binocular vision, and I learned to steer clear so as not to bump into them. (Touching a woman was taboo big time.) Kathy Lamoureux remembers that the only way to recognize many of these covered women was by their ankles!

Randolph W. Hobler

Libyan "One-Eyed" women: they always keep the left eye open

In this slow, easy-going society with no particular rush to do anything, villagers greeting one another would fill up the time with a dozen greeting statements back and forth, often with prescribed alternate responses, like:

"Salaamu aleekum" (Peace be upon you).

"Wa aleekum salaam" (And upon you peace).

"Sabah elkheer" (Good morning).

"Sabah an-nour" (Morning the light).

"Ween jeet?" (Where are you coming from?).

"Keef halik?" (How are you?).

162

"Ana kwayyis" (I'm fine).

"La baas" (Not too bad).

"Al hamdulillih" (Thanks to God). And on it would go.

I noticed that my village friends would pry open bottle caps from Pepsi bottles with their teeth. Speaking of teeth, I noticed that instead of toothbrushes, during the day, Libyan men would chew on light-brown (not a color to inspire confidence) *meswek* sticks. When you chew at the end of these sticks, they fray into fibrous strands with a pleasant fragrance. It turns out they are also surprisingly effective for flossing and for other medicinal purposes. And, not to put too fine a point on it, these chewing sticks are highly recommended by the Prophet Mohammed in the Koran!

Meswek chewing-stick vendor

Meswek stick ending

I noticed that villagers would forage for firewood with their donkeys and return with the donkeys laden down with branches and twigs. I noticed two miles away, on a hilltop I could see from my abode, a Roman watchtower. One day with principal Belgassim and others we went to visit. It was constructed around 200 A.D. with 10-ton marble blocks. I realized that this must be one of a string of watchtowers across North Africa corresponding to maps I had seen studying Roman history. I was living exactly on the southern border of the Roman Empire! What I didn't know then was that this network of towers was part of the *Limes Tripolitanus*—a frontier defense zone—and, like elsewhere in the ancient world, the watchtowers were constructed within eyeshot of one another. This meant that using fire signals, in a matter of minutes, the Romans could communicate across hundreds of miles.

Roman watchtower visible from my house

I noticed that framed photos of King Idris Senussi I and his much-despised dumb nephew and heir Crown Prince Hassan El Senussi graced the walls of every shop. (Idris had married four times but had no living children because they had all died in infancy.)

Scholarly, pious King Idris I

165

Much-despised nephew to King Idris, Hassan El Senussi

And it was only 50 years later that I noticed, in retrospect, that there were no street names or street signs in my village. Even the main paved road that sliced through the town at the hill's summit had no name.

In passing I learned that there were many similarities between whatever Hebrew words I happened to know and Arabic. "*Shalom*" equals "*Salaam.*" "*Rosh hashana,*" I noted, was "*Ras Isana*" (the head of the year) and "*Yom Kippur*" was "Yom Kibbir" (the big day").

I learned that the price of a camel was $1,000—way more than I ever would have guessed. In parallel, I was continuing Bibling. In the past I had snorted disdainfully that Job owned 1,000 camels. I now made the connection that in his time, this dude was a millionaire!

Speaking of money, as in any country, you acculturate to the coinage of the realm. The currency was the Libyan pound (the *junyah* in Arabic) pegged to the British pound, in bills of various colors in varying sizes. I noticed that King Idris was so self-effacing he'd prohibited his likeness on the Libyan currency.

Libyan quarter-pound note: English side

Quarter-Pound note: Arabic side

The Libyan men's wallets, of which I was one owner, were large, highly colorful ones. The coins in English were referred to as "piasters" and in Libyan Arabic as *gersh*. Two of the denominations sported scalloped edges.

Coins of the Realm

Some noticings took time, but through observation, language usage and reading I started to understand the belief that only Allah can know the future. In practical day-to-day terms, this means that agreeing to meet at a specific time or to be on time for an appointment has to do with the future—Allah's realm. Therefore, if one is late, it's not one's fault. It's up to Allah whether you're on time or not. You're chronologically off the hook. Punctuality kind of goes out the window. In language this is reflected in the word *inshallah* ("If God wills it"), which is invoked by Libyans and other Arabs literally dozens of times a day. This off-the-hookiness is reflected in another word *ma'lesh* ("it doesn't matter," but is stronger than that, meaning "it doesn't *really* matter"), also invoked multiple times daily to excuse most any failing.

In one case invoking *ma'lesh* did matter. One fine day, Ted Kelley was driving Jeff Taylor, Linda Dixon Williamson, Charlie Cross, Kathy McLean and John Legasy on a Tripoli highway in his Land Rover. As a car pulled alongside, Jeff decided to flip the finger at the occupants (Ah, youth!). They quickly saw that one of the passengers was a policeman. The Libyan vehicle started chasing the Americans. Kathy said "To the Embassy!" She said she knew a Marine guard there who could get them through the gate safely. Arriving breathlessly, the group saw a 6' 5" tall Marine with a revolver on his hip. The Libyan car screeched to a halt behind them. Out jumped the policeman who confronted the Marine guard asking what that gesture with the middle finger meant. The guard shrugged, said *"ma'lesh"* and that's all it took for the Libyans to demur.

I couldn't help but notice how hospitable and generous the villagers were. From the time of my arrival, I was invited to dinner and lunch almost daily. Many evenings Milaad would treat me to dinner with friends.

Principal Belgassim taught me how to make couscous. Beyond meals, friends would periodically stop by my place and give me food. A friend named Abdullah once dropped off a bushel of onions and four beers. Just a month in, I wrote to my grandparents, "The hospitality here is overwhelming. I've had two meals (at home) the whole last week here." I had read nothing in the U.S. press ever about how hospitable the Arabs were. This was the first of many a wake-up call. Mostly, Arabs were depicted in the U.S. press as terrorists, armed to the teeth. Many years later, reading T.E. Lawrence's *Seven Pillars of Wisdom*, I learned the origin of this hospitality. It emanates from the Bedouin's law of the desert, which recognizes that nomads are often in dire need of food and water after long treks in inhospitable wastelands of sand. The rule was if all you had left to your name was a handful of rice, you must give it to any visiting traveler. This is burned into the soul of every Arab to this day.

Along these lines, I also noticed that in photos in Arab newspapers and magazines, Arab leaders like Gamal Abdul Nasser and Yaasir Arafat were usually smiling. My recollection was that in the U.S. this was never the case. (My suspicions were confirmed when I got back to the States and sure enough, invariably, photos of Arab leaders did not depict them smiling. In fact, they were usually shown scowling.) This represented an enormously unethical practice on the part of U.S. press (and I'm not even talking about the huge bias against and misrepresentation of Arabs in the stories themselves.) Literally decades of demonization of Arabs. Really opened up my eyes!

What I didn't notice, because I couldn't have at the time (given that I'd never seen any Libyan woman's face), were the tattoos on Berber women's faces. While there are variations of locations, they were most commonly on the chin, the tip of the nose and the forehead. A huge profusion of designs—thousands of them—populate their visages, symbolizing such things as evil eyes, snakes, twigs, feathers, lizards, flies, seeds (for fertility) palm trees, flowers, amulets, sickles, amulets and many more. In the 21st century, such tattoos—the last vestiges of a pre-Islamic, pre-Christian animistic belief systems which nonetheless convey wondrously imaginative spiritual worlds—have evaporated.

Tattooed women teachers in Beida

Women might also choose to place letters of the 33-letter Berber alphabet on their faces. The letters would also be symbolic—for beauty, good luck, etc. I find these letters to be fascinating. You have to read the words from the bottom up. And it turns out they are derived from the Phoenician alphabet. Rabidly anti-Berber, Muammar Ghaddafi banned any public exposure of the Berber language.

The Berber alphabet

Berber girl with Berber letter tattoo

Among the many whose eyes were opened about Arab demonization was John Maclean. One of his neighbors was a highly-educated Palestinian doctor, who convinced John of how slanted the news in the U.S. was towards Palestinians. Like John, most of us were naively surprised to meet Palestinians who were doctors, lawyers, teachers, business people, professionals—not a terrorist among them! Kathy Lamoureux was assigned to the Tripoli Women's Teacher Training College where she had the most populous of all our classes in Libya—between 90 and 100 students in multiple locations across Tripoli. "I became friends with several Palestinian women who were as keen to share their language and religion as I was to learn about it." Diane Forasté: "The Palestinian women spoke English and were well educated. I was woefully unaware of the Palestinian history and perspective. These women took every opportunity to educate me."

The Forastés' next-door neighbor was Palestinian. In late December 1968, he and his wife "sent over a small plate of stuffed cabbage with a tiny piece of meat inside each roll. There was a small note attached that said 'Happy Christmas.'"

In Homs, the Petersons befriended a number of Palestinian families. In one case Rebecca knew a Palestinian woman who had lost her home on the West Bank and had a series of personal losses. Her father died. Then her son. Then her mother got quite ill. She was quite distressed. Rebecca accompanied her to a doctor in Tripoli who provided her with some pills. But ultimately the only R_X that helped was telling her, "Rebecca will sit and cry with you and make you feel better."

Richard Massey noticed something I never did. "Birthdays are not celebrated here in Libya, the main reason being that people don't know when their birthday is. Up until very recently, no one recorded the day of birth, much less the time."

Sensitive to a historical perspective and aware that oil had been discovered in Libya a mere nine years before, in 1959, Stoney Bird was noticing the ripple effects extending deep down into the Fezzan. A paved road was constructed. A public sector water supply was installed. Diesel water pumps were installed. And the Fezzan villages found themselves hosting dozens of American Peace Corps volunteers. By the time the Peace Corps arrived in Libya, annual per capita income had surged to $2,000 and the Kingdom had become the world's fourth most prolific source of oil.

Stoney noticed and marveled at a building in Ar-Rugeiba built by the Romans with blocks of marble that had been carted across the desert from the Mediterranean. He admired a still-standing old Roman fort, replete with towers and crenellations two thousand years old. And a local German archaeologist explained to Stoney that what looked to him like piles of rocks atop an escarpment were wind shelters 100,000 years old.

Bob Marshall's diary was replete with incisive descriptions of his Libyan friends. For example, of his fellow teacher Idris: "Idris is the clown, the character, the salt of the earth. 28, very dark, with teeth and eyes that sparkle, he is a beautifully real person. His capacity for enjoyment, his freedom from inhibition, enable others to simply watch him. Speaking to me, he uses a mixture of Yugoslavian, Italian, Arabic and English that he believes is perfectly comprehensible."

The staff "experts" at Clearfield had not warned us of an Arab-world-wide cultural quirk; if someone admires a possession of yours, you have to give it to them. John Lynch admired a Libyan friend's English-Arabic dictionary. The friend gave it to him. John kept trying to refuse the gift, but as the rule is you must take it, John finally did. From a female volunteer, "The first time I visited a teacher friend of mine, she showed me around her house. We stopped to look at a table that was inlaid with mother-of-pearl and I admired it. Two-and-a-half hours later, she presented it to me as a gift." On a trip to Algeria, Tunisia and Morocco, Lorraine Slawiak joined Jeanne Maurey, Shirley Greuel and other female volunteers renting a car to get around. In Algeria, they were conversing with an Algerian woman. Trying to be nice, Lorraine said, "I love your earrings!" The woman immediately took them off, gave them to Lorraine, absolutely refusing to take them back. Lorraine has these earrings to this day.

In Ar-Rugeiba, Stoney Bird had a short-wave radio. It was stolen. Well, "stolen" perhaps. A young man, following Arab tradition, expressed admiration for said radio, and thus expected Stoney to give it to him. When Stoney didn't comply, the young man just took possession of it.

■

Sometimes it takes a half-century to suss out a problem one is struggling with. Except for one of us, we all struggled mightily with privacy.

Spying Suspicions, Hyper Hyenas

My circle of friends enlarged during November. Milaad's brother, Abdul Magiid, settled into Al Gala and regularly had dinner with us. A friendly Tahir took to me as well and joined us for dinners. A very outgoing guy named El Haadi showed up. The Libyan 100-meter dash champion, he casually took up residence next door to me. I didn't know it at the time, but he had been dispatched by Tripoli to spy on me under cover of being a teacher, based on general suspicions that Peace Corps volunteers were CIA spies and more specifically perhaps triggered by the long antenna on my roof. For a while I wondered why anyone would imaging my spying upon this tiny, remote village. There were no military bases, no chemical labs, no institutes of higher learning. I then realized that, from the Libyans' point of view, if I were spying on them, there must, therefore, by definition, be something important in Al Gala worth being spied upon. El Haadi, iron-ically, turned out to be my best Libyan friend.

El Haadi, best Libyan friend

In Bin Gashir, near Tripoli Airport, the Libyan teachers accused Bill Cagle of being a CIA spy. One activity that prompted this suspicion was that periodically Bill and some fellow PCVs would go to the edge of the runway and get a rush when the planes roared over them. Every time the teachers confronted him about the CIA, Bill would say, "Hey, if I were a CIA spy, I wouldn't be sitting around drinking tea with you guys!"

In Al Gala, there was a third El Haadi, who drove a Toyota pickup truck. Well off by local standards, he could afford three wives. (The Koran allows four wives. All must be treated equally, right down to buying them equal amounts of gifts. By the way, if you decide, for whatever reason, as a Moslem man that you don't want a wife, here's the protocol for divorcing her. You simply say, "I divorce thee," three times in a row. That's it.)

Joshingly, I began to call this El Haadi "El Haadi Toyota." After a while, this caught on and all the villagers started calling him "El Haadi Toyota."

I made the acquaintance of Mohammed, the Chief of Police (and only policeman) in Al Gala. I started teaching English to him and to Sassi from the post office in my spare time. What with all this hanging out amongst friends, my Arabic improved.

In November 1968, before we got our motorcycles, Dan Peters crashed at my place three times. I was impressed with his nonchalant ten-mile walks each way to visit. On one occasion two snarling hyenas came after him. For a second, he didn't know what to do. ("What to Do When Attacked by Hyenas" was not in the Clearfield curriculum.) In sheer desperation, he grabbed some rocks (ubiquitous in the hardscrabble terrain), and started to throw them at the hyenas, yelling at the top of his lungs. Luckily, they dispersed. Over the course of these visits, I learned that this presumed Wisconsin rube had studied at Omani University in Hyderabad, India. He had traveled extensively in India, as well as to Iran, Turkey, Israel, Syria, Jordan, Lebanon, Greece and Austria. Then, it turns out he was born in Appleton, Wisconsin, where my great-grandfather, Edward Hobler, owned a factory. One of these Thursday evenings was Thanksgiving, but because of our remote situation (and lack of turkeys perhaps) my diary makes no mention of it. I just said it was good to see Dan and that we cooked up soup and couscous for dinner. After dinner, we played chess, with many more games to come. (I wish I'd known at the time the Arab contribution of chess to Europe by way of the Moors in Spain, having been adopted previously from the Persians and before that the Indians. I also wish I'd known that the term "check mate" originated from the Persian *shah mat*, and thence to the Arabic *sheikh mat* meaning "the king is helpless," i.e. unable to move.)

One Friday Dan and I wandered down to the very bottom of the valley. We saw a camel being butchered (they only kill camels when they're too old to do work; at that point their muscles are quite rangy). They gave Dan and me about three pounds of the meat for free. We ran into a friend and had a Pepsi in his house. As we were about to leave, we complained about what a trek it was to the top of the canyon. The friend said, "No problem, you can take the shortcut."

"Where's that?" He pointed at the nearly sheer face of an escarpment with a dusty switchback trail about two feet wide that zigged and zagged four hundred feet to the top. "Don't worry, I'll tell you where to go."

Foolish youth. We gamely started up this narrow trail. Every time it wasn't clear which way we should go, the friend shouted at us "Go that way!" or "Move to the left!" Every few minutes, when we looked back down at him, he got smaller and smaller. Somehow, we kept our footing the whole way and somehow blocked out fearsome acrophobia.

Of course, we had to cook the camel forthwith, but it was so tough we had to grind it up and we ended up chowing down on camel cheeseburgers. The taste? Like a mix of venison and beef. That evening, we listened to the Voice of America on my transistor radio. Other stations I would listen to included BBC, Radio Monaco, Tunisian Radio and Wheelus Radio, part of the American Armed Forces Radio and TV. They had a DJ with a daily middle-of-the-road music show named Howard David. The news announcer liked to josh with him, and when turning the microphone over, to tease him as "Mean old Howard David." (Bob Marshall enjoyed listening to Radio Luxembourg and Radio South Africa.) It was clear Dan would be coming regularly and after a few Thursday nights where I slept on the floor in deference to him, I decided to buy another mattress so we could both be comfortable going forward.

In mid-November, I started teaching the kids to write in English. Strange for them as Arabic is written from right to left. The dichotomy between the Al Gala and Um El Jersan kids continued. In Al Gala the kids were extremely bad. Unruly. On one day I reported that the "Um class was perfect today. Al Gala the worst yet." On another day the Al Gala class gave me the silent treatment. I threw one out of class. Then they responded well. Around this time my friend El Haadi hit an unruly Al Gala kid with a chair.

Andrea Murphy tells an egg story. A Libyan lady lived in a tin shack next door to them. She would sell eggs every day, and Andrea was such a soft touch she would always buy eggs from the woman even if she didn't need them. At one point she'd accumulated 30 eggs. She and John wearied of eating omelets! One night they heard an explosion in the backyard of the lady egg seller. A fire had broken out. The only running water available was in the Murphys' bathroom. So, the villagers and Murphys improvised a bucket brigade from the bathroom to the fire.

Over in Janzur, Victor Gramigna's students would regularly bring him fruits and vegetables. On one occasion a teacher brought his entire class over to Victor's place to help him plant a garden. Unlike any other volunteer, Victor had so many sweaters (complemented by even more that his mother would send him) that he was able to wear a different one each day. The students would regularly ooh and aah about this. Finally realizing that these kids had just two outfits to their name, Victor felt guilty of conspicuous consumption and halted the practice. In fact, he went even further: at the end of the school year he gave away all his sweaters to his students.

Periodically, Tom Weinz, a Peace Corps inspector whose job it was to inspect Libyan and Arab teachers teaching English, would stop by and spend the night in my humble lodgings. He also took the trouble to visit Dan Peters in desolate El Khozeur.

**Tom Weinz (second from right) hanging with
Dan Peters and friends in El Khozeur**

November 21 was the first day of Ramadan, a month of fasting where no food, drink or sex is allowed during the day, but extensive, late-into-the-night feasting occurs during the evening. It is one of the Five Pillars of

Islam, the other four being Faith, Prayer, Charity and the Hajj—the pilgrimage to Mecca. During this Ramadan season, Richard Massey visited many homes. "Since I'm inevitably the center of attention at these affairs and since my Arabic is limited, I have to spend a great deal of time just smiling. I smile so much that I have to frown for half an hour afterwards to get my face back to normal!"

Dan and I ventured out to Tripoli (we walked three miles before getting a hitchhike to Yifran, then grabbed a bus), the first of 13 trips I would take there. I needed a haircut, and as the barber was shaving my neck with a straight razor, I felt a sting up and down both sides of my neck. He started to apologize as he had made two four-inch-length cuts. He mopped it up and stanched the bleeding, but it was harshly sore for days.

I bought a Panasonic tape recorder, got a medical kit at the Peace Corps office, bought a Libyan flag, visited the fascinating, colorful covered bazaar in the old city and indulged myself with a dinner of filet mignon and Heinekens.

The next day Dan and I bought *holies* and hopped on a Yifran-bound bus. (Later, to complete my Libyan outfit, I purchased a *caboose* and a vest.) In the middle of nowhere, with no other roads in sight, no landmarks at all, Dan shouted at the driver to let him off. He hopped off, weighted down with his Tripoli purchases and started trudging off to El Khozeur. The Libyans on the bus watched through the windows wondering where the hell this crazy Westerner was going. It was four miles to his village.

I got three letters this day. One from my sister, Bassett, who was unhappy at college and a *long* letter from Jeanne Maurey. A most welcome piece of correspondence not just because it was from her, but it was already a month-and-a-half without any female companionship whatsoever, so such a letter was most warming. I, of course, wrote a letter back that very night. Not sure where this might lead, but it was a good start. I also was gratified to receive a two-page letter from Bob Steiner, the Regional Director, North Africa, Near East and South Asia at the Peace Corps, reacting to my long critique from October. Some excerpts:

> I think Al Wight would be the first to admit that administration is not his strongest point. He is clearly an

idea man and I cannot take issue with your criticism that he was miscast as the manager of the program. Another factor that tended to lower your FSI scores was our experimental use of language informants who also had to study English as part of their responsibilities. The last big point you raised was the so-called D-group. The questions you were asking me are types of questions usually associated with Volunteers who have been in-country over a year. The parts of the D-group sessions with which you take issue may have been nonsense or irrelevant or even damaging. If so, obviously, we should eliminate these parts.

I had thought they would deliver our Moto Guzzis to our doorsteps, but no! We had to go get them in Garian. So I walked quite a ways, then finally got a ride, picked up my cycle and rode it some 40 miles back to Al Gala. "Great to have the cycle."

My Moto Guzzi

Dan and his Moto Guzzi

Meanwhile, in Aujila, Bob Marshall, whose two schools in Aujila were three miles apart, was hoping to get a Land Rover. Bob Pearson, the Peace Corps Cyrenaica Director, nixed that. Then Bob started campaigning for a Moto Guzzi, claiming there was this enormous hill he had to climb between his two schools. At one point, Pearson walked up the hill with Bob, and grudgingly allowed that although it was, indeed, steep, he noted that the teachers and students themselves walked up the hill every day, and thought it wise for Bob to do the same. So Bob never got a Moto Guzzi, but did get in a lot of walking. (Ted Kelley, unlike the rest of us, got a Land Rover, probably because one of his schools was a full 30 miles away.) Various parts of Bill Cagle's Moto Guzzi would fall off regularly, as the Libyan mechanics didn't know how to assemble them. The Moto Guzzis had no air filter. So down in the Sahara heat, John Becker recalls, his cycle would just stop. Then, in the desert, sand would get stuck in the gears. One time he was zooming along a road and was about to hit a donkey pulling a cart. The throttle was stuck on full. In an instant he managed to reach over the headlamp, pull out the ignition pin and stop the engine just in time to avoid a collision. In a signal example of the collision between old and new technology, Bob Gausman, while cruising along a narrow path, hooked his Moto Guzzi handlebar through a donkey's saddlebag. The donkey lurched one way, Bob the other. He was flipped high into the air, but luckily, was unhurt. One day in Samnu, Bob Gausman was riding his Moto Guzzi back from school when a ghibli stormed up. He put a handkerchief over his mouth to keep out the pelleting sand. He couldn't see ten feet in front of him. He thought he'd never make it back home and was scared to death. Somehow, he persevered and made it.

One Saturday in Gara Bulli, on his Moto Guzzi, Neil McCabe was forced off the road by a truck passing another car on a curve. He was knocked out and came to in an ambulance. He was taken to a room in the local hospital with "the oldest X-ray machine in the world." While the X-ray technicians yammered away in Italian, trying to make the X-ray machine work, the police, oblivious to his injury, were grilling Neil about why he didn't have a motorcycle license. The X-ray machine wouldn't oblige, so they gurneyed Neil into another ambulance to transport him to Wheelus Hospital. Along the way, the back door of the ambulance blew open, swaying back and forth. Luckily, Neil was not swept out the back. At Wheelus examining the X-ray, the Palestinian doctor found a hairline fracture in his collarbone. Neil asked, "Am I gonna die?" The doctor replied, "No. Not today. Sunday."

A Moto Guzzi situation in late 1968 was no laughing matter. Bob Suzuki, who was stationed in El Marj near Tobruk (famous in WWII for having been taken by the Italians, then the British, then the Germans, then the British) suffered a motorcycle accident, fracturing his skull. Richard Massey and others took him to a local hospital where they gave blood to help him out. He was medevacked out to Wheelus and subsequently to an American military hospital in Germany to be treated.

John Maclean showed up in Gara Bulli on his Moto Guzzi, wearing a snazzy jumpsuit, a gleaming white helmet and a license plate that read *Hokoma* ("government"). So decked out, he was regularly saluted by policemen wherever he went.

For Bob Pearson, the issue with his vehicle was the cold. His jeep had no heat and he had to travel a lot. His feet would feel frozen. One time, he got home, took off his shoes and socks and put his feet up near the fire. However, because his feet were so numbed, he almost burned his soles. Despite Libya's desert climate, Chuck and Jane Beach reported that they counterintuitively suffered more from the cold than from the heat. And John Forasté wrote, "At night? It was *freezing*. We had to preheat the bedroom with a small hot plate in order to even tolerate getting into bed at night."

For Dan and me at the time, we had no idea what possessing Moto Guzzis would unleash. For the nonce, we just dutifully used them to go to and from our schools, and, in Dan's case, going to and from my place (when he didn't have a flat tire, which was most of the time).

The only way to keep in touch with my outside world in those pre-Internet days was the exchange of letters. There were days when I would receive no less than seven letters. To my surprise, one of those was from the Ministry of Defence, British Army Headquarters. They said they didn't issue medals, but referred me to the Joint Personnel Administration Centre (JPAC) in Glasgow, Scotland. I immediately shot off a letter.

Speaking of letters, I never was conscious of my incoming mail being censored, but clearly it was a regular practice of the Libyan Post Office system. (A girlfriend of Randy Melquist's sent a letter to him that mentioned she had enclosed a photo of herself in a bathing suit. It had been removed.)

In terms of keeping in touch with friends and villagers in Al Gala, I faced a difficult balancing act, as did every other Libyan Peace Corps volunteer. In Libyan culture, it's open house for everyone all the time. You drop in to visit anyone's house at any time. For Americans, there is such a thing as too much hospitality, as when the Libyans would expect you to hang around with them for hours at a stretch. While it was enjoyable to socialize up to a point, if followed according to their standards, I would have no time for anything else, including necessities like writing lesson plans for the next day's school classes. We Western volunteers, imbued with centuries of Protestant ethic, were colliding headlong with centuries of tribal customs. One night in November, I was at Milaad's from 6:30 PM to 10:00 PM. In my diary, "Ruined my night. No letters, no working, no reading." On another occasion, "Everyone over for tea here. By the time I'd cleaned up again it was 9:30. No studying, no reading, not much done. Feel very frustrated about today."

Privacy issues are compounded when you're in a compound with Libyans. Dan Peters complained, "There is almost no privacy here. My roommates want to be together all the time so if I go off by myself into my room, they come here, too. Sometimes I would like to be left alone, as when I want to listen to the news on the radio or type this letter." Dan Peters wrote home, "I naturally would like to be alone at times but they often come into my room, preventing me from reading or writing. The other day when I took my lamp and left the common room, I was confronted with, 'You think your room is better than ours.' So they decided to make a point of eating in my room."

Jeanne Maurey wrote, "Privacy. That's one thing Libyans don't have. They never want to be alone and they can't understand it when you do."

Bob Marshall was upset with the constant hanging out. His diary: "Talkative friends can take up all your time." He would try to excuse himself early, but it was tough because not only did he not want to appear rude, his problem was exacerbated by living with a 19-year-old Tunisian roommate, Mahdi. Since Tunisians speak a combination of French and Arabic, Bob said he conversed with Madhi in "Franglarabic." Due to tradition, the villagers had to invite both Bob and Mahdi together so as not to offend either one. So, if Bob took his leave early, that would force Mahdi to leave at the same time. Bob was further constrained within their household. "Then, the biggest problem is after dinner. Mahdi would like to sit and talk all night. I prefer to leave directly [for his own room] after tea."

We all wanted to be friendly, but we had other demands on our time. Unfortunately, I, and every other Libya PCV save one could never come up with an excuse that didn't come across as anti-social.

Fifty years after the fact, I learned from Frank Nicosia that he'd come up with the perfect solution. At 6 PM he would look at his watch and tell his Libyan friends, "Oh, gee, I have to go pray now for two hours." They were totally OK with that. If only we had known!

◾

Bob Gausman soon learned that maps had no place in the classroom.

Whacks, Games, Veils

The nearest place to gas up my cycle was Yifran. While doing so, one day in early December I met a French secondary school teacher, Gil, who roomed in Yifran with two other French teachers, named Denis and Pedro (don't ask). Turns out there were 100 French teachers scattered throughout Libya. Delighted to meet them, I looked forward to babbling away with them in French, but found myself tongue-tied. I had been so immersed in Arabic, that when I plumbed my brain for a French word, the Arabic word would pop up instead. Very disconcerting. On a future visit with them, they taught me how to make crepes. I then passed this forward by teaching same to my friend El Haadi. Also in Yifran, I used to chill with a sunnily engaging shopkeeper named Ayed.

Shopkeeper buddy Ayed with super-sized key in Yifran

187

Speaking of shops, out in the sticks there were no barber shops for these Berbers, whose practice was to go Yul Brynner. During breaks at school, a teacher would remove his *caboose*, another teacher would slather shaving cream on his pate, whip out a straight razor and shave it all off. (In a desire to look sharp for their much-anticipated winter vacation to Rome, Mike Lee and Craig Owens descended on a barbershop in the city of Garian. Sitting side-by-side in barber chairs, they asked each other "Gee, how would you say 'Not too much?' " They decided to tell their respective barbers *shweya* ("little"). Their intent was to convey this as "a little off," but the barbers interpreted this to mean "only leave a little." The barbers shaved off all their hair. So, much to their dismay they showed up in Rome as skinheads decades before this was at all fashionable.)

Surprisingly, one day at Um El Jersan I had to throw one of the students out of the classroom. And that same day, the Al Gala kids went so nuts I had to throw out a third of the class. For the Libyans, school discipline was meted out by whacking a student's palm with a eucalyptus switch. It was painful to watch.

Peter Hawkes remembers, "There were reddened hands. Sometimes tears. Once I saw blood." The Libyans sure took the expression "Spare the rod and spoil the child" from Proverbs literally. In some parts of Libya, another procedure was to slap the bare soles of students' feet with the stick. With rare exceptions, none of us Peace Corps Volunteers used the stick on students, despite the urging of our school principals, teachers and even the students. The Peace Corps had not alerted us about this practice, nor had they taught us one whit about how to cope with pupils' unruliness. It was only some time after starting school that we were admonished by Martin Sampson, who had been a volunteer in Libya I, that we were not to hit the children.

A Bedouin father of a student stopped by to see Malcolm Travelstead.

"How's my son doing?"

"He's smart. But sometimes he doesn't pay attention."

"You hit him, didn't you?"

"No, I'm not Libyan."

"But you're a teacher!"

"I'm not going to hit him."

"OK, then, I will."

And he did. The kid never gave Malcolm any more trouble.

On one occasion, Dennis Carlson told a very unruly student to come to the front of the room to be switched. He refused. So Dennis had to go back to his desk in the rear of the room to forcibly bring him forward. The student resisted, and even started swinging at Dennis. They got into a prolonged wrestling match, with the other kids laughing, placing bets on who would win. Eventually, Dennis managed to pin the student to the floor. After that, the student was never a problem.

Paul Rhodes had a student named Sassi Said who lived up to his name by making smart-ass remarks. At one point, he shredded a writing book to pieces. Angered, Paul started to chase Sassi around the classroom. Later, Sassi's father left a message for Paul, "It's OK to use your stick on my son. You have my permission to bang him on the head and neck." Paul, who was a Quaker, explained to his principal that it was against his religion to strike a student. However, he never had a scrap of trouble from that kid for the rest of the year.

Jack Seifert asked his students why they were so hard to control. They said, "Because you don't hit us with a ruler." Jack asked, "How am I supposed to do that?" They said, "The student puts his hand on the desk and you rap him." One of his students, a teenage boy, was a troublesome ringleader who mouthed off once too often for Jack, who reported him to the principal. The principal and the teachers beat the daylights out of him, including kicking. After that, he, too behaved.

Mike Lee's principal, Mohammed, summed up the Libyan pedagogical principle with some economy, "Without the stick, there is no learning."

According to Bob Gausman, the girls rarely, if ever, misbehaved. (Surprise!) Every morning in Samnu, after the singing of the Libyan National Anthem, the principal would call out all the kids who had misbehaved the previous day and give them a severe whacking. In his school, the teachers would pace up and down the aisles of the classrooms, brandishing a stick like a drill sergeant.

In Sabratha, Diane Forasté shared with her head teacher a problem she was having with one of her girls. "She called the girl into her small office and had me stand there as she hit the girl several times, very hard, on the knuckles. I was horrified! The girl bravely accepted the punishment."

To avoid hitting his students, Bill Cagle would send them home. This backfired, however, because once they got home, "the father would beat the shit out of them." The kids would give Bill the stick and say, "You have to hit us." Cagle's resourceful response to this situation was, in effect, to disarm the teachers without depriving them of a means of punishment. He stole all the sticks and replaced them with short lengths of much softer rubber hose. The teachers asked him, "Where are the sticks?" and Bill would say, "Use the rubber hose!" The Libyan teachers were none too pleased with this.

This form of discipline was not restricted to schools. Once in a Tripoli hotel lobby, Bill witnessed a concierge summoning a bellboy. He slapped the bellboy hard with a stick three times on the palm. In addition to the physical pain, the bellboy suffered public shaming.

Mark Lepori coped with the stick dilemma by sharply flicking the offending student's ear.

In his Shigran school, Peter Hawkes had two strapping 18-year-olds in his class. One of them was acting up repeatedly, severely trying Peter's temper. The kid then yelled *emshi nayick!* ("Go fuck yourself!") and for the only time in Libya, Peter lost it. He punched the student in the stomach. At that point the other 18-year-old jumped out the window. Peter grabbed the offending kid by the ear and dragged him out to meet the *mudir*.

One woman volunteer witnessed three of her charges being hit ten times on the palm of each hand by her *mudira*. "She then asked me who else had been bad. I answered 'all of them,' sure that this would save any more from the stick. Instead she proceeded to go down each aisle as each of my 34 girls screamed in pain until the whole class was sitting, heads in arms, sobbing. The bell rang and I left the room in tears."

I know of only a few exceptions in the realm of stickdom on the part of volunteers. One was Greg Strick's experience in the village of Sidi Mahius. He had a student who was an "ornery fart" who didn't want to learn. He persistently challenged Greg. Finally, Greg sent him to the headmaster, who swatted his palms. But the kid persisted. The headmaster told Greg, "You have to assert yourself. You have to hit this child." The headmaster beat the wayward student sharply on the legs with a pointer, then handed the pointer to Greg. Greg swatted the kid twice ("the hardest thing to do"). Another was John Ziolkowski in Sebha, who would occasionally whack misbehaving kids. But he had an excuse. Having grown up Catholic, one of his long-remembered pearls of wisdom was, "You can't mess with the nuns." One particularly strict nun at his school used to throttle kids by the neck, earning the moniker "Sister Choker."

In Tarhuna, while one Peace Corps female volunteer was teaching in a girls' school, Jane Beach was teaching fifth grade in a boys' grade school. This arrangement was not trouble-free. The students in Jane's class ranged in age from 10 to 17. On one occasion, one of those 17-year-old boys exposed himself in class. Chuck told Jane's headmaster what happened. As Jane related it, "The next day, men from the boy's extended family came to the school to try to resolve the boy's future at the school. The young man was expelled."

Neil McCabe never had a discipline problem with his students. He'd make the lesson entertaining, having conversations with himself as he took his hat on and off. He had two brothers who were shepherds in his class, but they were never in the school at the same time. They would alternate weeks, with one brother going to school and the other tending to their flock of sheep. One day two mothers came to the school, unveiled. At this point, Neil was so acculturated that he couldn't look them in the face, but simply looked down.

Before we Americans arrived, Libyan students were totally acculturated to rote memorization and passively sitting in class listening to teachers. By contrast, Rebecca Peterson taught in the highly participatory TEFL style (as we all did) where the kids speak 50% of the time. Her fellow women Libyan teachers did not understand this. But the kids got it. Rebecca says "The kids naturally enjoyed English class more than any of the other subjects."

George Carter was assigned to the town of Derna on the Mediterranean coast. His fifth-grade students ranged in age from 7 to 23. They were intrigued by his blond hair and would keep touching it. Once an 18-year-old in the class started to masturbate. For some reason, this wasn't covered in Clearfield and George didn't know what to do. So, he said, "OK, then, let's do some writing now." When teaching counting in English, George initially started using his thumb to designate "one." However, it turns out that this means "Up yours" in Libya (also not covered in Clearfield), so he used his index finger from then on. Another cultural behavior difference was that when his students blew their noses, they would lean over a desk and blow the snot straight out onto the floor. On the other hand, George would pull out a handkerchief, blow his nose and put the handkerchief back in his pocket. One student piped up, "Mr. George, why are you saving your snot?"

In the 5th grade class in Wadi Al Kerwa in Tripolitania, Roy Douthitt was impressed by the dedication of his "super" kids just to get to school. "Some of those kids rode a donkey three miles to school every morning. They were real Bedouins, living in tents, all of them. By the end of the year, they could talk to each other in English."

In Farzougha, Richard Massey was taken aback as every time he, or any teacher, entered the room, all the children would jump to their feet. He had brought a magic slate which was a big hit. As was his Frisbee that "caused quite a sensation." In addition to his two 5th grade classes, his headmaster Younis asked him to teach English to the 50 students in the 6th grade, which Richard agreed to.

As in most of our classes, Jim Putnam had younger kids and then some in their late teens. The late teens would regularly jump out the window and run away. As for the teachers and staff at his school, he says they could not have been more dedicated or peaceful. And they were grateful for Jim and his wife Judy's presence and skills. Since Judy and Jim taught both in Aljmail and in Hamda ten miles away, she would ride sidesaddle on the back of their Moto Guzzi to get to and from Hamda.

In Trudy Swartzentruber's and Cathy Kaiser's school in Derna, the Libyans separated the two 4th and 5th grades by tribe, the only instance of this organization I've heard of.

In Ghemines, some of Peter Crall's students were Bedouins who lived in tents. "They would show up in class with straw and grass in their hair."

Harold McElhinny observed that the only two topics his fellow teachers talked about were Israel and sex. After a while, Harold couldn't help but let his mischievous sense of humor gain the upper hand. He told them, "You know, American men can't have children because their penises are too small."

Libyan teacher, "Where do all your American children come from, then?"

Harold explained, "From Canada. We buy all our children from the

Canadians. That's why in November we have Thanksgiving Day. That's the day we celebrate getting all our children from Canada."

Well. We're talking about a tribal, oral society and a relatively small town. The word in Arabic for "small penis" is *zib sereer*. The rumor spread quickly and from the ground, from the rooftops, from house to house the phrase of the day was *zib sereer!* No doubt to this day, 50 years later, the citizens of Zawia, Libya still believe Harold's explanation of our Thanksgiving.

Israel came up rather abruptly for Cathy Kaiser. Early in her stint, she walked into an apothecary. Before she could utter a word, the pharmacist angrily blurted out, "Why do you sell jets to Israel?" Cathy thought, "Mm, gee, I don't recall selling any jets to Israel recently."

In Misurata one day, drinking tea and chatting with Libyan friends, one Libyan told Randy Melquist that the U.S. had 51 states. "What? No, we have 50 states." The Libyan replied, "No, you have 51." Randy asked, "OK, which one is the 51st?" The answer: "Israel".

In the Fezzan, one of Stoney Bird's students approached him one day and extended two doves to him. The student said, "Mr. Stoney, I hope you'll remember me for a good grade."

Ed Quinlan's school custodian in Benghazi kind of overdid the hospitality bit. As Ed describes him, he was an "older fellow, skinny as a rail, tall, swarthy, with a handlebar mustache, clear eyes and an eager-to-please countenance." But month in and month out, he waited on "Mr. Edward" hand and foot when it came to tea, sweets, and the occasional tuna fish sandwich. Towards the end of the year, on the verge of final exams, the custodian's attentions became more pronounced. "Each day, my classroom door would burst open and the old man would stick his grizzly fist through the opening with something to eat or drink." Final exams were conducted. Then, in public, Ed had to announced by name who had passed and who had not. At one point, announcing a boy's name who had failed abysmally, the headmaster pled to have the boy pass, "followed by a cacophony of protest from everywhere." "You cannot let this boy fail!" they said. It turns out the boy was the son of the obsequious custodian. Ed argued. The whole body of teachers persisted. Finally, Ed caved and passed the boy.

The old man sitting next to me leapt to his feet, threw his hands to the heavens and proclaimed, in Arabic, "Thanks be to God!" The others offered enthusiastic congratulations and assured me I had done the right thing. On the motorbike back home and for days thereafter, I criticized my decision relentlessly. The insight came only later. English class made no difference. It wasn't important. What was important was the child's standing in the village, and that of his family and father. He wasn't likely to use English in his life, let alone obtain a Ph.D. in it. For them, it was only the joy of victory and relief that counted. I smile inside whenever I think of the gift of joy given to me on that day.

PCV John Lynch taught a prestigious 5th grade class at the Al-Noor School in Derna which included two royal princes who were sons of the Derna Minister of Education Fatia Ashura. Due to his bright red hair, his students called him "Tomato sauce." Student Elie Boudt (whose family had come to Libya from the Turkish Empire in 1567 and whose parents were merchants) was fascinated with this archetypal, healthy American with his shock of red hair, his red face and sporting big boots. He vividly remembers how very deliberate and thoughtful John was. At the start of every school day, after the ritual singing of the Libyan National Anthem, a chosen student would address the school at a microphone set up for the occasion. John helped Elie write a speech in English which he then delivered before the mike. On several occasions he invited John, proud to show him off, to his family's for dinner.

In Sabratha, teaching at the Men's Teachers Training School, John Forasté was self-conscious about how young he looked ("more like 16 than 22"). He grew a mustache to try to look older. Anything to convey some small dollop of machismo. A fly was buzzing around the classroom. "Then came the fly—right for me—and flew into my mouth as I was speaking. What could I do? Only one thing. I swallowed it whole, without letting on to my extreme embarrassment. I wasn't about to give up what little control I had of the class."

Inspector and near-professional entomologist Jay Shetterly was assigned to an apartment in Tobruk with two high-falutin' Oxford grads who were teaching English at the local high school. They were uber-knowledgeable across a range of topics, including literature, music and art, impressing even Jay. They delighted in playing a game that Jay always lost, called "Leonardo Trivia." This would include the most obscure trivia questions you can imagine. For example, one question was "What was Hamlet wearing in Act III, Scene 2?" They knew. Turns out that Jay was assigned to inspect *them*. When he informed them, they laughed. In their Oxonian supercilious accents they sniveled, "Why, Jay, you don't even speak English!" Horrified at the prospect of a mere Harvard-educated American going to rate them, they protested mightily to the local school authorities. Jay fought back and won. They needn't have worried, however, since Jay found them to be fine teachers.

John Peterson in Homs had one student in his mud-hut school room with a photographic memory. He was "a pleasure to teach." At the end of the year, John gave him a special dictionary.

One single female Peace Corps teacher reflected on her experience inside and outside the classroom:

> The girls go home and tell their parents about their blonde young teacher who is teaching them English and who doesn't beat them, and who rewards them for work well done instead. It is so important to install a sense of achievement and competition in the girls; this has been sorely overlooked. I have found that much of the difficulty is overcome when you set an example of "learning is fun." There are frustrations and heartbreaks when a good student is taken out of class by her parents to be married; when a class is one hell of a discipline problem; when you think that the results of your two years' teaching won't be seen for maybe a decade. But you can also share the warmth of friendship with the women, you can feel the love given to you by a family, you can suddenly forget the antics of your class when they do the lessons well or give you presents from their hearts. There *is* a place for us here.

Dan Peters sent an Aerogram to a grade school class in his hometown of Menasha, Wisconsin and had some of his Libyan students sign their names in English. While the pen strokes are relatively crude compared to their dexterous Arabic signatures, what is remarkable is that here they were writing in English after only two months' study.

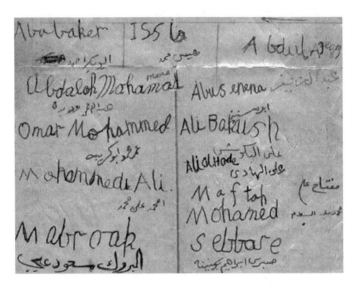

Letter from Libyan students to students in Menasha, Wisconsin

Dan also wrote home about the power of "show" not "tell":

Today I had to teach the sentence, "I clean my teeth every day." So I took my toothbrush and toothpaste and brushed my teeth in class. It was really funny leading a drill with a mouth full of toothpaste. Blub! Blub! No doubt it was the first time they ever saw anything like that toothbrush.

Dan Peters and his class in El Khozeur

(Note that, as illustrated in Dan Peters' photo, all the male Peace Corps teachers were required, for professional appearance, to wear a shirt, a tie and long pants in the classroom. No matter what the temperature.)

Bob Gausman observed that after 6th grade, when puberty hit, the girls no longer attended class. They would take to the veil. When he asked why bother sending the girls to school at all, he was told that even a little education helped raise the bride price. And, speaking of brides, the 5th grade boys used to constantly inspect the girls' faces, knowing this was the last chance to see them before they were veiled, anticipating that one of them might very well be a future wife.

Speaking of puberty, Bob had asked friends and family back in the States to send him magazines that he could cut out images from to teach English. One friend sent him a Sears catalog. The boys, of course, were mesmerized by the women's lingerie to the exclusion of all else.

In this same school, Bob once visited the *mudir's* office and was shown a locked closet filled with gorgeous wall maps. Bob: "Why can't we put those in the classroom?" "Oh, no, the maps'll get ruined."

My walking trips to Um El Jersan were much foreshortened by dint of the Moto Guzzi. It was what we would now call a dirt bike, designed for the off-road. While riding it, I wore my grey Air Force flight suit and a helmet. And, to carry my books and teaching materials, I bought a colorful *khurj* (donkey bag), a woven multicolored bag with two big pockets on either side connected with a double strap that you throw over the back of the donkey. This caused no end of mirth on the part of kids and villagers, as I toodled to and from the school. They would shout, "Mr. Randy, that's not supposed to go on a motorcycle, that's supposed to go on a donkey!" I told them I didn't care.

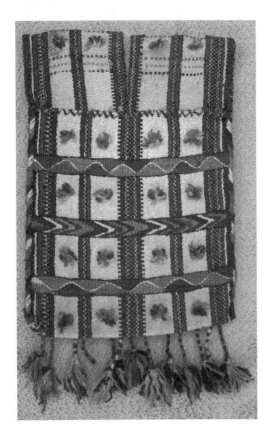

The donkey bag I lashed over my Moto Guzzi

There comes an exhilarating time when, as a bicycle rider, you reach the point that you can pedal with no hands. The corresponding moment with a motorcycle is when you can do a wheelie (a wheelstand, i.e. you jerk up on the handlebars and throw your weight back so that you're riding along on just the back wheel). I trained myself to do that and would show it off from time to time. But that was the wildest thing I ever did. (Had I opted to emulate Evel Knievel, maybe I would have tried to fly over 17 camels.)

On arrival at Um each day, Abdullah would continue to flap his arms saying "Freddo! Freddo!" (It was, indeed, cold now; inside my apartment I could see my breath each day.) While the Clearfield dorm-storm of nicknaming had faded with our dispersal to the far reaches of the Libyan countryside, that didn't stop me from continuing the tradition. On a lark, upon my arrivals at the school I started calling Abdullah "Freddo." I'd say, "Freddo, *keef halik*!" ("How are you?"). And he would laugh. Others over-heard me doing this and started calling him "Freddo" too. After a while the whole village forgot his name was Abdullah and called him "Freddo."

We had been taught that mixing in the teaching of songs creates interest and variety. Among other songs, I picked the catchy children's song with fun nonsense syllables, "This Old Man," because it also helped with counting. ("This old man, He plays three, He plays knick-knack on my knee, With a knick-knack paddy-whack, Give the dog a bone, This old man went rolling home.") I had no sooner started teaching this song to the class at Um when they started snickering and sniggering. I didn't know why, so charged ahead anyway to teach them the whole song. Later, I learned that the culprit was the words "knick" and "knack," both of which are almost the same as the word for "fuck" in Arabic. Needless to say, I didn't bother reprising that song at Um, much less teach it to the Al Gala kids. Sue Glover had been explicitly told not to say the word "neck." But she forgot and in demonstrating the parts of the body, she included "neck." This resulted in much tittering among her girl students. She was the talk of that week among the Libyan teachers.

Sue Glover's girls' class with teachers. Surman, Libya

Going forward, I had no idea I could help people win bets with my contact lenses.

Booze, Baseball and Bulgarians

Speaking of songs, my increasingly close friend Tahir scratched out the lyrics to the Libyan national anthem on a scrap of paper, and taught me how to sing it, wired into my noggin to this day.

On December 8, I received another long letter from Jeanne. I most definitely reciprocated. By long distance we were getting to know one another better. I also received a letter from JPAC saying they were not the source for issuing medals. They referred me to the Army Medal Office in Droitwich, Worcestershire, UK. I typed up a letter to them.

In early December I jerry-rigged a rudimentary backgammon set. Dan (who had been attacked *twice* by dogs on the way over) and I played three games that very day. We had couscous for supper, where he told me he listened to Arabic newscasts and when he heard words he didn't know, he'd write them down. He was also studying 1st grade Arabic books so he could systematically get a good grounding in the language. It reached the point where he started thinking in Arabic. We then went next door where El Haadi had organized an event that included singing, dancing, and playlets put on by the Al Gala and the Um El Jersan children. Some of it genuinely funny, but it went on far too long…till 1:30 AM.

With respect to games, Kevin Hunt used to play a card game called Scanbeke every night with his four Libyan roommates. The idea of the game involved cheating. Even rules about how to cheat. If you winked at your partner, it meant you had a queen. If you pulled the lobe of your left ear, it meant you had a king. But the double trick was you had to convey these signals without your opponents seeing them. This made for a very elaborate form of subversiveness. On Dan's next visit, we had boiled meat, peas, potatoes, onions, and cheese for supper. This night I also inaugurated a bedtime ritual. I took my trumpet up on the roof. It was, of course, incredibly quiet. Inky dark. I was at the very top of a vertiginous series of canyons. I put the trumpet to my lips and played Taps. What I didn't expect was the resounding echoing of these forlorn notes bouncing off the canyon walls for miles.

The next morning, I felt some slight pain in my lower belly, wondering if it was coming from the pressure there from my trumpet playing. At this stage of my life, where the amount of time available seemed infinite to my young mind, I vowed that the next instrument I would learn would be trombone, and then more. As unrealistic as this was, I also aimed at learning more languages. German was next on my list. In light of these ambitions that I did not shed until much too late in life, I wish I could go back to my younger self and tell myself "You're spreading yourself too thin! Focus!"

Also in early December, over in Aujila, the two Bobs—Bob Pearson and Bob Marshall—continued what was the most unusual bonding activity in Peace Corps Libya. Both being avid professional baseball fans, and both having memorized the batting order of all the teams from their childhood and teenhood, they played a series of Fantasy Wiffle Ball games. One would pitch. The other would bat. Marshall chose the Pittsburgh Pirates from 1960. Pearson's team was the Detroit Tigers from another year. Depending on how far they hit the wiffle ball, it could be a single, a double, a triple and if it hit the back of an abandoned Libyan courthouse it was a home run. Somehow they kept track of the score and the innings as they went along.

Both Bobs were also into soccer. Bob Marshall often played soccer with the young men in his village. Because he was tall, they made him goalie. Because Bob grew up playing baseball and touch football, he had many years of using his hands in sports, whereas the Libyans were skilled with their feet. He still treasures their comment *yimsik kwayyis* ("he catches well"). Conversely, when Bob Pearson had been a soccer coach in Peace Corps Afghanistan, he inadvertently crossed over a line. In typical American style, he barked out to his players to do this, to do that. He paced up and down the sidelines, yelling encouragement to his team. An acquaintance then came up to Bob, jabbed the stem of a flower in his mouth and peremptorily told Bob to stop yelling.

"Why should I stop yelling?"

"Because you're trying to affect the outcome of the game."

"What's wrong with that?"

"You are trying to affect Allah's intent. Allah already knows how the game will turn out."

Down in Samnu, Bob Gausman was startled to witness a fully-staffed Bulgarian construction crew descending upon the village with the remit to build a huge community outhouse. The crew included short-sleeved, tractor-driving Bulgarian women—eye candy for the local Libyan men. The thing is, these Bulgarians spoke no English. So, when they invited Bob over for dinner the only way they could communicate was through mutually familiar proper names. After dinner the Bulgarians poured out the schnapps. One raised his shot glass and shouted, "Eisenhower!" Bulgarian custom dictated that everyone down the entire glass. So, everyone else shouted back, "Eisenhower!" and downed their glasses. On the heels of this, someone shouted "Montgomery!" Everyone shouted back, "Montgomery!" and downed another shot. Then "General Patton!" Shots downed. Dozens more shots ensued, climaxing with "Studebaker Packard!" By this time, Bob was totally schnookered.

Field Marshal Montgomery, "Monty", icon beloved by Bulgarians

National Archives and Records Administration

As I proceeded through my days, I couldn't help but continue to roll up more layers of knowledge about the culture I was immersed in. For example, I noticed that Arab men hold hands. But you can't be squeamish about this when they hold yours, as it's not an indication of homosexuality. It turns out that when you're in a tightly monitored society with sexual segregation, unmarried men have zero female companionship. But the need for touch does not go away. So they hold hands with other males, even dance with one another. Arab men rationalize this as a sign of solidarity and kinship. John Forasté recalls, "It was uncomfortable for me, very uncomfortable. Here was my colleague, who was also a neighbor, and I chatting in our neighborhood while holding hands. He was a very friendly Palestinian—a hefty guy with very big hands, I might add."

I noticed that there were three beasts of burden in Libyan society: camels, donkeys and women. Women carry brushwood in baskets strapped to their heads and water in tanks on their backs—every day. Other activities include picking vegetables in the garden, baking bread, milking goats or sheep, preparing meals. Oh, and when there's time left over, maybe weaving palm frond baskets. And just to rub it in, when transporting chattel in a pickup truck, the men sit in the front seat and the women sit in the back with the sheep. Dan Peters commented, "When going to the fields or coming from them, the man will ride a donkey and the woman will walk about 20 paces behind. Even if there is another donkey available, the women will never ride it."

In Benghazi, Jeanne Maurey noticed, "The Libyan women are all huge and love it because it is a desired trait here." The thinking being that if you are overweight, you can afford a lot of food.

I noticed, via many discussions and reading, that *nowhere* in the Koran does it say that women must veil their faces. Mohammed does call for women to cover their heads. It turns out that the veiling of faces was a *cultural* practice spread throughout the Turkish Empire. It was so widespread and ingrained that to this day, millions of Moslem Arabs will tell you that the Koran demands women cover their face.

I learned what a clever community organizer Mohammed was. As he went about proselytizing his new religion, he knew that there were hundreds of minor deities (a God in Arabic is *lah*) worshipped across what became the Arab Empire. He knitted all this together under one umbrella, as he explained that all these individual gods were manifestations of "The God" ("Al" meaning "the"), namely Allah. He also observed that many of these communities worshipped rocks. Instead of dismissing the idea of rocks altogether (which he realized would be a fruitless effort), he embraced the idea by narrowing down, for example, the number of rocks at the Kaaba building in Mecca from 360 to one, calling it "The Black Stone" now so central to Hajj celebrations.

Many of these discussions took place in Abdu-Salaam's shop over tea. On two occasions I felt like a Connecticut Yankee in King Arthur's Court when it came to some Western technical developments unknown in Libya at the time. One was when, to the shock of everyone in the shop, I dropped my Timex watch into a bucket of water. After a while, I retrieved it, and it was still working. They had never seen a waterproof watch. The other had to do with my contact lenses. Bob Marshall also wore them, and I had learned from him at Andover that if you get a painful dust mote in your eye and you have no access to a sink, much less contact lens solution, the fallback is to take the lens out of your eye, carefully place it in your mouth, let your tongue rinse the lens, then put it back in.

Libya being dusty, I found myself having to remove a contact lens in Abdu-Salaam's shop one day, then putting it back in my eye. When I looked up, everyone was staring slack-jawed at me. I immediately intuited why, so I explained, "You see, in the United States we have developed these tiny pieces of plastic that are like little eyeglasses. You put them in your eyes and it helps you see better." They didn't believe it, so I took a lens out, placed it in my palm and showed it around the shop to murmurs of amazement.

About a half-hour after I put the lens back in, a fellow named Mohammed ambled into the shop.

"Hey, Mohammed," said Abdu-Salaam, "Guess what? Mr. Randy has little pieces of glass in his eye for eyeglasses. He takes them out of his eyes, then puts them back in."

Mohammed replied, "Oh, no, this is not possible."

Another in the shop chirped up, "Oh, yes, Mr. Randy does this. He just showed us."

Mohammed still didn't believe. "No, no. That's crazy."

Another in the shop said, "Yes, yes, it's true, isn't it, Mr. Randy?"

I nodded.

Mohammed said, "I don't believe it."

Abdu-Salaam countered, "You wanna bet?"

Mohammed stepped up to the plate. "Sure. How much?"

Abdu-Salaam threw out, "Thirty pounds." (Thirty Libyan pounds was one month's salary for Mohammed.)

Mohammed was cool with that. "OK."

Abdu Salaam shook Mohammed's hand, smiled craftily and looked my way. "Mr. Randy....?"

I promptly removed a contact lens, placed it in the palm of my right hand and leaned over to show it to a crestfallen Mohammed who had to fork over the money on the spot.

While I enjoyed these socializations, I balanced my life by not hanging around all day in the shop. I would've gone stir crazy. In my diary: "Nobody reads here. All day they listen to the radio, talk, play cards, drink tea. Their indolence is a little exasperating but I keep it to myself."

On December 19, Dan and I grabbed a cab from Yifran for the 85-mile trip to Tripoli. Cost? $1.80. We checked into the Hotel Haiti. Cost? $13 per person per night. At the Peace Corps office, I ran into a bunch of us fellow volunteers. Terrific to see them. And after two months of monastic existence, it was wonderful to see some of the Bisbee women. Most terrific of all was luxuriating in a *hot* shower at the hotel before turning in.

In such a strict Islamist country, Tripoli was hardly a hot spot. The best you could do was illustrated by Randy Melquist's accidental discovery of an Italian night club frequented by Italian women. The only catch? They were heavily chaperoned by their families. You could ask a woman to dance, then carefully walk her back to her family table. At least you could talk to and touch a woman, however chastely. Ted Kelley frequented so many bars in Tripoli he had ratings for them all which he incorporated later into a manual he wrote for Libya III. His favorite activity was to sit on a rooftop bar and sip whiskey sours while watching the sun set on the Mediterranean.

Over the next few days, Dan and I took a bus fifty miles to the west of Tripoli, standing all the way, to visit the extensive Roman ruins at Sabratha, most notably the still-intact amphitheater, which used to seat 5,000 people.

Randy at Sabratha Amphitheater

After a night in Tripoli, we hopped on another bus (much jostling and pushing to get on, you just have to go with the flow) to travel 75 miles to the east to Homs, where we checked into a hotel and then visited the nearby, much more magnificent Roman city of Leptis Magna, considered one of the most impressive Roman ruins in the world. The ruins had been buried under sand until 1911, when the newly arrived Italians excavated the city as a symbol of the past grandeur of the Roman Empire. Baths, an amphitheater, buildings, still-intact roads, arches, colonnades, mosaics. I noticed colorful marble cladding. I had never seen such a thing in any Greek or Roman ruin before. I subsequently inquired about this and discovered that many Roman columns were clad tip-to-toe in beautiful colored marble, but that over the centuries, vandals had stripped away all the valuable marble. (In the case of Leptis Magna, this cladding had been sourced from Italy, Greece, Asia Minor and Egypt.) This meant that all the renderings in epic movies of Roman columns depicted as plain white were plain wrong. More relevantly, this extends to U.S. examples of this kind of architecture, like our Supreme Court.

Roman column cladding at Leptis Magna

A month later, Bob Marshall visited Leptis. His diary notes, "Leptis Magna is one of the sensational sights of the world, about which I could never say too much. The ruins are overwhelming in both their grandeur and their preservation." And unlike the rest of us, Bob, as a birder, was overwhelmed (I could tell from his two exclamation marks) by the birds he sighted there. "I almost cried for my binoculars, the birds were so great: shrikes, warblers, thrushes, crows, doves, hawks, curlews—and hoopoes!!" (Don't rush off to dive into Wikipedia, here's the dope: Hoopoes are colorful, display a distinctive crown of feathers, have long, narrow, sharp beaks, and are mentioned in the Bible in the Book of Solomon, in Leviticus and in Deuteronomy. To top it off, the hoopoe is the national bird of Israel.) For me, the birds of Leptis totally escaped my notice.

Hoopoe

On a different occasion, John Lynch ran into Bob at Leptis. He recalls that Bob pulled out his wallet and showed John a picture of Elvis Presley. Bob had his idiosyncrasies!

Bob Gausman visited Leptis and was blown away by a 100-hole-long marble latrine. (Tourists at Leptis and Sabratha never fail to take photos of these facilities.) The Romans had resourcefully leveraged the nearby Mediterranean to pipe in sea water that would wash away the waste. Later, Bob leaned up against a random column and spent the night there. (In Sabratha, Joe Connor would snuggle four feet down in one of its ancient mosaic baths to do weekly lesson plans. "I was smiling that here I was in a place all my own in a two-thousand-year-old bath.")

Leptis Magna was the hometown of the only Roman Emperor from Libya, a Berber named Lucius Septimius Severus (193 A.D.–211 A.D.). Once emperor, he greatly enhanced the whole city, making it the third most important city in North Africa, after Carthage and Alexandria. He notably expanded the Roman Empire in 202 A.D. in southeast Libya.

Leptis Magna

Over the next three days, Dan and I hitchhiked to Suug El Xumis, Zlieten, Misurata (stayed overnight at PCV Dick Kean's), Tummino, then to Homs to spend night with PCV Peter Hawkes, then to Tarhuna and finally back to Tripoli on Christmas Eve. (Unbeknownst to us at the time, this was the very day that Libyan television debuted.) On Christmas Day, Dan Peters, Mike Culkin and I went shopping. At an Indian shop with many ivory carvings Dan explained the fascinating hidden meanings of the various pieces.

Because it was Christmas, I went to the huge post office to make a call home. To do so you had to go to a teller and get assigned to one in a long row of booths. The line quality was terrible and the service so unreliable that you could be cut off at any time. So you had to talk fast.

In my diary I said the only thing I wanted for Christmas was Chapstick (nowhere to be found in Libya) to help me playing the trumpet when my lips got too dry. As our winter vacation was going to start January 10 and Dan and I were going to travel to Tunisia and Algeria, we visited the Algerian Embassy to make sure we had our visas. Instead of a turkey Christmas dinner, I consumed couscous, chased down with beer.

In one instance in the Tripoli *souk* (bazaar) Kathy Lamoureux did her part for Americans' reputations. She was helping some Westerners there to bargain at length for some ornamental brass plates of camels. At the last minute, "the Westerners walked away. I felt so bad about the situation that I bought the plates. I still have them now in Sydney, Australia. My one other souvenir is a book of Libyan proverbs which fits snugly in my bookcase."

Tom Weinz went to this same Tripoli post office late one night and put in his request to call the States. "It was late. I was tired. I was alone in the room. I put my feet up on a small table and dozed off. Suddenly, I heard the lone Libyan operator yelling at me. Too late, I realized that the heels of my feet were directly across from a portrait of King Idris." So much for Tom's call to the U.S. that day!

(In a similar vein, some ten years later while touring the exclusive boardroom of the Ministry of the Interior in Riyadh, Saudi Arabia, a friend ushered me into the royal bathroom. Needless to say, it was liberally embellished with all things gold—like spigots, handles, and the toilet appurtenances. "This is not how the toilet was originally situated," he said. I asked what he meant. "Originally this toilet was facing Mecca. So we had to rip up the floor tiling and redo the plumbing to pivot the whole kit-and-kaboodle 90 degrees away.")

Another Bob—Marshall—met two Irish lads, Pat and Terry, on his way back from his second school one day. They told Bob their job was to construct an electric plant for Aujila. Bob noticed that their main furniture was cases of beer and asked about that. They told Bob that the first couple of Guinesses were just to get the sand out of their throats. Then the real drinking (for which they seemed to have an unlimited supply) would begin.

Over in Derna, in Cyrenaica, Christmas made the PCVs feel homesick so they cobbled together a Christmas of sorts. George Carter brought poinsettias to the women's (Trudy Swartzentruber, Mary Buelt and Cathy Kaiser) apartment and strung them on the wrought iron stairway leading to the door. (He had been walking down an alleyway the day before with some students, and had admired some poinsettia plants he saw. An hour later, his students brought him a gunny sack filled with the blossoms.) Mark Lepori brought a ragged "Charlie Brown" Christmas tree. Mary Buelt had been saving up foil candy wrappers for months and used these to decorate the tree. They all—one Mennonite, two Catholics, an Assembly of God, a Methodist and an atheist—went to midnight mass at the Catholic Church in Derna.

In Aujila Bob Marshall was able to indulge in a right-proper Christmas dinner of a dozen dishes with free-flowing booze at the Occidental Petroleum facility there. These oil companies, of course, regularly flew in fresh supplies of food and drink. Their budgets exceeded that of the entire Peace Corps. Bob had made friends of several of the oil workers, most notably a tough, robust, hail-fellow-well-met Irv Welch. With only one small store in his oasis with a limited supply of Bulgarian canned vegetables, Egyptian pasta (and no bread), Bob had worried how he would eat for two years. Thanks to the concern and generosity of the Occidental quartermaster, he was able to score filet mignon, duckling, and other goodies from time to time (not to mention peanut butter and jelly). In addition, some villagers who commuted out to the oil camps would return to the village every afternoon, bringing him bread from the Occidental camp.

December 26th was *Istiklal* ("Independence") Day. The Peace Corps physician, Dr. Coulson, examined me. He said I had a left inguinal hernia that would have to be operated on in the near future. With Dan and PCV Joe Conner I visited Wheelus Air Base for the first time. While Dan and Joe had dental work done, I got a haircut. We had a great meal in the mess hall, a room equipped with slot machines. Couscous again for dinner.

On this same day in Aujila, Bob Marshall sat in the front row, next to the regional governor from Jalo, for a three-hour celebration attended by everyone in the village. The village elders paraded in; students sang the Libyan National Anthem; a teacher related the history of Libya (including numerous references to Omar Mukhtar and King Idris) and intoned an invocation; the students performed two skits and two games; tea and juice were served. The ceremony was punctuated by frequent enthusiastic clapping and wrapped up with another singing of the national anthem.

New Year's Eve? I decided that I wanted the inside of my main room to feel like a Bedouin tent and proceeded to festoon colorful blue, gray and white striped cloth billowing down from the ceiling.

In Libya, January 1 is the Feast of the Tree. Part of the celebrations included all the teachers giving little speeches. I donned my *holie, farmla* and *caboose* and gave a little speech of my own.

On January 2, with nails holding the material in place, I draped my main room ceiling with the "tent" material, removing the rectangular hard edges of a modern building and with the cloth billowing from the ceiling, making it feel that I was indeed, in a Bedouin tent.

January 11 was our day to start our winter vacation. Unfortunately I threw up nine times. What a miserable way to start a vacay!

And who could have guessed that scattered about Tunisia there were "Châlets de Nécessités"?

Catacombs, Cones and Camels

On January 12, Dan and I each got a five-cc shot of gamma globulin, obtained our Libyan exit visas and jammed ourselves into the cramped back of a shared Peugeot 404 taxi. We were super excited to have a full two weeks of vacation. Eleven hours later we arrived at Sfax, Tunisia, on the Mediterranean coast, dog tired, but with the fatigue offset a bit by good-hearted joking with all the passengers.

The next day we explored the old city of beautiful Sfax, then took a train to Sousse, halfway up the coast towards Tunis. After a night at the Claridge Hotel, we visited the vast Grand Mosque of Sousse, the first mosque I had entered. Next, we visited an underground museum. Escorted by an old guide and holding white candles, we descended into 40-mile-long catacombs where 15,000 Christians are entombed.

The following day, we took a train to Tunis. At an intermediary train station where we briefly we got off, I was first perplexed then convulsed with laughter at a sign on a door: "Châlet de Nécessité" (an exquisite euphemism for a toilet). In Tunis, went to a Turkish bath for the first time, then visited the El Bardo Museum, the second largest museum in Africa after The Egyptian Museum in Cairo and known for its Roman mosaics.

We took a side trip to the ruins of Carthage, visited the incredibly picturesque town of Sidi Bou Said, then had supper in an Arab greasy spoon.

(Richard Massey, Victor Gramigna and Pat Hilliard found their way to Tunis during this same vacation. Their five-course meal with wine and tip put them back $1.30 each. And the hotel? $1.80 a night per person.)

Dan and I hopped on a train which took us to Souk Al Ahras in Algeria. I had expected the scenery to be dusty and desert-like, as in Libya, but the terrain was mountainous, forested, with rushing streams. Breathtaking sights. On the train we met some hunters who had bagged 12 wild boars. We hitched two rides to get to the spectacular medieval city of Constantine. Like something out of a Hobbit movie. The city is a series of wide volcano cones that have petrified, the outer body of the volcanoes having eroded away over the eons. These cones are connected with picturesque swinging bridges over deep chasms. Stunning panoramas, and the Arab quarter was fascinating, right down to prostitutes sitting in caged windows reminiscent of Amsterdam's red-light district displays. I remember many cave-like dwellings with bulky, worn, centuries-old doors.

Randy and Algerian road signs

Then we hitched a ride to Timgad, a spacious Roman city 150 miles inland from the Mediterranean. Like Leptis Magna, all the roads, lined with columns, were intact, triumphal arches still standing, an intact amphitheater. It had been built as a retirement community for Roman soldiers. Awe-inspiring.

I was unaware of it at the time, but Dan and I turned out to be highly compatible traveling companions. In retrospect, I suppose, we were both highly traveled. We were both adventurous and loved trying new things, new foods, etc. And, coming from the bare existence we were used to in Libya, just staying in a run-down hotel that had electricity and maybe some running cold water was a luxury. "What are we going to grab for dinner?" "Sardines." "OK."

Then back to Tunisia and the town of Gafsa (my first oasis!), where boys dove for coins in a Roman pool and girls wove intricately designed cloths

216

on looms. We took our first camel ride out to another oasis, a three-mile trip. Very exotic locale and eerily quiet in the desert, where all you hear is the soft padding of the camels' feet on the sand. A train to Sfax. We were so tired during a two-hour layover that we just slept on hard stone benches. Another train to Sousse. Dan and I clambered up on the luggage racks to sleep which didn't go down well with the locals. Taxi to Kairouan, home of The Great Mosque, built in 670 A.D. Occupying almost 100,000 square feet, it's one of the largest Islamic monuments in North Africa.

As we meandered about Kairouan, we noticed a delightful consistency of ribbed domes throughout the city—i.e., instead of a smooth surface, bricks were deployed corners-out to create a unique effect. At lunch we encountered an architect with Peace Corps Tunisia. I expressed my admiration for the ribbed domes. "I'm afraid that's my fault," he said, and went on to explain that when he first arrived, he had seen one example of such a dome and he recommended to the city fathers that they convert all their other domes to the ribbed variety, as it was authentic to the city. They put him in charge of making it happen.

Next day, a bus to Tunis and we got a Swissair flight to Tripoli. On the plane, I finished reading *The Idiot*, just one of the 250 paperback books supplied to us by the Peace Corps. It was only 49 years later, in reading Bob Marshall's diary, that I discovered he was reading this very same book less than a month before.

We took a bus from the airport to Tripoli, coincidentally sitting with Peace Corps Libya Director Bill Whitman and his wife. We crashed that night in the Hotel Haiti, our vacation over. The next day, January 24th, I returned to my "home away from home," Al Gala.

Bob Marshall had left me a note. Turns out that, unfairly, the Peace Corps had allowed Dan and me to gallivant all over Tunisia and Algeria, while the Ministry of Education in Benghazi had not allowed Bob, who was psyched to visit Tunisia, to leave the country for winter vacation. Bob had quite resourcefully arranged to travel about Libya, dropping in on various PCVs' homes, in Homs, Zawia, Azzazia and Al Gala. He had dutifully hung out at Belgassim's shop all day, hoping someone would invite him to dinner. But, uncharacteristically, it never happened. With a combination of hitchhiking and busing, Bob had covered 360 miles. Total transportation expense? Four dollars.

During this vacation, John Becker visited Malta. Aboard a small plane on his return towards Tripoli, he found himself seated next to a loud-mouthed, ugly-American Texas oilman. The oilman spoke to John several times, and each time, John responded to him in Arabic. Finally, it dawned on the Texan that not only was John not swarthy, he was fair skinned even for an American. He blurted out, "Hey, you ain't no Ay-rab!" Undeterred, John again responded to him in Arabic. After that, the oilman never bothered John again.

Also visiting Malta were six women PCVs, including Jeanne Maurey. For four days they stayed at a three-bedroom place. The cost per person was $1.92/day.

Malta was a popular destination, as Greg Strick, Angus Todd (Fairleigh Dickinson College) and Bob O'Keefe decided to go there by freighter. On January 9, 1969, going through Benghazi customs, they were told they needed to produce their WHO cards (yellow World Health Organization documents) with their necessary smallpox vaccinations registered before they could debark. They had so very conveniently—all three of them—left their cards in their villages.

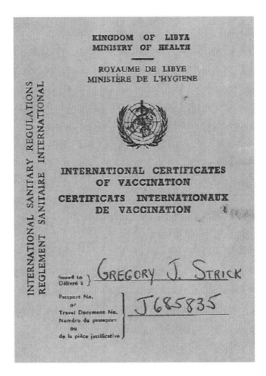

Greg Strick's on-the-fly WHO card

There was just one hour to go before their freighter weighed anchor. They rushed to the Ministry of Health to get the necessary vaccinations. As the minutes ticked by, an official sitting behind a larger desk laid out three WHO cards. Opening up a desk drawer, he drew out a stamp, summarily stamped all three cards and said, "That's it! Have a great trip!" They had not bothered to administer the requisite vaccinations. While they made the departure just in time, a great trip it was not. The high seas nauseated them the whole way to Valletta.

An example of splitting hairs occurred when Trudy Swartzentruber, Dave Munro and Cathy Kaiser were returning from vacation in Tunisia. When they reached the Tunisia-Libya border, the taxi driver ordered them to get out. Trudy said, "Hey, you said you would take us to Tripoli!" He said, "No, I promised to take you to *Tripolitania*." Upset, Trudy shouted, "What would Allah think of you?" Allah didn't think much of this so they had to settle for another taxi to Tripoli.

■

Going to sleep that January 24, I didn't know that on the very next day a remarkable, touching event would play out in Um El Jersan.

Critters

A word or two about insects and animals, should you ever venture into the hinterlands of an underdeveloped country. There is no parallel to visiting Europe, where your observations and interactions with dogs on the streets of Paris or deer in the Black Forest do not require adjustment. If you are an experienced First-World traveler, you may be tempted to extrapolate from the First World to the Third World, just one word. Don't.

Let's start from the smallest to the largest critters in Libya.

First, microscopic parasitic flatworm eggs. They thrive in freshwater. No, it's not like Europe, where you drink water and get Montezuma's Revenge and merely suffer from debilitating diarrhea for a few days. These eggs trigger a dread disease called schistosomiasis that kills 200,000 people a year. The eggs invade your urinary tract or your intestines. Symptoms include blood in the stool and urine and abdominal pain, and often enough, death by kidney failure.

Luckily, in their sometime wisdom, Clearfield management warned us to never drink fresh water from a stream, lake or cistern. Or if you had to, boil the hell out of it first. Otherwise stick to bottled water, beer, wine, fruit juice.

This brings us up to sand flies. (Or maybe they were midges?) They're not microscopic, but unlike skeeters, they're well-nigh invisible to the human eye. And therein lies the problem. There ain't no screen small enough to keep'em out! According to my diary, the sand flies/midges started in on me February 24, 1969. The problem is they bite, resulting in welts smaller than mosquito bites, but just as itchy. It was terribly hard not to scratch, which made things worse.

And since they also outnumber mosquito bites, they inflict many more welts. After a bit, the insides of both my forearms were literally coated with bites. It took years for all the scarring to go away. I suppose I could've used Off! or something, but maybe it wasn't available or I just didn't think of it. Plus, consider the nuisance of applying it daily.

Ants. Never a problem for me. And for Bob Marshall, they were insectivore saviors. From his diary, "Ants are fantastic! Patrolling my courtyard. I see trains of them leading to and from my kitchen. Now they are lighting on winged greenies that fall to earth stunned by my lamp."

Giant fleas. Jay and Nancy Corrin lived above a camel market in Misurata. And not any old camel market, but the second largest camel market in Libya. (The largest is Kufra, deep in the Sahara.) Their bed was "frequently frequented by giant fleas from the camels. It was a chore to keep the sheets from getting bloody."

Flies. (The Libyan ones are like our houseflies, but on steroids.) For Bob Marshall they were a scourge. "Flies come in every time the door is opened, and my stomach prohibits extreme spraying while a room is occupied." Bob bought two kinds of poison, Rapkill and Rotex "which turn a room full of flies into a buzzing morgue in a matter of mere minutes."

From Dennis Carlson: "The big desert flies, the kind that stick to your body and even bite, circled me like furies as I made the walk back and forth from Genobee."

Ted Kelley referred to the fly as the National Bird of Libya. When motorcycling in the winter, he would periodically stop to warm his hands near the hot exhaust pipe, only to be assailed on his lips and in his eyes by flies. His Libyan friends would say to him, "Flies are our friends."

Flies didn't get into my house much, but outside they were ubiquitous. I remember going to the sole Al Gala butcher shop down in the hot valley. No screens, no electricity to keep the meat cool. Not only was the air thick with buzzing flies inside, they literally covered entire slabs of meat hanging on hooks. The butcher would ask which part of the meat I wanted. I would indicate the part. He'd have to swat away the flies from that part of the carcass, slice away with his knife, wrap it in paper and give it to me. Needless to say, I was at pains to cook such meat to a fare-thee-well.

Cathy Kaiser asked her mother to send her flypaper. It came. She hung it up. In only a half-our, it was totally coated with flies.

Flies also carry a dread disease: trachoma. The flies alight on Libyans' faces, randomly crawling around. When they touch the surface of an eye (Jim Putnam reports the flies are attracted to the moisture) the trachoma takes root, at first as a small grey dot in the eye, then gradually expanding over time until the entire surface of the eye is a milky gray and the victim is blind. Yugoslavian doctors examined the teachers and students in Al Gala and found that most of the pupils and the teachers had trachoma of one stage or another. In a 1968 survey of 2,800 patients at a Tripoli hospital, 100% of them were found to have trachoma. Victor Gramigna rode a bus to Tripoli twice a week to give English lessons at the Institute of the Blind. Many of them had gone blind due to trachoma. (Unbeknownst to Victor at the time, Tom Furth regularly motored to Tripoli to teach English to blind elementary school students.)

While sitting around with Libyans and watching in horror as they allowed flies to migrate all over their face, into their noses, mouths, and eyes, Jim Putnam remembers seeing up to four flies at once in a student's eyes. He remembers that every day in Aljmail after singing the national anthem, the children in the school would all line up, close their eyes and teachers would spray some kind of medication on their faces. John Forasté reported seeing flies walking on babies' eyelids. "Their mothers didn't swat them away. They seemed oblivious to the flies. I couldn't comprehend how that was possible and never learned to accept it."

In Al Gala, I swatted flies away like a son of a bitch. I asked my friends why they didn't do likewise. They said, "Allah meant for the flies to be on our faces. If we were to swat them away, we would be disobeying Allah." I countered "Well, if Allah is all powerful and does not want me to swat away the flies, He would have stopped me." This argument did not gain any traction. They couldn't see beyond the grip of fatalism they were embedded in.

I had been casting about for what my second-year project would be. I soon zeroed in on eradicating trachoma from my village. It turns out the treatment involves the application of a Chapstick-like tube of tetracycline to the eyelids, with a repeat application six weeks later. I was inspired by two heroic Western doctors of recent renown, Dr. Albert Schweitzer and Dr. Tom Dooley. (Schweitzer was a German theologian, musician, philosopher and physician who won the Nobel Peace Prize in 1952 for his dedicated work in Gabon. Dooley built many clinics and hospitals in Laos.) I felt that this would be a much more satisfying contribution to humankind than just teaching.

Spiders. On May 20, 1969 I killed a super-weird-looking spider in my apartment.

Black beetles. One night, Bob Marshall noticed a thin strand of sand spilling down from the ceiling. He wondered where it was coming from. After several nights he discovered it was hideous black beetles, scraping sand out from the junction of a ceiling beam and a wall. "The black beetles are ugly enough to look at, and their after-lights-out scraping gives me the creeps, but it is the killing them that turns my intestines the most."

Dung beetles. A dung beetle made Neil McCabe a half-hour late to school. He was walking to school one morning and spied a dung beetle approaching a large roll of donkey dung that was much larger than the beetle. For a half-hour Neil watched fascinated as the beetle managed to roll the dung down the street.

Cockroaches. Alan Frank coped with gigantic cockroaches that "lived in my Libya-style toilet." In Brak, Martin Sampson declared there were two seasons: Cockroaches and No Cockroaches. When he first arrived in his dorm, he heard what sounded like a hailstorm inside a wooden cabinet. It was a ton of cockroaches. They were so tough, he'd smash them hard and still they'd walk away. Dave Dittman's bed was on the floor. Three-inch-long cockroaches would crawl over him at night. One night he threw a board at a cockroach. The cockroach was so big it moved the board.

When Mark and Maggie Brossoit arrived at their Tripoli apartment, they were appalled to see literally thousands of cockroaches clinging to the walls. They washed the place down from stem to stern. That was not enough to deter all their visitors. They dreaded turning on the light in the kitchen every morning. They would find four-inch-long cockroaches in the sink.

In Derna, Cathy, Mary and Trudy called it, "The Battle of the Cockroaches." As they had no furniture, they took advantage of free furniture available at the Ministry of Education's warehouse. So, they brought back a kitchen cupboard. They opened it. Out burst hundreds of cockroaches! The women grabbed brooms and starting slamming the bugs as hard and as fast as they could.

In Sabratha, the Forastés were initially living in some empty British troop barracks that had running water. The water in the bathroom attracted giant cockroaches. John wrote, "So, when duty called, we would accompany each other and take a deep—very deep—breath and enter the bathroom with a flashlight to not very successfully shoo away as many of the swarming—yes, swarming— giant insects as we could. It was a God-awful experience."

Worms. One of the cooking challenges for Diane Forasté was worms in the flour. Even with a large sifter recommended by Libyan friends, "to my dismay, it only sifted out the one-inch or larger worms. We learned to accept the tiny worms, but were sure to thoroughly cook them from then on." However, she could not abide these creatures in fresh oranges, "… which, when cut in half, were swarming with tiny worms inside."

Scorpions? Their stings are debilitating and can be lethal. Since scorpions like to nestle in shoes overnight, the Peace Corps counseled us to shake out our shoes vigorously each morning. I did so religiously for the rest of my Libyan stay, and, by force of habit, for years later back in the States. In the village of Edri, deep in the Sahara, Chip Chandler reports that two toddlers didn't shake out their shoes and died after being stung. After a huge dust storm that drifted sand on Chip Chandler's patio like snow, a five-inch-long scorpion crawled out. Chip threw lamp oil on it, then a match.

Teaching school the summer of 1969, Frank Reese stepped on something that made a huge noise that scared the crap out of him. Turned out it was a chameleon. He ended up keeping it on a tree branch on the wall, as a kind of pet. He then found scorpions, cut off their stingers and fed them to the chameleon.

Another piece of Peace Corps advice remembered by Rufus Cadigan was to place our beds in the middle of the room, as scorpions skittered around at the tops of walls and might fall on us in bed and attack.

At Clearfield they'd also warned us about scorpions under rocks. Angus Todd, in Ganfuda, used to enjoy purposely lifting up rocks and making note of how many black versus yellow (the most poisonous) scorpions there were beneath.

One day, Paul Rhodes, in Al Beida in Cyrenaica, was stretching a laundry line across the courtyard of his house and needed a rock to anchor it. He gingerly lifted a rock, and sure enough, there were three scorpions twitching about there. Paul started to take slow steps backward. Something grazed his calf and he leapt up in fright. He looked down to see what it was. A blade of grass.

John Becker was posted deep in the Fezzan in the village of Gira. At night, it got cold. One night, having put on a sweatshirt, he felt something crawling up his sleeve. Whoops! He immediately worried that this could be a scorpion. He ever so slowly slipped the sweatshirt off, then shook it thoroughly, and out came...a praying mantis.

Just before the 1969 summer vacation, Victor Gramigna's students gave him some watermelons, more than he could eat. He left them in the house. Upon his return, the melons were disintegrated and the house was infested with literally hundreds of scorpions. Victor pounded as many as he could to death, but couldn't handle them all. The school custodians came to the rescue by spraying the rest and removing their carcasses.

Back in Libya I in Brak, Martin Sampson was sitting outside his house with friends, drinking tea. He spied a scorpion and luckily remembered the name for it in Arabic and shouted *agreb*! One of his friends smashed the scorpion to smithereens with his sandal. The summer previous to his arrival, ten people had died in Brak from scorpion bites.

Frogs. One evening a frog came bounding into Richard Massey's bedroom. This is the only instance I've heard of about these amphibians in Libya.

Mouse in the house. (Mice in the hice? Why isn't the plural of "house" "hice"?) My battle with mice was ongoing. My first encounter was in November 1968 when I threw one out of my house. In January, I bought a mousetrap and duly placed some cheese on it. The mice never went for it. The cheese went stale. I killed a mouse with a broomstick in February and again in March. In the month of May, 1969, Richard Massey caught 20 mice in his house. Bob Marshall, by contrast, trapped a mouse just five minutes after setting a trap. Initially he was trapping a score of mice each night!

The other problem with mice is sound—it's hard to sleep when even one of them is scratching around all night. So, in April I cemented up every

226

possible hole and crack in the place to stop the mice. Around that time, my flimsy aluminum bed had collapsed, so I was sleeping very close to the floor. Just behind my head was a low-lying table I'd built for eating on while sitting cross-legged on the floor. Very late one night, I felt something skittering up my foot, my calf, my thigh, my back, then right across my face. It was a goddamn mouse. I began to wonder why the mouse wanted to walk all over me, then it occurred to me that he was using me as an on-ramp to get some bread I had left on the table.

Canaries. Well, one canary. Don and Lani Leydig bought one. Having brought it home during a roaring ghibli, the canary was traumatized and didn't sing or peep. A month later, Lani turned on her hair dryer. Over the sound of it she heard something. As soon as she turned it off, the sound stopped. After several iterations of this, she realized that their canary was singing along with the hair dryer.

Chameleons. In Jado in July of 1969, while teaching English for his summer project, Dan Peters acquired one as a pet. As he described it,

> It's an ugly chameleon about 10 inches long. Enlarged, it would make a good horror movie monster. Its tongue is as long as its body. And each night you can see the ridiculous spectacle of five or six Peace Corps men gathered around this animal watching it eat. We ooh and aah each time it snatches a bug from an ever-greater distance. The other night we gave him a scorpion and had an even bigger thrill. Our friend's name is Baloney.

Bittern (a kind of heron). Someone brought a small bittern to one of Bob Marshall's schools. Worried it would be ill-treated, like a faithful birder, he took it home. A Libyan friend told him to feed it soup, meat, cold water, but not Pepsi. (I'm sure that's how it reads in *Peterson's Field Guide to Birds.*) In Bob's diary, "I figured on leaving it in the spare room during the day, then letting it fly off when night came." But it turned out it didn't seem to know how to fly or want to. It paced about then hid behind some palm fronds. "I'd have been very content to have him as a pet, if he drank my water and ate beetles from the courtyard." He did neither. So after three days of this, Bob decided to chase him away after supper. But he was already gone.

Non-Pepsi-drinking bittern

Hens. One day, Dan and I rode our motorcycles 22 miles to Alasaba where PCVs Ed Collier and Gary Dallman lived. They had a dog named Atlanta (that Dan used as a pillow that night) and had purchased two hens, which they had dubbed "Minneapolis" and "St. Paul." Jack Seifert set up a chicken hutch—three hens and a rooster. At one point the rooster started eating the eggs. So Jack ate the rooster.

Speaking of Jack and roosters, one night in Ghat a rooster started to crow. Not at dawn, when he was supposed to. Like at 3 AM. This triggered barking from every feral dog within earshot. That, in turn, triggered all the other roosters to crow. That in turn triggered every donkey in town to bray at full force. An unholy racket.

Right after arriving in Sabratha, Diane Forasté relates, "One morning, some grazing chickens started to chase me. I screamed and ran, much to the amusement of those watching."

Snakes. They're all over Libya. One PCV knew some French teachers who captured and beheaded snakes, then embedded their heads in plastic as paperweights. One day, during English class, an asp invaded Kevin Hunt's classroom. Everyone evacuated. A Libyan teacher came to the rescue and beat the snake to death.

Cats. Jim and Joyce Swanson asked their landlord's daughter for a cat. She brought them a cute little kitten that they promptly dubbed "Ralph."

Later they belatedly discovered that Ralph was a girl cat, thereby certainly causing gender identification problems for the pet.

Stoney Bird somehow took in a kitten. At one point it was bitten by a scorpion. Hoping against hope, Stoney raced her on his Moto Guzzi the 24 miles to Taiwanese doctors in Sebha. They declared they were not vets and didn't know what to do. Stoney insisted they do something. They said, "OK, we'll give it a medication that works on humans, but it might not work." It didn't.

Rabbits. John Peterson was invited to be the guest of honor to rabbit shoot with fellow teachers. He got to carry the only gun they had, a single-shot shotgun. John had rabbit-hunted where he grew up in Western Pennsylvania. They would deploy beagles to flush the rabbits out into the open. Needless to say, without beagles, the Libyan teachers resorted to running about wildly waving their arms. Finally, they scared up a rabbit. John took his best shot—and missed. The Libyans decided to take the gun away from him.

Partridges. While I never saw a partridge, Richard Massey, way over in Farzougha, did. He went partridge hunting with his headmaster, Younis. Richard didn't do any shooting himself; he just rode shotgun (so to speak) while Younis zoomed around the countryside in his VW with one hand on the wheel and another holding a gun. When he saw partridges, he'd stop the car. But instead of getting out to shoot, he would just shoot through the window. At one point he killed two of them and gave them both to Richard as a gift.

Dogs. For Libyans, and Arabs in general, they're rarely pets. They're feral. They run wild. The reason for this lies in the Koran. Dogs' fur and saliva are considered unclean and impure. If you touch a dog, you must ritually wash your hands seven times. When visiting Peter Hawkes, I saw local villagers throwing rocks at a dog. (Years later, in Saudi Arabia, I was walking our dog Poppins. Some kids started throwing rocks at her. One hit her and she looked up at me with the most plaintive, pitiable, forlorn look, as if to say, "How could anyone possibly do this to me?")

One night I was down in the village after supper with friends. It was pitch black, of course. I mounted my Moto Guzzi and started up the hill. Out of nowhere, a feral dog was upon me, snarling and barking. It scared the bejesus out of me. It's not like I could hear him coming from a hundred yards away, he was suddenly just there. While trying to maintain control of the bike, I kicked away at the dog who was snapping away at me. I finally sped up enough to get away. In Zawia, Charlie Cross reports lots of wild dogs. They would lurk in the hedges, then suddenly attack. In self-defense he always carried rocks in his pockets to throw at the mongrels.

Up in Azzizia, someone gave Tom Furth a beagle. He called it "Meshuganeh." He didn't dare tell anyone it was a Yiddish word, but since the Yiddish word means "crazy person," and the Arabic word for crazy is *mejnoon*, he just told people it meant a "crazy dog."

Jack Seifert was given a female whippet puppy. He named her "Mickey." Mickey loved to run around super fast and would get in trouble from time to time. When Jack left for his summer project (teaching Libyan teachers TEFL in Jado), he had the caretaker watch Mickey while he was gone. One day, she got loose and a local policeman shot her to death.

One time, Richard Massey found a dead dog in the well he used for drinking water.

African Wolves. Occasionally these coyote-like creatures would chase after John Farranto on his Moto Guzzi.

Goats. Although very useful as garbage disposals—goats took care of all my garbage—they were a large factor in the erosion of valuable Libyan topsoil into the Mediterranean Sea. This was the fertile topsoil that was the basis of Libya's having been the granary of the Roman Empire. Goats have no top front teeth, so when they graze, they don't chomp off the grass, but rather yank it out by the roots. It is the roots that retain the topsoil. Sheep, on the other hand, have upper front teeth and when they eat grass, they chop it off neatly, leaving the roots intact. The Libyans never put two and two together.

Sheep. How could a sheep be life-threatening? Read on. Peter Hawkes was riding his Moto Guzzi to the house of a Libyan friend. As he approached, he noticed a large sheep in the yard, tethered to a tall stake in the ground via a rope laying squiggly on the ground. Spooked by the sound of the motorcycle, the sheep bolted, thereby snapping the rope up taut to the level of Peter's neck. Peter squeezed on his cycle brakes, but everything happened too quickly. The rope hit Peter right in the neck. The motorcycle was still running and the sheep was running, panicked, in circles, thus wrapping the rope around Peter's neck. Now Peter was panicked, too, not knowing whether he should cut off the engine first, or use his hands to somehow loosen the choking rope. In desperation, he dropped off the Moto Guzzi and started to charge at the sheep, which started running in the opposite direction, still tethered. By so running, the sheep was unraveling the rope from Peter's neck. He escaped murder by sheep but did suffer severe rope burns.

Donkeys. A major form of transportation and beast of burden. Amiable, friendly, docile. Also, a source of vociferous nighttime braying, especially while echoing about the canyons of Al Gala. You can see where they get their volume if you just watch. When a donkey inhales, his whole body bloats up with air, and as he brays, it all collapses down.

Gusbi taught us that if anything strange happens in class, instead of being thrown off, make it a teaching moment. One day, in Al Gala, a donkey stuck its head through the window of my classroom. The class froze, hoping I'd freak out. Remembering Gusbi's advice I calmly walked over to the donkey, said, "What is this?" and self-replied, "This is a donkey." The class repeated, "This is a donkey!" I patted it on the snout and we repeated this exchange a couple of times. The students were deeply disappointed that I had handled it in stride.

Al Gala: My students laugh at me onboard a donkey

Gazelles. I never saw a gazelle but they were common in other parts of Libya. The Libyans loved to hunt them. Because gazelles are so fleet of foot, humans need some speed to get within range. Jim Seroogy accompanied Libyan friends in a Land Rover who chased gazelles until they were exhausted. His friends would then slit the gazelle's throats, cut them up and cook them on the spot. In one case related by Paul Rhodes, his Libyan friends couldn't catch up to the gazelles, but seeing some about a mile away fruitlessly shot off their shotguns in that direction. All they were able to bag that day was an unfortunate porcupine, which they proceeded to flay and eat. Who knows if they used its own quills as skewers?

Cows. I never saw one, but beef was often available in various parts of Libya. Dave Goff was scared out of his wits one night, drawing water from a well when a big dark shape came up behind him. He turned around and shouted. Richard Massey relates, "I didn't know who was more startled—Dave or the cow." Richard had a clothesline outside his house. One time a cow came up and ate his underwear right off the line while he watched.

Horses. Ed Collier bought one. I imagine this required quite a bit of upkeep.

Camels. A delicacy for them? Cactus pears. Their lips and tongues are so thick the spines don't bother them one whit. They are quite independent (as mentioned in the plowing incident). I experienced another example 10 years later in Riyadh, Saudi Arabia. I attended a camel race on the day that King Khalid was hosting Prince Philip of the UK, clearly aiming to impress. The track is much longer than for typical horse racing, and racing camels have smaller heads, all the better to reduce wind resistance. The race started well enough, as 18 camels thundered off counter-clockwise on the oval. About a third of the way through the race, one camel decided that he didn't really want to run in that direction, and despite pulling and yanking by his jockey, he pulled a 180 and charged off clockwise. Needless to say, the immediately amped-up roar from the stands was in anticipation of what would happen when the maverick camel inevitably crashed into the herd. The King must have been mortified. I laughed at the lunacy of it all. Sure enough, the errant camel smashed head-on into about four other camels, riders spilling about, a total disaster.

Present-day camels have become inadvertent victims of World War II. It appears that a disproportionate number of dropped Italian Air Force bombs were duds. Many were covered up by shifting sands over the years. In fact, there were literally hundreds of thousands of land mines scattered about Libya by the end of the war. To this day, from time to time, a camel will step on one of these bombs or mines and it will blow the camel to shreds.

In April of 1969 my friend Tahir and I went to Yifran Hospital to see a friend of his. The friend had stopped in the desert, made a fire in the sand above a WWII bomb and it blew up on him. Peter Crall in Ghemines recalls, "Many land mines remained from the war and we would hear periodic reports that a camel or donkey had been suddenly reduced to dinner-size pieces." Angus Todd had a 5th grade student who was missing an arm and an eye. When he eventually asked the boy about it, it turns out he'd picked up a grenade from WWII that was still live that blew up on him. To illustrate this problem a bit more dramatically, Wheelus photographer James Voris was Land Rovering about the desert when his shotgun-toting friend Rejeb bragged that he knew about the location of mines in the area. Voris challenged him. Rejeb then shot three times, once to a spot 40 yards, away, then a spot 35 yards away, then to a spot 20 yards away. Boom! Boom! Boom!

In April 1969, Dan Peters and I hitchhiked to Garian. We had to sit in the back in the back of a pickup truck with a spittling camel. When the truck went around curves, the half-ton beast would slide towards me. My only defense was to brace both my feet against his side to fend him off. He didn't like that much and tried to crane his neck around to bite me.

Of course, camels could be glorious as well. On one beautiful sunny day, I saw a sight from my house that took my breath away. A half-mile-long camel caravan was moving with stately grace on the main road a hundred yards away. The snarfling camels were colorfully caparisoned, men walking along with them, with decked-out horses and tinkling of bells. I watched in wonder for it all to pass, feeling a first-hand taste of history. Jack Seifert not only witnessed two caravans while in Ghat, he engaged with the traders, buying a handful of peanuts, a couple of kilos of unidentified dried meat (he had to pound it with a hammer to get it to cook) and a beautiful decorated goatskin traveling bag. Ghat is the oldest of the Libyan caravan routes. In the day, the largest caravans boasted up to 12,000 camels. Camels as beasts of burden in Libya go back to around 500 A.D. Before that it was donkey caravans that ruled the routes.

In Tarhuna one night, Jim and Joyce Swanson were awakened by horrible roaring outside their house. A sound they had never heard before. They were scared to death. The next day they asked around the village as to what it was. A female camel in heat!

In a similar vein, John and Peggy Ziolkowski were startled out of their bed early on the first Friday of their stay in Sebha by groaning, grunting, roaring, blubbering camels. (The sound of a camel is very close to the sound of Chewbacca the Wookie.) Their house was right next to the Friday camel market. At the market they periodically saw some hapless Libyan walk behind a camel, only to receive a vicious kick that would send him sprawling and rolling in the sand. One time, John saw a camel kick a Libyan right off the back of a pickup truck.

Given that a typical Libyan farmer would have a couple of camels, a donkey or two, some sheep and some goats, he has to have a method to give commands to one set of animals without having all the animals follow the same direction (camels can understand dozens of commands). So, Libyan farmers have developed different basic commands for "Go away/back off, come here, and stop" for each of the types of animals. *Zah!*, for example, was the word for "go away" for camels. For sheep and goats, it was *khkh!* And for donkeys, it was *kanife*. I witnessed one farmer with his menagerie out in a field shout "Zah!" to the group. Only the camels moved.

Who needs aspirin when you could can whip out a razor blade? I was soon to find out.

Side Trips and Blood Lettings

January 25, 1969 dawned cold and sunny. I went to the post office where a small box awaited me, postmarked from Scotland. Could it be? Upon opening it, I was at first astonished, then deeply gratified to see, nesting in the box, Ahmed's three long-deserved World War II medals. I rushed over to Um El Jersan, tracked Ahmed down and offered him the box. He was overwhelmed, tears moisting his eyes, thanking me profusely. He wanted to put the medals on his *holie* and asked me to help. I managed to pin all three on, in the upper left chest section where I figured medals should go.

He marched about the village, chest puffed with pride, explaining to his friends that the stories he'd told them for decades about the medals were now fulfilled. The word swept through the village like wildfire and soon everyone was clapping and cheering as he continued his tour, especially the ragamuffins circling him like small planets. I felt touched by history. The whole village felt touched by history.

Also in the mail, a letter from my parents, from Gram, from a classmate at Princeton who had dated my sister Debbie and was in the Peace Corps in Micronesia and from Nancy Waddoups (finally). And I sent yet another letter to Jeanne.

Speaking of mail, over in Derna George Carter got a big box in the mail. It had sat in customs for four months. It was from his self-deselected buddy David Kermani. Contents? 144 rolls of toilet paper.

Over in Dariana in Cyrenaica, many of George Carter's students rode donkeys to school. Some came on foot. Many on bicycles. The problem was, however, that the moonscape terrain they had to cycle over meant that *all* the kids that rode bikes to school had perennial flat tires. So they would pump the tires up before going to school. By the time they got to school, they were again deflated. Same routine for the trip home. Another reflection of the toughness of the terrain: Dan Peters had a total of 15 flats with his Moto Guzzi while in Libya.

Over in Derna, Mark Lepori's Moto Guzzi broke down repeatedly. In one case it took literally months to repair, forcing him in the meantime to hitchhike to school. Just like for all of our Moto Guzzis, Mark's license plate included the word *Hokoma* ("government") on it. Anticipating any problems the Peace Corps volunteers in Derna might have, Minister of Education Fatia Ashura provided Mark and the others a letter to whip out any time they might get in trouble. Sure enough, once Mark was accosted by a policeman. "What are you doing driving a Libyan Government motorcycle? You are a spy!" Mark whipped out Fatia's letter and he backed down in a nanosecond.

Speaking of Fatia, once on a visit to her office, Dave Munro casually mentioned he needed a little more furniture. She immediately summoned a huge truck from the Ministry of Education warehouse, ordered the workers to stuff it with beds, desks, chairs and lighting fixtures to be delivered forthwith to Dave's house. As this was far more than Dave needed, most of these items languished the rest of his time in a back room. In a subsequent discussion, Fatia regaled Dave with a tale of some French teachers who were always complaining. Her breaking point was when they requested blankets—that had to be pink! "I sent them to the Fezzan!" she confided with a wicked snarl.

In Misurata, housemates Dick Kean, Randy Melquist, Sam Cangemi and Tim Vollman learned a cultural lesson we were not warned about in Clearfield. They invited over some Libyans and Italians for dinner on the same night. When the Libyans heard about this, they refused to come if the Italians were there.

Bob O'Keefe learned a humiliating lesson in not making assumptions. One day in his village, he observed a man with a woman who carried a baby in her arms. He assumed it was a new baby being brought back from the hospital, so he waltzed up to them and offered spirited congratulations. However, it turned out the baby was dead and was being brought home to be buried.

In Benghazi Lorraine Slawiak noted a routine among her fellow female teachers. They would be driven to school while bundled up head-to-toe in burkas, skirts and head scarves. Once in the school, they would roll up their skirts above the knee, roll their shirt sleeves, remove their head scarves and put on make-up. During breaks between classes they'd listen to music on the radio and dance about the teachers' room. At the end of the day, the skirts and sleeves would be unrolled, the make-up would come off, the head scarf would go on and they would primly travel back home.

Also, in Benghazi, on the occasion of King Idris I's birthday celebrations on March 12, Jeanne Maurey's fifth-grade girls participated joyously.

Jeanne Maurey's fifth graders celebrate the king's birthday

Jeanne's students in the parade

Despite Clearfield psychologist Benne Williams' reassurances, John Becker got a notice from his local draft board: "We hereby deny you permission to leave the U.S. You must return now." John asked Fezzan Associate Director Al Nehoda for help. Nehoda interceded so forcefully that the draft board backed off. But they insisted he take an Army physical to be eligible to be a conscientious objector. Why not take an Air Force physical right there in Libya, at Wheelus Air Base, the largest U.S. military hospital in the world outside the U.S.? Oh, no, the draft board insisted, it has to be an *Army* physical. As the nearest U.S. Army base was in Livorno, Italy, the Army said they'd pay John to travel there for his physical. (Your tax dollars at work!) Before John left, John and Peggy Ziolkowski asked him to buy three things for them in Italy: a flyswatter, a bottle of whiskey and a current issue of *Playboy*, all of which he delivered on.

By late January, there were visible signs of progress in Al Gala and Um El Jersan: the students could spell, they started to recognize whole words and learned to figure out pronunciations from the spelling. I started them on really short homework assignments, but I increased it gradually so they'd have to work an hour each night, something to which they were wholly unaccustomed.

The devils-and-angels split between Al Gala continued. Some of the Al Gala kids were so bad I had to up the punishment ante.

"Al Gala kids awful. Kicked Kamal Ali out for the rest of the year." Two days later, I kicked out Hassan for the year. Then, a day later I kicked out another one. The teachers were all upset. In late February, the Al Gala class was awful, in an uproar. Principal Belgassim meted out caning and yelled at six students.

The Ummers were so much more placid, a joy to teach. The two black adults in the back row were still reserved and quiet, in contrast to the rest of the students, who really got into my rhythmic teaching style. On January 27, in addition to teaching the Um El Jersan teachers English, I agreed to teach them French. I simply used the TEFL model, a totally portable method that can be used to teach any language. (So, in effect, TFFL—Teaching French as a Foreign Language. Of course, extendable to TGFL for German or TSCFL for Serbo-Croatian.) Two weeks later, I got a letter from Bob Marshall in which he mentioned *he* was commandeered to teach French to the 6th grade in one of his schools. Plus, his fellow teachers pressured him relentlessly to teach them English in the evenings. He eventually caved. He also mentioned that, in a reflection of the granary-of-the-Roman-Empire history of Libya, he had spilled some water outside his house, and the very next day there was a small patch of grass growing in that spot. He saw this as evidence not only the fertility of the soil, but of the fact that some seeds can lie fallow for many centuries. All they need to be activated is a small dose of water. (For the skeptics among you: in 2020 scientists grew six date palm plants from 2000-year-old seeds found in the Judean Desert in Israel.)

Dan Peters wrote home of continuing trials and tribulations with his Libyan roommates. They would not allow him to use the toilet inside the house because it made it too smelly. He was forced, even in the dead of winter, to do as they did and do his business outside. "I have been taking care of nature's call outside. I still haven't substituted stones for toilet paper, though." Khazam, the school principal, "has a habit of poking me in the ribs." And, "Because we only have one kerosene lamp, it is impossible for me to do any writing or reading at night." And, "My roommates still enjoy going through my trunk." In one letter, he related, "I was visited by the director of the Peace Corps in Libya the other day. He couldn't get out of here fast enough."

Using my guitar and my battery-driven Panasonic tape recorder, I recorded a song for my family I dubbed "Hello, Family," to the tune of "Hello, Dolly" using new words and Louis Armstrong's gravelly voice. On another occasion, I changed the words of the novelty song "Hello Muddah, Hello Fadduh" by Allan Sherman. It's a comic sung letter from a tweener to his parents from Camp Grenada. I adapted it to my situation:

Hello Muddah, Hello Faddah
You know I'm not in Grenada
Coconut palms you cannot find
And the camels here are not the cigarette kind.

We've got sandstorms, dust is legion
No mosquitoes in this region
Air is hot here, Pater, Mater
Please don't question me on how I ever got here.

Bob Marshall had the opportunity to meet, befriend and observe some field interviews of an American anthropologist, John Mason, who just happened to choose Berber tribes in Aujila among the hundreds of potential towns in Libya as the subject of his Boston University Ph.D. thesis. The results were later published as *Island of the Blest: Islam in a Libyan Oasis Community*. At the time I was oblivious to the existence of tribes in Libya. I had spent hundreds of hours talking with Libyan friends in both villages and never once did anyone mention they were part of a tribe. Nor did the Clearfield staff or the Clearfield Libyans ever tell us about tribes. It was only many years later when Ghaddafi was killed and Libya descended into tribal warfare that I first heard of them. I discovered there are no less than 140 tribes in Libya, falling into four major ethnic groups: the Berbers (as in my village), The Arabs, the Tuaregs and the Toubou. In Al Gala, there are two tribes, those that live at the bottom of the canyon (the lower tribe, more specifically the Alwadi) and those at the top (the upper tribe, the Albhour.)

In mid-February, Dan and I had a Duh!/V-8 moment. Dan had been riding his motorcycle in order to get to Al Gala and back instead of walking ten miles. I had been dutifully riding my Moto Guzzi daily between the Al Gala and Um El Jersan schools. That was it. We realized, hey, it's a Friday, our day off, and we both have motorcycles, we can go anywhere we want! On February 14, we cycled out to the remote town Swadna. This little village was on an unpaved path. It had a spring, palm trees, beautiful flowers. And one villager invited us to lunch for couscous. The next week we motored out to Kikla with beautiful views over grassy meadows that extended into brown valleys, illuminated in spots by shafts of sunlight. Then we ventured via an all-dirt road to Jahish, a small, barely accessible, quaint village on a ridge. The folks there served us tea and a meal with Libyan bread.

One day in February, on the spur of the moment, Steve Hughes, Paul Rhodes and Roy Douthitt decided to hitchhike 300 miles from Al Beida to Brega aboard a large Italian truck. After finagling their way into the highly secure Brega Oil Terminal, they were greeted by Chif Crawford, a Canadian PR guy who gave them the royal tour and even hosted them for lunch. (Another coincidence: 18 years later while working for Booz Allen Hamilton in Saudi Arabia on a Saudi Royal Navy project, Roy ran into the very same Chif Crawford!)

Bob Gausman also used his cycle to visit. One day, he cruised to Sebha to visit John and Peggy Ziolkowski. Half the village was crowding around the Ziolkowskis' house. They had called their landlord because their toilet was totally clogged up. Their landlord was digging a hole out in the street to get to their sewer pipe. He took off the top of the pipe and found that the pipe was clogged with tampons. Neither the landlord nor any of the Libyans had any idea what these were. The landlord was yelling at them for causing the clog.

On March 7th, in Aujila, Bob Marshall was thrilled to bird-spot a brilliantly yellow black-headed wagtail poking around outside his house.

On March 11, Dan and I cruised to Jado, dropping in on Michael and Judy Crowley who had trained in Bisbee. Another coincidence: Judy had seen my rock group, The Nightwatch, in Newport, Rhode Island the summer of 1966! They let us crash in their living room. The next morning, fortified with a breakfast of bacon, eggs and toast, we motored to the small village of Mizou, then Riana.

March 13. I rode my cycle out to El Khozeur to Dan's place. His roommates were incredibly trying on the nerves, singing and shouting well into the wee hours. A torrent of teasing and cajoling. "I don't see how Dan takes it," I noted. In Dan's letter home he wrote:

> Randy, my friend in the Peace Corps, came on Thursday and claimed that his stay was very enlightening. He got an impression of what it is like to live with several Libyans; the lack of privacy and constant BS which is usually child-ish. He felt that it is best to fight fire with fire and it was really a noisy riot all the while he was here.

On March 27, we traveled to Alasaba. I saw villagers throwing rocks at a stray dog that they'd cornered in a fenced lot.

In mid-March, while I was chewing the fat with villagers outside the Al Gala Post Office, one of them started strongly criticizing Americans. "But I'm an American," I protested. "Oh, Mr. Randy, *wallahi alatheem,* ("God Almighty") you're different. We really like you."

March 28 was my birthday, and after the fact I learned that it became a Libyan holiday, *Al Jalal*, beginning in 1970. "British Evacuation Day" they called it, celebrating the final pull-out of British troops from Libya. (I'm relieved they didn't declare my own final departure date from Libya a holiday!) After a breakfast of bread and butter (if you're wondering how I could have butter with no refrigeration, it was canned butter, which can keep fresh for up to two years!), we drove our bikes to Garian, then to Rebta 90 minutes away, down the mountain, off onto the plain, driving by an abandoned Italian train station, over springs, through palm trees. Most of the road was rocky and jarring, causing my hands to fall asleep on the motorcycle handles. We visited Bill Fligeltaub, who was happy to see us and fed us some oatmeal. Then to Chuck Smith and Tom Weinz's house in Garian for the night. I enjoyed a birthday meal of beef stroganoff and banana bread. The next day we drove to Stu Magee's place in Al Kaleebah ("Village of the Dogs").

These mini-trips were exhilarating explorations, imbuing us with a deeper understanding of the warp and woof of Libyan society. Dan and I bonded even further in sharing these excursions. With so much time on the seat of a Moto Guzzi, riding became an easy, fluid, organic second nature to us both. A terrific feeling of command.

During this period, we also got around by hitchhiking. In late February, Dan and I went to Jeff Taylor's house in Zawia and had the closest thing to a blow-out during my entire Libyan adventure. A bunch of other PCVs had come down from Tripoli. There were some women. We downed 15 bottles of booze. John Maclean made out with Jeff's girlfriend. I got smashed, Dan got sick. And the noise brought down the wrath of the local police.

The next day we went to Azzizia to visit Tom Furth and Jack Hoffman. Azzizia's claim to fame is the highest recorded temperature in history, on September 13, 1922: 136.4° F. They served us pork chops and rice for supper. Years later, we wondered how a Moslem country could have had pork. Since Randy Melquist in Misurata regularly bought pork chops from an Italian butcher, that's my best guess as to the source in Azzizia.

One day, as I arrived in Um El Jersan, I saw old Freddo standing, holding his *holie* robes up by his waist. His legs were streaming bright red blood.

"What happened?" I asked.

"My legs hurt, so I cut them," replied Freddo.

Forgoing cultural sensitivities, I said, "Freddo, stop that right now! Cutting your legs will not make them feel better. It will make them feel worse. This is something from long ago and modern doctors no longer do it."

Surprisingly, he complied, saying, "Oh, sorry, I'm just a stupid Arab."

I reassured him he was not stupid, but got him to promise not to cut his legs any more. Some weeks later, I came upon another Ummer named Ahmed. He was sitting with a razor blade in his hand, blood pouring from his ankle. I gave him the same lecture. I also asked him about this practice. He pointed at multiple vertical scars on his forehead that I had until then assumed were tribal markings (as I had seen on the faces of various Sudanese in Libya).

"Whenever I get a headache, I cut my forehead with a razor to make it feel better."

Just months before our stint in Libya, the folks at Occidental Petroleum near Bob Marshall's oasis in Aujila got the surprise of their lives.

Magrunas, Ullulations and Aquifers

Relations with my Libyan friends continued to evolve. For example, in addition to hanging out, having tea and meals, along the way I taught El Haadi to play backgammon, chess and ping pong. El Haadi got better and better in chess, and soon all my Libyan friends clamored to be taught. The only drawback to the ping pong table I had constructed and painted green was there was no plywood available so I had to make do with 3"-wide planks of wood. Whenever the ping pong ball hit one of the plank edges it would career off at an angle.

Along the way, of course, one absorbs cultural lessons. I learned (not explained to us in Clearfield) that like the Japanese, Arab societies are face-saving; they are ashamed if you directly contradict them or tell them they are wrong. One must therefore master the art of indirection. Ten years later, I was able to leverage this knowledge to good effect in Saudi Arabia. I was working at the Ministry of Education. An American consultant working for me had left a report with an executive named Hamid El Abdulli and wanted to get it back. He repeatedly demanded this report back, insisting that Hamid had it, and Hamid repeatedly told him he did not have it. The consultant complained to me and I said, "Don't worry, I'll take care of it."

I sauntered into Hamid's office, made some small talk, then said, "Hey, you know, Hamid, I'm so stupid."

"What?"

"I'm so stupid, I don't know what's wrong with me."

"What are you talking about?"

"I don't know, I get forgetful."

"About what?"

"Well, I somehow lost that report, I'm sorry."

Hamid immediately pulled open his top desk drawer, drew out the report with a flourish, and said, "You mean this?" and promptly gave it to me.

Another interesting insight was the alacrity with which Libyans respond to your talking to them in Arabic. Their enthusiastic reaction was far and above the reaction of a French- or Spanish-speaking native hearing you speak their language. At some point it was explained to me that the Arabs consider Arabic to be the language of Allah. The Koran was written in Arabic because God's first language is Arabic. So, speaking their language is not only a linguistic affirmation, but a virtual endorsement of their revered Islam.

I noticed there was such a difference in altitude between the bottom of Al Gala and the top that the climate was literally different. Palm trees grew in the valley, but couldn't above.

Al Gala: palm tree climate at the base of the canyon

Above were olive trees, spaced about 100 yards apart. The villagers in Al Gala referred to this area as "the forest."

Al Gala: Cooler-climate olive trees atop mountain: "The Forest"

(Over in Al Gaigab near Derna, there were small patches of trees next to Mark Lepori's school. He soon dubbed them the "Al Gaigab National Forest.") Speaking of the canyons' miles-long vertical walls, far and above my experience in trumpeting Taps was the opportunity to experience Al Gala's women wailing during a funeral. I remember sitting for some hours in a villager's house when a bevy of women outside began to ululate at high volume. (Ululation being eerie howls accompanied by trilling.) Their voices echoed with plaintive force up and down the canyon for miles. A sound I will never forget.

Dan visited a half dozen times in February and March. Once he brought a donkey so he could walk back the four miles with an ample pack of supplies. In this time frame I built a ladder for easy access to the roof. Dan and I would clamber up there for lunches and dinners. One night we had fried steak, French fries and beets, downed with Mirinda orange soda. Another night it was just Spam downed with Heinekens. Another night, just soybeans and potatoes. Whatever was available. We were young. We didn't care. I didn't know it at the time, but Dan was corresponding regularly with a Wisconsin woman he was close to, Betty Klasen. In a letter home he wrote, "I got two Valentines from Betty. We are writing each other regularly."

Periodically, inspector Tom Weinz would drop by unannounced (what was he supposed to do, text me?). One night I served him Spam sandwiches.

On another I cooked up some Libyan soup. On another occasion, we ambled down to the village and were served great soup and couscous. On the way back we happened upon a Libyan wedding in the fifth of its seven days. We were invited right down in front of a large circle of participants. As we sat down cross-legged on the ground, we watched three black dancers, two drummers, Libyan girls sit-swaying back and forth to the rhythms, and the roofs of the surrounding houses lined with Libyan boys.

We learned that the groom was 17 years old and the bride just 13. (Standard operating procedure.) We learned that they, as was the custom, had never met one another before their wedding night—an arranged marriage. What I didn't learn at the time, Dan Peters had: "It is the custom here for parents to choose cousins as marriage partners."

After the consummation indoors (with the whole village waiting outside—talk about pressure) a family member brings out and waves a bloody wedding-bed sheet to prove that the wife was a virgin. (This is actually sheep's blood and everyone knows it.) The throngs cheer heartily at this. (Cathy Kaiser witnessed a wedding in Derna where, after the "consummation," the male wedding guests would take a white, blood-soaked pennant, mount it on a car and drive it all around town.)

Much to our delight, a walk-about three-man band—the wedding orchestra, in effect—started to perform. One drummer, tat-tat-tatting up a catchy rhythmic storm, and two magruna players. Magrunas are basically bagpipes with the bag made of goatskin, and two reed pipes with five holes in each pipe, with bell-shaped horns at the end. They were blowing out exotic, sinuous Arabic melodies. Since no party planners are involved, and neither bride nor groom pay for this band, they must solicit payment from the guests. Luckily, we saw how this was done before they came to us, so we could join in appropriately. Instead of a tip jar or a hat on the ground into which one might throw money, the band would approach a guest in the circle, play to him while retreating then approaching for some two minutes of individualized attention. Then, the guest would take a Libyan one-pound note and neatly slide it under the performer's hat.

Typical wedding band

In case you're wondering what Libyans do on the other of seven days of a wedding, one of them is designated *Al Layl El Henna* ("Evening of the Henna"). The bride and female relatives fête themselves by dipping their hands and feet in red henna dye. On another day, in some locales, the bride is conveyed to her new home on a camel, and an egg is ceremoniously broken on the camel's knee.

Down in Ghat, before going to a wedding, his friends dressed Jack Seifert up as a Tuareg. Many women did a double-take upon seeing a 235-pound Tuareg. The bride and groom arrived on camels. To the infectious rhythms of magruna music, the attendees danced in trances, long into the night.

John Lynch was lucky enough to attend a Bedouin wedding, replete with many tents out in the desert. Before the meal, attendees set up a chant. Then individual Libyans would spontaneously recite poetry about the groom. Lots of clapping, energetic dancing. Another male PCV waxed poetic over a Bedouin wedding:

The tent was huge. It had quilt walls and a roof made from a huge blanket of wool and goat fur. The walls were laced with twine to the roof and hung freely to the ground. Two long wooden poles, spaced six feet apart, formed peaks in

249

the center of the roof. On the poles hung dried sheepskins used for storing sour milk. After tea, everyone went outside for the dancing. The bright moon seemed to hang almost directly over the tent. A woman dancer of medium height, holding a short stick, stepped out of the tent. She wore a wide-sleeved, purple-and-gold-striped blouse, a long, bulky white shirt, red stockings and white shoes. The headlights of several Land Rovers showed through her sheer red veil. The dancer moved to one end of the line of men, raising her arms about waist high, spreading her fingers and holding the stick between her thumbs. She began shaking her hips in rhythm to the men's clapping. The rhythm gradually increased as the dancer continued to walk from one end of the line to the other. Suddenly, there was a burst of speed in clapping. Her hips vibrating wildly, the dancer tilted her head to one side and held the stick high overhead. We were entertained until midnight. A few men clapped so continuously that the palms of their hands were bruised and bleeding.

Dan Peters attended his roommate Khazam's wedding in El Khozeur. He learned:

The bride price is paid in jewels, dresses, incense, oil, barley and money. Several veiled women broke out in a weird hooting wailing sound which, I am told, demonstrated their satisfaction and excitement. The bride fainted three times on her way to the bridal chamber.

Around this time in Ghemines, Peter Crall went to an otherwise unexceptional Bedouin wedding that became most exceptional only in retrospect. Sitting one man over to the left from Peter was an unknown military colonel named Muammar Ghaddafi. Peter describes the scene: "Though he didn't talk much, he regarded me with keen and skeptical interest as I rambled on in my bad Arabic about various local and international issues. I like to think I was the last Westerner he met before he staged his revolution."

Jeanne Maurey shared her memories of a Libyan wedding that reflected another angle—that of the bride and the women around her. Traditionally, during the wedding Libya brides can neither speak nor laugh.

Sad bride

The bride does not smile because this is a time of sadness—she is leaving her family. She doesn't eat or drink. She sits, wearing all the jewelry she has been given. (In this case, the groom reportedly had to pay $5,600 to the bride's family—a princely sum in such a poor country.) Some women dance, some ululate. Later, tea, nuts and candy are served. The dancing continues. Around two or three in the morning, the songs become very mournful. And the calls become very deep, almost like a wounded animal's death sounds. This is just the first of seven days of parties, with the men partying separately. The next day the bride and groom are shown into a bedroom and left alone for one-half hour. This is the first time they have laid eyes on one another. The husband then comes out to his brother, who then shoots off a gun signifying the girl is a virgin. (Without the virginal pretense, were the bride not in fact a virgin, she would be cast out of her family. They would have beaten her or even killed her.) The bride's sisters enter the bedroom, crying hysterically. One of the sisters then sprinkles perfume on everyone. The bride's mother then advises her that she will cook for her new husband, sew for him, weep for him, bear children for him.

One Cyrenaican volunteer remembers other details:

At Jameela's wedding, to show off her dowry, she started off wearing a white wedding gown, then changed into nine different evening dresses. Later, I walked into Jameela's bedroom. She was dressed in her negligee. The women were happy, throwing cologne, singing, yelling. Jameela was crying. When I got ready to leave, Jameela threw her arms around me and really started crying. A shocking experience for me. I walked back to the tent in a daze.

One of Diane Forasté's students was 13 and to be married at the end of the school year and would not be returning to school. "I gave her a small gift (talcum powder and lotion) and asked her how she felt about the marriage. She only looked at me, shrugged and looked down. I still remember those eyes."

Down in Ghat, Jack Seifert witnessed a remarkable ceremony around a holiday they called "Revenge and Forgiveness." Villagers from all three sub-villages in Ghat dressed up, covering their heads to be somewhat anonymous. A group of musicians led the entire population into a circle around the village. Then, if you had a bone to pick with anyone you were allowed to whack that person repeatedly, while shouting your grudges against them, but with a soft reed-like plant that didn't hurt. Both men and women got to vent, get it out of their system. (Maybe we should inaugurate such an annual event for Democrats and Republicans!)

On a more somber note, Dennis Carlson describes a Libyan funeral he attended.

> Soon, about 70 men and boys had gathered around the shallow grave, with the body of the dead man wrapped in a white shroud lying beside the grave. After a *shebanee* (old man) led a brief prayer, several young men lifted and lowered the body into the grave and shoved sandy dirt over it. Everyone stood silently for another minute or so, at which point the deceased man's young sons along with… cousins…began a dervish-like spinning on the ground, kicking their feet, crying loudly and shaking and twisting in a chaotic dance of tears.

Thanks to an essay from one of the Cyrenaican male volunteers and the observations of his wife, a much more comprehensive description about Libyan funerals is revealed. In this case another man had died:

> The body was immediately buried with a three-day period of mourning to follow. I entered the living room, where the Koran was played on a portable phonograph and everyone solemnly listened. Between five-minute stretches of silence, someone would point out that the small white flag flying three houses away meant someone was away on the Hajj. Another person commented that the man I had just greeted was the best tooth puller in town.

> When my wife entered the deceased man's house, she was greeted by the sound of wailing. The women had been scratching their faces in sorrow for 24 hours, and were a sorry sight with their faces scabbed and swollen.

During this time, I continued to devour books (the *Koran*, *L'Exile et le Royaume* by Camus) and magazines. Letters from Jeanne continued, including an eight-pager with a Valentine. I continued to practice guitar, trumpet and Arabic. Bob Marshall and I also exchanged letters. We'd decided to travel together for the summer vacation and were making preliminary plans. In one of these letters Bob told me that an Occidental oil drilling crew near Aujila had struck—water—back in March. A *lot* of fresh water. I've since learned that they'd discovered a gigantic fresh-water aquifer, the largest in the world, beneath the Sahara Desert containing more water than all the Great Lakes! An astounding 7,000 cubic miles of water. As much water as flows through the Nile in two hundred years. Bedouins would have to revise their long-held belief that the Sahara was a "waterless sea." Occidental realized that with an unlimited supply of sunshine, an unlimited supply of fresh water, and a vast area of fertile soil that used to be a savanna (as reflected in the sprouting Bob had witnessed) they could grow crops with amazing efficiency. So starting right when Bob arrived, they planted wheat, barley and alfalfa. The system was so productive, they began harvesting the alfalfa four times a year.

They then expanded the land under cultivation to 8,500 acres—13 square miles. They deployed circular irrigation machines whose arms were a kilometer long (it took three days for one complete revolution). To create a complete system, they fed the alfalfa to sheep, slaughtered the sheep, then raised more sheep, a complete agricultural cycle.

Gigantic irrigation circles

Kilometer-long irrigation machine

Unbeknownst to me, come March two remarkable school exploits would play out.

Finger Shadows, Fast Alphabets and Feasts

Now we arrive at the period of March 4 to April 30.

As a kid, I made crude finger shadows, you know, like ducks. But in Libya, one evening after Dan and I had feasted on bouillon and hash for dinner, we hosted Milaad, Abdul Majiid, Al Haadi, Dan's roomies Issa and Ahmed, and two other Libyan villagers. We were having an engaging talk. The light from my kerosene lamp threw sharp shadows and just fooling around, I accidentally created a camel. And was somehow able to replicate it. And make the mouth move. It still never fails to delight kids and mildly amuse adults.

On March 4 my students started to gain more significant traction in English with some experiencing breakthroughs. (Appropriate, no doubt because it's the only date in the year that is a sentence—"March Forth.")

To keep things lively with the back-and-forth TEFL method, e.g. teaching the students the alphabet, I made it rapid and rhythmic:

Me: "A!"

Students: "A!"

Me: "B!"

Students: "B!"

I would keep this going while walking around the room. Sometimes I'd go outside and keep it going while I was outside the window and they were inside.

On March 5 one student in my Um El Jersan class recited the English alphabet in two seconds! Crisply, clearly, without error. Diary: "*I* can't even do that. Hard to stop smiling in appreciation."

Lest you assume that the unruly, rowdy Al Gala kids were not learning English through the bedlam, they were, in fact, absorbing a lot. Hussein Solliman was able to read most of the English for Libya 1 reader faultlessly. It continued to be a madhouse, however. One day I had to yell my head off to keep order while giving exams at Al Gala, giving me a sore throat. On another occasion, Tahir Said tore up his English book. The Um kids were usually nice, sweet, and sometimes funny. And the two tall black men in the back row continued to be very quiet and unparticipative. One day I played dodge ball with the Um students. That never happened at Al Gala. (For a rogues' gallery of the Al Gala students, see their all sweet faces in the Appendix to this book. They didn't like to smile for the camera, but the old "cheese" trick worked like a charm.)

Never having been a teacher before and not having been alerted to this during our training, I was pleasantly surprised when I developed "teacher's ear." This is where you reach the point of familiarity with the voice of all the kids in your class, so that even with your back turned, you can identify exactly who is talking. It helps with the discipline to be able to swirl around and say "Hussein, be quiet!"

At Um one day, the two reticent black young men in the back had a breakthrough. Having laid the groundwork for the structure and vocabulary of increasingly varied sentence structures, the time had come to introduce the notion of "not." They had already mastered the verb "to go" and they knew the word "home" and they knew the pronouns. So, with a theatrical slash of my arm, I declared, "I am *not* going home!"

All the students in the class dutifully repeated this sentence except for the two black young men. They had hesitated for a beat. Then, they both jumped up, slashed their own arms down dramatically, and yelled "I AM <u>NOT</u> GOING HOME!" I had to tamp down a desire to convulse with laughter. The next day, I realized that they had had their own breakthrough. They were really taken with the idea of "not."

Depending on our personalities, teaching ability and other characteristics, we all inevitably affected our students in idiosyncratic ways. One day Dave Munro was traveling in northern Libya and just happened to stop in a small village for a bathroom break. He was approached by a young boy who recognized what might be an American. He said, "Hey thayre! How are yeew?"

"Do you, by any chance," asked Dave, "have an English teacher named Clarence?"

"Thaas ryeet! I deeu," he replied with a big, surprised smile.

Dave had pegged the kid to have North Carolinian-drawlin' Clarence Young as his teacher. No doubt there still live a couple dozen sixty-ish Libyan men running around speaking English with a thick North Carolina accent.

Dan crashed at my place six times in March and April. I would take my small low table to the roof and we would dine on more camel cheeseburgers, spinach and OEA beer. Another night it was corned beef hash, beans, bread and Heinekens. Whether local or Dutch beer, we had to consume it English style—warm. I guess we didn't care, what choice did we have? Needless to say, neither shop in Al Gala sold beer, so I'd have to lug back beer whenever I could hit Tripoli. We'd play chess, checkers, ping pong. One night we borrowed El Haadi's binoculars to marvel at the stars. One day we walked the six miles to Um El Jersan, with much banter along the way, then hopped a ride back on a tractor.

Tripoli: Window shopping without windows

Tripoli: camel market

I continued studying Arabic as much as I could squeeze in. The three moments that gave me a feeling that Arabic was seeping into my brain were 1) after six months in country, and mightily trying to master it, I was finally able to pronounce the Arabic "ayn." Other than what I understand as the clicks in click languages, it is the most difficult sound to conjure up that I can think of. 2) I found myself inadvertently counting the hours

260

in Arabic as I wound up my alarm clock, and 3) I found myself able to spontaneously make fun by speaking Arabic in an Italian accent.

I continued to absorb observations about this society with which I was growing increasingly comfortable. After shaking hands, the men would make a fist, kiss the knuckle of their right index finger, then touch their hand to their chest. A quaint respectful elaboration of greetings. (A woman volunteer remembers, "When you get to the house, the women greet you by shaking your hand and then kissing your hand or cheek.") I noticed that the Libyans washed their hands, feet and face a number of times each day (this was associated with the five daily prayers). With the exception of school desks and perhaps one at the Post Office, there were no chairs in Al Gala or Um El Jersan. I noticed they automatically docked my $168 dollar-a-month pay by two Libyan pounds (about $5) that went to El Fatah, a faction of the PLO—The Palestine Liberation Organization. I didn't care, I guess, one way or the other, but some of my fellow PCVs did. One woman PCV was upset and demanded her money back. She declared that the Peace Corps was not meant to be political. She never was able to stop the deductions. For Dan Peters, "I was about to be paid last week minus $5.40 which was to go to the Palestinian guerillas. I told them this was illegal, dictatorial and undiplomatic. Unexpectedly, my fellow teachers agreed completely with what I said and even offered to make up the $5.40 from their own pockets."

Peter Hawkes objected that El Fatah was a terrorist organization and he was part of a team of peace, not a team of war. His solution was to simply stop picking up his checks. Martin Sampson advised Peter not to rock the boat, but Peter dug in his heels, and set off a stream of events by writing to his sister about the El Fatah discounts. She was married to an official at the Defense Communications Agency, who promptly wrote a letter to President Nixon. Peace Corps Tripoli was inundated with diplomatic cables from Washington. Two anti-Peace Corps senators were already attacking the Peace Corps and this letter could be used as ammunition.

Shortly thereafter, country director Bill Whitman descended upon Peter's school. The teachers threw together an impromptu lunch for him. Afterwards, Whitman says,

"Peter, take a walk with me." They walk.

"Peter, do you know somebody who knows Nixon?"

"No."

"We've been besieged by cables. There's this volunteer out here some-place who hasn't been picking up his checks. Is that you?"

Now on the defensive, Peter said, "Yes," but then explained his anti-war rationale.

"I hope you understand that this could result in everyone in Peace Corps Libya getting expelled from the country?"

"I don't want that."

"Who did you tell about not picking up your checks?"

"My brother-in-law."

"Can you write to him and get him to stop pursuing this?"

"OK." (What else could he say?) "But what about the checks?"

"Just go there and get them from here on out."

When Peter went to pick up his checks, he was met with a barrage of yelling. In anger, one Libyan kicked a chair violently across the room. It turned out that Whitman had spoken to Mustafa Gusbi who put a halt to the El Fatah discount practice. Clearly, some people had paid the price, but Peter got his past and latest checks in full.

In Tarhuna, teachers, including Peace Corps volunteers, were paid in cash. At the end of a table, a PLO representative collected funds. When asked how much he was going to contribute, Chuck Beach simply declined. In a more overt vein, John Forasté refused to contribute to El Fatah and declared he would make his contributions to UNICEF (United Nations Children's Fund).

Speaking of money, I learned that the average Libyan in 1968 made $50 a month. Given the standard of living in my village, this was enough to get by—for food, mostly. No one was buying much in the way of new clothes, just wearing the same traditional garb all the time. They already had a roof over their head. They weren't buying books or radios or games or toys. They didn't pay for water. They didn't pay for electricity. No in-surance. They had no monthly cable bill. A simple, happy existence. They had no inkling that they were living far below the poverty level. There's a message in there somewhere.

Except for the occasional car or pickup truck, they were living exactly as their forebears had some two thousand years before. At the time, I deeply appreciated that. I felt like I was in a time capsule, whisked back to Biblical times.

I was able to observe a lot by being invited to 24 hours of El-Haadi-the-Um-El-Jersan-school-principal's seven days of feasting after his going on the Hajj in Mecca. This is a huge deal for Moslems, and especially for a Moslem from a small, out-of-the-way village in a poverty-stricken land. Thenceforth, for the rest of his life, he could append the honorific "Hajj" to his name. So, he became "Hajj El Haadi."

On March 16 I arrived at Hajj El Haadi's house. In a letter I wrote:

When Hajj El Haadi returned from the Hajj, he had to grow a beard. Then, for a week upon his return, he had to entertain constantly at his house. Each house has an entertainment room with no women allowed covered with new rugs, lined with pillows and cushions. No chairs. Soon after my arrival, we were served sugar-coated almonds, dates and drink made from water and a white-colored liquid. Libyan tea was served constantly and soon couscous, completely covered with fresh lamb on bones, was served. One man lifted a pitcher up in the air while the man on his left held a bar of soap beneath it. He washed his hands with brisk, smooth motions, then put some of the suds in his mouth, brushing his teeth with his index finger. He then cupped his hand for more water, then spat it out in a long stream into the bowl, shielding his mouth with this right hand while he passed the bar of soap over to the next man on his left. Then, all the men muttered *bismillahi* ("in the name of Allah") and dug in. The meat had to be consumed at the same time by everyone, excursions into the couscous being forbidden until the meat was finished. As usual, fruit was served afterwards (bananas and oranges and apples).

Then El Haadi led a prayer. He stood facing the east. He murmured *allaho el akbar* and bent at the waist, and five friends followed suit. Each then said a pre-memorized prayer, with just their lips moving, no sound. Then El Haadi straightened up, and uttered another religious formula. Then he knelt in prayer, groaning this time, as others followed him. He then touched his forehead to the floor (signifying a sign of the ephemeral nature of wisdom) and resumed his standing position. The whole procedure was repeated about five times and then he says "Salaam aleekum" about three times, and everyone has what looks like free prayer for three minutes, sitting down by himself, and moving his lips to the unspoken words he is uttering. This whole cycle of tea, food and prayer was repeated about four times in eight hours, with a constant influx and outflux of friends. Outside there was a makeshift corral holding about 12 sheep, each awaiting his turn. The underground house they lived in was filled with women, meeting with the wives and doing all the cooking. Whenever something was ready for serving, his wife would knock on the wall and he would somehow hear it through the cement and run out to bring it in. I was drawn into a religious discussion. They asked me why I didn't become a Moslem. I replied that if Allah wanted me to be a Moslem, I would be one. That gambit didn't work! They said "No, Mr. Randy, it's up to you!"

Then, from my diary, "Hajj El Haadi gave me a watch—I was overwhelmed. So great to be living Libyan." The next day I was up at 7:30 AM and was served delicious bsisa, biscuits, coffee and tea. Bsisa is a Bedouin dish, consisting of a base of roasted barley, combined with fenugreek, aniseed, cumin and sugar. As a born-and-bred Presbyterian whose only contribution to the church was a nominal collection-plate bill or two, I could not imagine the cost and sacrifice of feeding dozens of people all their meals for an entire week.

(At another Hajj feast, Phil Akre witnessed a man dancing to a frenzy who stuck a dagger in his stomach and pulled it out. Phil figured at the time that this had to be sleight of hand, but it looked real to him at the time.)

Speaking of converting to Islam, in Azzizia, Tom Furth's teachers in Azzizia told him in jest they were going to convert him. The first requirement was he must change his name from Tom to Barka ("blessed"). Then they said if he wanted to be a Moslem, they'd have to circumcise him. Little did they know that would be unnecessary. And Dan Peters noted, "My roommates have been trying to get me to become a Moslem so that we can all go to Heaven together."

Given this immersion in Libyan village culture for five months, the molasses-like rhythms of life began to imprint themselves upon me. I was still very active, but mentally I found myself not racing about like a 20th-century American Type-A, needing to jam every nook and cranny of my life with productive work. I clearly remember one afternoon succumbing to the languor. I squatted outside, allowing my mind to dull and dim and just wallow, realizing that this was essentially how Libyan villagers feel.

Mail. On March 17 I got a large envelope of 30 1968 Christmas cards from the entire second grade at Hunter's Point Navajo School. The reason for the delay? The Navajo teacher had failed to put the country on the package. From the stamps I could see that it had originally been sent to Lebanon and some bright mail handler in Beirut figured out Al Gala was in Libya. I got a letter from Norma Salem, a Smith college undergrad and the daughter of Michel Salem, inviting Bob Marshall and me to come to Cairo in the summer. Our connection with her was my grandfather, Atherton Hobler who had, in 1961, established an international athletic scholarship at Smith College, the Virginia Hobler Redpath Foreign Student Fund, in honor of his daughter, who had died after childbirth in 1947. Norma, a physics major, was the recipient of that scholarship for this school year. Then there was the ongoing long-distance postal correspondence with Jeanne, 700 miles away in Benghazi. We exchanged long letters in March and April. I don't recall how we figured this was going to play out with so few opportunities to get together. We were just twenty-somethings operating on a wing and a prayer!

One evening, after a meal of spaghetti and mackerel, I had a wide-ranging discussion with El Haadi. Initially, I asked him what village he was originally from in Libya and asked him to show me on the map of Africa on the wall where it was. Instead of immediately pointing his index finger to the village, he placed his finger randomly on the map of Libya, and leaning in close, began to trace a random zig-zag pattern on the map. After several long minutes, he finally came upon his village. I realized that he was not only unfamiliar with maps, but had never learned spatial relations, nor how to consider the set, subset and sub-sub- set of geographies in order to quickly identify his home town. I realized that we Americans just took it for granted, with many elementary-school classroom hours behind us. We then had a long discussion about marriage, and along the way he asked me for advice on sex. Turns out he (and by extension most Libyan men!) was totally unaware of the notion of foreplay. His eyes widened in surprise and appreciation as I walked him through all the ins-and-outs, so to speak. I later learned from one of the women PCVs that at the hospital where she volunteered, every week a number of Libyan wives would come in with vaginal abrasions because their wham-bam-thank-you-ma'am Libyan husbands had no idea what they were doing.

Hospitality, continued: On April 7, I "bought ten eggs from a woman in Um El Jersan. Unveiled! Talked to me yet! Progressive little town!" (Bob Gausman thought he'd get in big trouble in Samnu when he looked at the face of an unveiled woman with disheveled hair in the street. She began talking to him and he was at a loss as to what do to. Turns out she was mentally disturbed and the village couldn't have cared less. In Aujila, Bob Marshall only saw a woman unveiled once. She was talking to him openly. Bob soon realized she was blind, so it didn't make any difference.)

"Went down to village [Al Gala]—fun bulling with people. God how they sit around and do nothing!" On the way back up the hill, a man gave me two 10-inch-wide round, warm loaves of bread right from his wife's oven. "The best bread I've had yet in Libya. Had that for supper with four fried eggs." I was not the only one who savored Libyan bread. Among many RPCVs' similar recollections, Jim and Joyce Swanson often ate loaves right out of the oven.

Also in early April, electricity was finally available in the village below. Mohammed, the hefty Chief of Police and BMOC about town invited me to a delicious dinner and declared he was getting a TV. He was going to be the first person in history in the village with a TV. He wanted me to help him with it. A week later he summarily summoned me to his house. He was installing the antenna on the roof and I instructed him to align it so as to receive the TV signals from Tripoli in the north. Downstairs, a gaggle of kids sat cross-legged on the floor waiting to see. Like a latter-day Margaret Mead, I couldn't wait to see how they would react to this new technology. A couple of adults were randomly fiddling with the knobs, not knowing what they were doing. I turned the fuzz adjustment knob to the right and on came the picture. And the kids? They just watched, as if it were nothing new.

In Qawassim, Mike Lee and Craig Owens' school principal had a TV. After serving them dinner, they were subject to a confusing mishmash. The show was *The Fugitive*, which Mike and Craig were looking forward to enjoying. However, it was dubbed in Italian, had Arabic subtitles, and all the teachers in the room were shouting out all the subtitles aloud.

The only impact electricity had on me was that shopkeeper Belgassim bought a Frigidaire and I would occasionally buy pear juice that, instead of being warm, was frosty cool.

They had electricity in nearby Yifran. Among other things, this powered the gas station where I gassed up the Moto Guzzi. After visiting friend Ibrahim's son there in the hospital, I visited my French friends again. They served me a delicious dinner accompanied with beer, and topped with scrumptious crepes. It was great to periodically refresh my French. On this occasion, I walked to the edge of Yifran, which brought me to an escarpment on the northernmost rim of the Nefusa Mountains. Spread out before me, as far as the eye could see was hardscrabble pre-desert, like a magnificent scene from *Lawrence of Arabia*. Breathtaking.

**John Meynink and friend in the Fezzan
with Yifran-like landscape behind**

On April 26 Dan and I hitchhiked and bused 50 miles to Qawassim to visit Mike Lee and Craig Owens. They weren't there. So, of course, we hopped their back wall and snuck in a window. We cleaned dishes. We cleaned the kitchen. We listened to their tapes. We cooked 13 crepes which we wolfed down along with some of their coffee. We played chess with their "cool bottle-can chess set." We left no message, other than our indirect *pièce de résistance*, when I retuned Craig's guitar to a G-tuning, so he could suss out which RPCVs had burgled their house.

I started to skywatch, memorizing various constellation names. "Stars and moon magnificent—awe inspiring, frightening as if in outer space looking at them. Can see about 20 times more stars." The Libyans thought I was crazy to want to learn about the stars. For yet another coincidence, during this exact same time period Bob Marshall took up skywatching. However, his comprehensiveness and dedication put my efforts to shame. From his diary: "Took half an hour out to stargaze—it's a gas! Spotted Auriga and Taurus, cemented Gemini and Canis Minor and added them to Orion to block out that portion of the sky." On a later occasion, he writes, "Then I have laboriously tracked Hydra almost to its tail, identified Corvus the Crow, and grasped for Crater the Cup. Bootes is an airy, horizontal strongman lying above the oil field fires, and Draco faintly but distinctly fits between the two Dippers. Canes Venatici and Coma Berenices are found resting unobtrusively between Ursa's tail and Virgo, the representative of the Zodiac. Jupiter shines brightly from the Virgin's right vertical and a rising filling-out crescent lights up the northwestern sky, where Auriga, Orion and Canis Major are still important figures."

I soon found out about some women who were never allowed out of the house.

Gripes, Gropes and Grabs

In another example of befuddled decision-making and lack of institutional memory, there was no fully thought-through policy on how to deal with the go/no-go policy on single women serving in Peace Corps Libya. This was on the heels of the aforementioned situation with Libya I trainees Colleen Ehart's and Karen Southard's diversion to Tunisia for fear of sexual harassment in Libya.

In 1968, Peace Corps Washington advised the Bisbee staff not to send any single women to Libya. And some of the Libya I volunteers training in Bisbee also told the single women they shouldn't be sent to Libya. But Bisbee management went ahead anyway and sent 18 of them. And despite the troubles most of these women experienced in Libya, 20 single women were recruited for the Libya III training. Clearly, the level of sexism, sexual harassment or sexual violence in Libya had not changed in a mere two years. One factor in having the single women come was the influence of Minister of Education in Derna, Fatia Ashura. She supported the idea of single Peace Corps women teaching in Libya and said she would be responsible for them. Another factor was the desire not to favor boys in Libya over girls—to give the girls an equal shot at an English education.

On a superficial level, one might have assumed that given the relatively uneventful experiences of Peace Corps women in nearby Tunisia and Morocco for many years, the experience would be similar in Libya. They were all countries in North Africa, all Arabic in culture. However, when comparing American single women's experiences in Libya vs. those in Tunisia and Morocco, a clear difference emerges. King Idris I of Libya descended from pious and pristine scriptural Sunni ancestors, going back to Mohammed ibn Ali Senussi, born in 1787 in Mustaganem, Algeria.

By 1856, the Senussis ended up in Al Jaghbub near the Egyptian border where they founded a *zawia* (religious lodge) that grew into Africa's second largest university, after Cairo's Al Azhar. From this base of operations, the puritanical reigned. Separation of men and women was strictly enforced. The consequence of this policy was a society of single males with enormous bottled up sexual frustration whose frequent outlet was harassment of Western women.

In more enlightened Tunisia and Morocco, with many years of experience with Europeans and their ways, it sufficed for the PCV women to dress conservatively, covering their arms, legs and heads, adapting to the relatively mild sexism there. They kept a low profile in public, not shopping, eating after the men, etc. While these activities are unfair, they don't physically hurt you. In this way they could have a positive Peace Corps experience. Tunisia had always prided itself on being the most advanced Arab country when it comes to women's rights. Women there had long had the right to divorce and gain custody of their children. Polygamy was even abolished there in 1957. Bob Marshall, having subsequently gone to teach in Tunisia, weighed in many years later, "Tunisia is vastly different. Remember, it is a French culture there, as much as Arab. A single woman wouldn't stick out in Tunisia, let alone be assumed to be a prostitute."

Libya III's Dotty Hanson (formerly Dukehart) felt safe in downtown Tunis. Most urban Tunisian women would cover their heads, but not their faces. Classes were mixed gender. Tunisian men would sometimes rub against Dotty on the bus, but she points out that this happens in the U.S. as well. Tunisian women were far more subservient to their husbands than in the U.S. But Dotty never once met any of her friends' husbands over two years.

Since Libyans could not understand an adult single woman living alone—all Libyan women married in their early teens—Peace Corps Libya arranged to house single women in groups. In Benghazi, for example, one group of single American women living together were called "The Barclay Girls" (after the Barclays Bank branch on the ground floor). The Peace Corps advised the single women not to look a man in the eye, because this would be interpreted as an invitation to bed. So, Cathy Della Penta wore dark glasses all the time. And a trench coat. And a long skirt. One day she was walking down a sandy alleyway with her friend Hamida. As they passed a man in the street Hamida did not acknowledge him at all. Later, she turned to Cathy and said, "Do you know who that was?" Cathy said, "No." Hamida said, "That was my brother."

Another example: "We walked into a restaurant one afternoon dressed, as usual, in our overcoats, scarves and dark glasses. I overheard one of two British women at a nearby table say 'Look, here come the Hungarians.' "

The social constrictions on the American women were oppressive, as Jeanne Maurey recently shared with me, contrasting my male recollection of Benghazi with that of her American women friends.

> We never saw the "beautiful city" with your eyes. We couldn't walk the lovely El Nasr Street corniche; we couldn't go to the movies; we couldn't walk the streets to see the camel or sheep markets or speak with the merchants; we couldn't interact with our students or their families. To visit a woman, one of her young brothers or sisters would have to walk us to their house and back. It makes me sad to realize how much I missed of Libya because of my gender.

One day kids came by the Derna women's apartment with an adorable short-haired terrier puppy in a basket. They adopted it and dubbed it Tonja ("Victor"). Tonja had a bit of a jolt when she was shoved into Mary Buelt's wardrobe by a robber who burst through their front door, ransacked their apartment and stole every American-made item they had (radio, cameras, jeans, tape recorder, etc.) Mary lost cash. The landlord came to examine the scene of the crime. He grabbed a pack of cards, saying, "I'd better take this as evidence." After the robbing a protective Mme. Fatia Ashura said, "You have to move. If you can be robbed, you can be raped." So they moved to the 8ᵗʰ floor of another building that had a security guard.

"It is only the men in the street that are disgusting," wrote Jeanne Maurey. "You can never go out without having them stare at you, make comments, and force you off the street. At times I would love to haul off and smack one of them in the face." At the end of her stint,

I was very happy to leave Benghazi. The environment became increasingly more hostile to women. It was dangerous to walk the street, to go to the market or visit friends. One was always in danger of being grabbed by the breast, jostled and derided. Ugly, ugly, ugly.

One female volunteer underlined that buses were particularly dangerous places to be: "I was literally thrown off a bus in Benghazi, skinning my hands and knees as I landed, with school books flying in all directions." But the street was dangerous, too. "Many times men grabbed my breasts as I walked home. Men would wave money under my nose and say 'You'd do it for Americans!' Then there was the time I bit a guy to get him to let go of my crotch." And she experienced a carry-over effect. Soon after her return to the U.S. she was on a New York City bus and was reflexively seized with fear because "men were looking at me." She had to get off the bus. Despite these predations she says, "I'm really not angry or resentful about my PC experience. I'm very glad I went. I learned a lot—about myself, about the Arab world—that has helped me immensely since."

A more poignant situation involving the sexes is the issue of what happens was when you combine an American nun and a Greek ship captain in Libya. The nun in question was Mary Buelt, who at 40 was the oldest of all Libya II volunteers. She had big brown eyes, was by all accounts a very funny person with "a ready laugh and quick with a joke." She was also well-respected by volunteers as a leader. Her formal convent name was Sister Mary Joseph Bernadine. She had taught for over two decades at the Sisters of St. Joseph of Carondolet congregation in St. Louis. And she had a Masters in French. By the late 1960s she had become disillusioned with religious life and applied to the Peace Corps. (One contributing factor: She had had a fierce argument with her Mother Superior who insisted that she punish a boy for retrieving a ball from a roof when Mary had expressly given the boy permission to do so.) Having been cloistered, she was naïve when it came to relations with men. Posted to Derna, she got to know and fall in love with a Greek ship captain who lived in their building. He told her to quit the Peace Corps, go back to the U.S., get a job, save up money, and then come back to marry him. Luckily, she had several conversations with Peace Corps friends and with Bob Pearson who all cautioned her on the inadvisability of this whole idea.

In a nice turn of events, Maggie Brossoit's Men's Teacher College students became protective of her. They'd create teams that would ride with her on the bus on the way home. If any aggressive male approached her, they would yell at him and he'd beat a hasty retreat. However, when not under the protection of her students, she was bumped into by Libyan men all the time, even though she was dressed modestly, with her neck demurely covered. When she was with her husband Mark on buses, she'd read a book, head down, to avoid looking directly at any Libyan men. Once, a man approached her, not even speaking, and had his face two inches from hers, just staring. Mark said, "Take it easy!" Maggie took it a step further and yelled at the guy in Arabic, "Yes, I can read and you turn around!" And he did.

On another occasion, having just disembarked from the bus at the square near the cathedral, Maggie noticed a Libyan man whom she concluded was following her, because when she switched sides of the street, he did likewise. That afternoon she was hot, tired and crabby. The man bumped into her. Her usual response would be to grumble and walk away. But this time, she saw red and yelled in Arabic, "You pig!" She was appalled in spite of herself. She kept moving away, thinking the guy would keep following her. But the guy was so shocked he stood stock-still in the middle of the road, slack-jawed with honking traffic flowing around him.

One Cyrenaican female volunteer remembers, "Staring at women is a national pastime, ranking only below tea drinking. It can be hazardous, though. I saw one bicycler ogling so much he ran into the back of a parked car."

Nancy Corrin's introduction to Libya's harassment culture did not go well. Since she was teaching in Misurata in an all-boys school and the faculty was all-male, they didn't know what to do with her. So, between classes she was holed up in a tiny closet stuffed with mops, brooms and buckets. And she was never offered any tea the whole year.

On her very first day of classes, Nancy endured a double whammy. First, some of the boys in her classroom started fighting, hitting each other with rulers, protractors and fists. "Some of the boys jumped out the window and all hell broke loose." Second, on the way home from school that day, while walking through the *souk*, she heard

> Strange, high-pitched clicking and yelling sounds. I saw up to fifty boys from their young teens into their early twenties running in my direction. I then heard stones zinging through the air near me. Some were hitting my head and back. I started running very fast, right into the center of the market and jumped into the nearest merchant's white-washed tiny hut. There was only room for two of us in the hut. In a flash, the mob of boys was outside screaming, yelling and knocking pots and pans off the carefully arranged display of wares. At this, the merchant got angry with the boys, yelling and throwing stones at them. The boys went scurrying off like a pack of wild animals. The merchant told me that the boys said I was a witch and that I ate babies.

Sometime later, Nancy and her husband Jay were dining with the official in charge of keeping order in Misurata. As Jay recounts it, "He assured us that Nancy wouldn't have any trouble in the future, since they found the 15-year old boy responsible for the attack. He was sentenced to hard labor for life in a Benghazi prison where he would break up rocks in the hot sun."

Jay also recounts a weird incident for PCV Carol Evans, a friend of Jay and Nancy's. Carol taught boys ranging from 12 to 19 years old. Although she took great care to wear modest clothing, including long stockings, scarves, and long sleeves, on one particularly hot day she made the mistake of rolling up her sleeves, thereby exposing her elbows. "Given the fact that these boys had never seen a woman past puberty, the image of Carol with exposed elbows was apparently overwhelming. Carol, to her great shock, discovered that one of the older boys in the back of the room was unable to contain his excitement and began auto-eroticism right there in the classroom. Carol quickly rolled her sleeves back down, thereby putting an end to a rather strong dose of cultural misunderstanding."

The degree of sexual harassment varied due to location, deportment

and just plain luck. It was no-win overall for the female PCVs. If seques-
tered in their apartments it was isolating. But when out and about it was
being constantly ogled and hassled.

For Andrea Murphy, "I was stared at a lot, as if I were not totally
human." Cathy Kaiser says, "I was ogled even wearing a raincoat and a
babushka on my head. I almost felt like a zoo animal." She added that they
learned quickly not to ever turn on the lights in their bedrooms as there
were always Peeping Toms in the street. Once the three Derna women decided to go shopping in Tobruk. They went to a taxi stand where taxicabs
were waiting for customers and hopped into one of the ubiquitous Peugeot
404s and proceeded with the ride on steep switchback mountain roads.
Another taxi driver from the taxi stand was angry that these three unveiled
women were not in *his* taxi. So he gave chase, trying to force the women's
taxi off the road! When the women finally reached Tobruk, their reward
was being able to purchase a plastic-coated wire dish drainer.

Another time, Cathy, Mary and Trudy went to the local Derna hospital that was run by Italian nuns to visit a Libyan student of Dave Munro's,
Ayid Mohammed, who had appendicitis and required immediate surgery.
Because the surgeon was a famously drunk Brazilian, Dave had banged
on his door a few mornings earlier and threatened to kill him if he were
drunk the day of Ayid's operation. The women brought Ayid a Donald
Duck comic book in Arabic that the boy loved. Their reward for this as
they left the hospital? Being pelted with stones thrown by boys who were
shouting in Arabic, "Whores! Hookers! Jezebels!"

In Homs, Rebecca Peterson walked daily about a half mile across a
wadi to her girls' school. This took her past a boys' boarding school. All
was well until one day a klatch of boys spotted her. They started shouting
out obscenities. They started to throw rocks and closed in around her in a
circle. Her adrenalin kicked in. She decided to address the biggest of the
boys and shouted in perfect Arabic, "*Haram aleek*! ("Shame upon you!")
You have brought shame upon your mother! You have brought shame
upon your sisters! You have brought shame upon your grandmother!"

The boys were taken aback, shocked that this white woman spoke
Arabic. They couldn't deal, thinking she was some kind of witch. They
ran away!

Things were, of course, much worse for Libyan women. Women not only had to ride in the rear of the bus, they had to sit on the floor. Libyan women were not allowed to drive cars or even bicycles. Bill Cagle reports that one of his Libyan friends literally *never* let his wife out of the house. When Bill asked why, his friend said, "I'm a poor man. If I let her out of the house, she'll see things she wants to buy. I can't afford to buy them." Charlie Cross and roommate Jeff Taylor in Zawia had a neighboring family where the father was a police lieutenant, there was a housewife, three small children and an older woman. When they passed by, typically the wife was sweeping the front stoop, and she would flee indoors, put a scarf on her head and stare shyly at them out the window. Eventually, she got more relaxed and she said "Hello" to Charlie and Jeff. The older woman, who turned out to be the lieutenant's other wife, reported this to her husband. For this, the younger wife got beaten.

Lorraine Slawiak, in addition to her teaching duties, volunteered at the Benghazi Hospital where they would periodically treat Libyan wives for burns. The cause was always the same. These wives would prepare meals for their families over charcoal stoves that, rather than being waist-high on a counter, were on the floor, which entailed much bending over. Husbands would get upset that a meal wasn't ready on time and would summarily kick over the charcoal stove, sending hot coals flying in all directions, and inevitably the wives' clothes would catch fire.

One female volunteer recounts, "One day in a teacher's room, I mentioned that my student Shemsa was not returning to school. The teachers recounted that, in fact, she can never again come to school. Why? One day while her parents were away a man on the street came into her house. When her father found out, he forbade her to go to school, declaring she must remain in the house for the rest of her life."

On the positive side, all over Libya, we found a deep, bonding sense of community between us Peace Corps volunteers and our friends, colleagues and villagers.

Libyan Duds and Buds

Ⅰf you dress up like the French, The Brits or the Germans, you'll be basically indistinguishable from Americans. However, in Libya the everyday dress is exotic so many of us had fun buying *holies*, vests and *cabooses* or colorful *barracans*, headwear and brass jewelry.

Dan Peters and fellow teachers mostly wearing *holies*

Randolph W. Hobler

**Benghazi roomies Jeanne Maurey and Cathy
Friberg in Libyan wedding dresses**

Judy Putnam, in Ajmail, in traditional Libyan wedding dress

278

Diane Forasté's women friends asked her to teach them the Twist—pretty hard with Arabic music. "But there was one song that had a good Twist beat for the first few measures, so we played that part over and over while everyone tried twisting. It was wonderful to be part of this happy group."

For almost all of us, we easily made friends with our fellow Libyan teachers and villagers, hanging out, going on picnics, sharing tea, sharing meals. A formal part of the Peace Corps mission is to cultivate positive community bonds, but it was hardly necessary for us to formalize, we just were naturally drawn to these friendly, hospitable, generous people. Here are five of my Libyan friends in Al Gala. Note they are hanging out in a 6' x 10' hovel still having fun!

Clockwise from bottom: Milaad, Tahir, El Haadi, Abdul Magiid and Masoud

Dan Peters, with roommates Khazam and Issa

Richard Massey, hanging out with friends in Farzougha

Mark Broissoit (in the back) enjoying
lunch with friends in Sharshara

Chip Chandler's friends in Edri in the Fezzan

John Meynink and Libyan friends in the Fezzan

Sue Glover with neighbors and teacher Aisha Bosefi in Surman

Alan Frank in Zliten, imbibing Libyan tea and Mirinda with friends

For an overnight picnic, Joe Connor's fellow teachers joined a couple of goats with them in the back of a Toyota pickup truck. After dinner:

> We sat around an open fire while some of the guys sang these lovely songs of longing and lament. I was then told it was my turn to sing. What could I sing that was in the same mood as their songs? Then I thought of Elvis. I sang "Love Me Tender" slowly and sweetly. Under a desert sky full of stars, my audience was transfixed. Then my Libyan buddies wrapped themselves in their robes to sleep. And I crawled into my sleeping bag.

Kathy Lamoureux with Bedouin women friends in Derna

The most ambitious effort at making Libyan friends was when Ern Snook, John Meynink and Bob Gausman set forth on an eight-hour trek around Christmas-time to the remote oasis of Mindera during *Eid Al Kabir* (the "big feast"). Escorted by a guide, they shuffled along in sandals, across the gigantic Ubari Sand Sea, suffering mightily from bloody toenails. The Sand Sea was so formidable you could only reach Mindera by foot. "Just in time for dinner, we crested a dune and saw the most incredible sight." Amid huge rolling dunes, they descended upon the oasis in all its glory—smoke emanating from mud huts, dogs barking, palm trees and a double line of men racing towards them, singing, grabbing their arms in a loving embrace and ushering us joyously into the center of the village to the dwelling of the Sheik. He had fought with King Idris in World War I against the Italians. This was the only time in living memory that any American had set foot in this village. The camaraderie for anyone to visit this village—much less Americans—was palpable. Luckily, John Meynink was the most comfortable among them with Arabic and shared natural laughter and many stories with the Sheik while they—entranced with wonderment—crowded the room as the trio drank Libyan tea. Ern, John and Bob spent three full days in Mindera with the village men arguing over who had the honor of hosting them for the next meal.

Ern Snook's Libyan friends literally hanging around

An inadvertent bonding resulted from a long, surprisingly poignant story involving Bob Conway. One night, Bob answered a knock on the door. It was a policeman who jammed a gun up to his nose demanding to search the house. Bob was sweating bullets. This was compounded by double-confusion because his eyes were stuck shut by gunk generated by local sandstorms at the time. The policeman ransacked his Peace Corps locker, but confiscated nothing. He was, however, fascinated by a spatula. Bob reported the incident and a week later was escorted by Land Rover to Sebha, 37 miles away, to ID the perp in a line-up. Turns out the offending cop was a teenager who was drunk, and that the gun had been a toy.

To make amends, a few days later, the teenager's father had Bob over for tea and offered to buy something for Bob on his upcoming trip to

Cairo by way of "compensation for your trouble." Bob asked for an *oud* (a guitar-like instrument) but never got one. At that point, he realized the sharing of tea and the offering of a present was "a ritual way of mending fences without literally any intent to give gifts." A while later, Bob came upon the father in the Brak market, struggling to carry a heavy shopping bag. Bob offered to help, grabbing one handle while the father took the other. As they lugged the bag down the street, the crazy town poet began walking behind them. The whole way back to the father's house, the poet improvised couplets about the whole situation, praising Bob for being so helpful in the face of the distress caused to him by the teenage policeman.

And in a mixed bag example of bonding in Sabratha, neighbor Mohammed Younis took John Forasté out to a sparrow-like bird sleeping in a tree. As Diane Forasté describes it, Mohammed shined "…a flashlight into the bird's eyes, temporarily stunning it. He used a slingshot to kill the bird. They plucked the feathers and brought it home to fry in a pan. The bird was so tiny it hardly offered any meat but Mohammed chewed on the bones as well. It seemed better to me to have left that little bird to sing another day, but we realized this was a special treat offered to us in friendship."

My stargazing and moonwatching soon intersected comically with my villagers amid the excitement of the upcoming American Apollo moon mission.

Arab Astronauts, Shepherds, Exams

One night in early May, strolling through dark downtown Al Gala with friends, I looked up, pointed at the moon and said "What's that?"

"Why, Mr. Randy, that's the moon!"

"Really? We don't have that in America."

On May 25, 1969, Apollo X, with astronauts Thomas Stafford, Eugene Cernan and John Young not only circled the moon but tested the lunar module which detached from the main command module and dropped to within eight miles of the lunar surface. (Who knew I'd meet Young just three years later while making a film for Encyclopaedia Britannica?) This was the last mission before Apollo XI, which was scheduled to land on the moon later in July 1969. Needless to say, the whole world was agog in anticipation of the moon landing—the most significant event in the history of mankind. Over 500 million people worldwide watched the Apollo moon landing.

So, Tom Furth asked his students if they'd like to go to the moon.

"No."

"OK, then, would you like to go to America?"

"No."

"Well, then, would you like to go to Paris?

They all shook their heads.

"All right, would you like to go to Tripoli?"

"Well, maybe."

I brought up the topic sitting cross-legged on the dirt floor in Belgassim's shop, sipping tea with a handful of Libyan men.

"What's going to happen when the first Arabs go to the moon?"

Belgassim sparked to this. "Yes! Arabs on the moon!"

The others picked up the cry and started chanting "Arabs on the moon! Arabs on the moon! Arabs on the moon!"

I said, "No, no, I have a question about Arabs on the moon."

"What?"

"How are they going to pray?"

"What do you mean, how are they going to pray?"

I asked, "How are they going to pray up?"

"Pray up?"

"Yes, Mecca will be up, so if you're on the moon praying on your knees, you won't be facing Mecca."

A roomful of quizzical looks. OK, further explanation is needed.

"You see, when you're on the Earth," I gestured upward, "the moon is up there. But when you're on the moon (I gestured up again) the Earth is up there."

"Oh, no, Mr. Randy, the Earth is down here!"

I tried to demonstrate with my hands—this hand is the moon, this hand is the Earth. "You see how when you're up on the moon, when you look up, you'll see the Earth in the sky."

More adamant, and thrusting their hands towards the ground, "Oh, noooo, the earth is down here!"

"You know, up on the moon, you'd have to bring a ramp along and kneel on the ramp so you'd be facing up towards Mecca. Up there on the Earth."

Most adamant, stabbing their fingers towards the ground, "No, no, no! The Earth is down *here!*" I gave up. But I did make a mental note that when the first Arab astronauts are preparing to fly to the moon, the trainers should give them a heads-up (so to speak) on spatial relations. (*Nota bene:* 16 years after the first moon landing, there *was,* in fact, an Arab astronaut. While he didn't go to the moon, he did orbit the earth on the space shuttle Discovery. And he was a royal: a Saudi named Prince Sultan bin Salman Al-Saud.)

Upon the actual landing of Neil Armstrong & Co. on the moon, on July 21 (Libya time), PCV Frank Reese was listening on a transistor radio to the news with Jack Seifert and some Libyans. The Libyans asked what was being said. When he told them, they said, "No way. The moon is sacred to Allah. Allah would not allow humans to travel there."

In Cairo, the Russian director of the Aswan Dam project invited Victor Gramigna, Pat Hilliard and Richard Massey to his hotel lobby for drinks and to watch Apollo XI land. He was gracious enough to toast the Americans for being first to the moon. The event was doubly meaningful for Victor—July 21 was his birthday.

In Benghazi, John and Andrea Murphy recall that the principal of their local junior high school had warned them the moon mission would fail because, "Man may reach for the moon and the stars, but only Allah will get there."

Marge Amerud, the wife of a Wheelus plumber said, "I watched the moon walk and listened to the Arabs say it was a Hollywood stunt."

Also in Benghazi, Don and Lani Leydig were watching the landing in a shop window on TV. A Libyan next to them intoned, "You have to be careful, because sometimes the moon is not there." In Athrun, Dave Munro and his best friend and fellow teacher Shaeb found in the moon landing an opportunity to bring swaggering local police chief Hajj down a peg or two. They hatched a plot that they shared with Hajj's superiors at the police department who agreed to play along. They called in Hajj and with great gravity informed him that the Apollo XI astronauts were going to splash down just off the coast between Athrun and Ras El-Hillal, and that Hajj was being deputized to pluck them out of the ocean and take care of them. "The honor and reputation of Libya are riding on this!" Dave describes the rest.

> He rushed to my house, saying "What should I do? What should I *do?*" Hajj summoned Shaeb to help and the three of us agreed that he and his wife would prepare appropriate food and lodging. Shaeb and I would scout the coastline for the re-entry vehicle. After all his preparations, later in the day the police informed Hajj that the astronauts had landed elsewhere and that he was off the

hook. Hajj was exhausted but immensely relieved. We had
a terrific party, with lots of excellent food. It's a shame Neil
Armstrong and Buzz Aldrin missed the chance to sample
home-cooked Libyan fare!

While much has been made of the famous "Earthrise" photograph
taken December 25, 1968 by the Apollo VIII crew, dramatizing mankind's
new perception of "lifeboat Earth," more particularly, in retrospect, our
relationship to the moon tied back into the Peace Corps. Precisely in 1968,
not only were we living JFK's dream of a world united in peace, but living
his dream of landing a man on the moon. Two inspiring visions of oneness
with mankind impacting us.

And as long as we're talking moon and Libya we might as well discuss
the Libyan flag which adorned my humble apartment in Al Gala and to
this day adorns my humble condo in Connecticut. It sports a crescent
moon and a star (much as the Islamic flags of Turkey, Algeria, Tunisia and
11 other nations do). While the origins of this symbol date to Roman
times, the more recent borrowing emanates from the flag of the Ottoman
Empire, illustrating the start of the lunar month. Astronomically, these
two celestial bodies constitute the conjunction of the crescent moon with
Venus. Symbolically, for Moslems, the crescent moon stands for the beginning of the lunar month.

Not to dive too much into arcana, but the colors of the Libyan flag are
not random. The red stands for the blood sacrificed for the liberation of
Libya. The black represents the dark days of occupation under the Italians.
And the green represents Libya's agriculture, harking back to its status as
the breadbasket of the Roman and Ottoman Empires.

The Libyan flag. Pre- and post-Ghaddafi

Imagine my surprise, while flying at night across the Atlantic from Europe several decades later, to see outside the airplane's window that very conjunction of the crescent moon with Venus. Given my familiarity with the Libyan flag it spooked me, this cosmic connection. I stared in wonder at the phenomenon for some time.

Venus right at the edge of the moon's penumbra

In early May, I experienced my first *ghibli*. This colorful local term, designates a huge south-to-southeasterly sandstorm that can reach hurricane velocity and last for up to nine days at a time. *Ghiblis* can transport huge quantities of sand, often burying entire villages. For me it was simply "incredible." One hit John Maclean's home. The sand was so fine and the wind so strong, piles of sand accumulated inside beneath the windows. To top it off, he was then pummeled the very next day by a giant hailstorm.

Playing chess with Dan was such a regular occurrence, we fancied it would be fun to enhance the experience by increasing the size and tangibility of the game. Inspired by Mike Lee and Craig Owens' outsized chess set, I bought a straw mat about eight times the size of a normal chess board, and using a stencil technique, painted black and white squares on it. For each kind of playing piece, we chose clear glass bottles of different shapes and sizes—e.g. for the pawns, little pear juice bottles; for bishops, Pepsi bottles; for the king, a tall milk bottle, etc. The really cool esthetic for us was instead of painting the outside of the bottles with white/black paint, we put the paint *inside* the bottles, shaking them up and dripping out the excess. The result was enticingly shiny pawns, bishops and rooks. It was a joy just to feel the heft of each piece as we moved them around. Dan: "Randy and I finished our chess set and it works beautifully." I can't count the number of games we played with that set.

The opposite of esthetics kicked in when I tried to show some Libyan friends how backgammon worked. Easy, just take a stick and form a backgammon board in the dirt, grab some rocks for the counters, imagine the dice and start to play. Easy and no fun at all. That's when I realized how much the mechanics of games and sports are only a part of the fun. It's the colors, the textures, the materials, the feel, the smell, the sound of the game or sport. In the case of backgammon, how much more I now appreciate the texture of the corkboard, the heft, beauty and sound of the counters as they click one another; the rattling sound of the dice; the soft feel and men's-club smell of the leather dice cups.

From the beginning of May through the Ides of June Dan visited five times. We played chess on every visit, once accompanied by popcorn, with Dan usually beating me. One night we had a long talk on religion, on marriage, and he regaled me with stories of stacking pea-vines on his family farm in Wisconsin.

293

Dan Peters at far right on family farm stacking pea vines

We'd continue to play ping pong. Another night we stayed up till midnight talking about Peace Corps policies. On another visit, Dan brought fruitcake (I have no idea from where) and much-needed Off! to help me fend off sand flies.

I felt compelled to reciprocate his onerous visits. One Thursday afternoon, constrained from riding my Moto Guzzi on non-official business, I determined to walk the ten-plus miles to El Khozeur. There were zero roads between Al Gala and El Khozeur. No pathways, even. No signs. No landmarks. Just undifferentiated hardscrabble. (We're talking decades before GPS.) I knew the general direction and gamely marched forth. After a few miles I came upon a shepherd with his sheep. I asked him where El Khozeur was. I expected some sort of direction like "Oh, go two kilometers this way and when you see a big rock on the right that looks like a lion, go to the right." All he did was gaze off into the distance, raise his right hand and slowly wave it vaguely in a general direction. I went through this exercise every few miles with other shepherds (sometimes with goats) who also did these slow waves, but pointing in different directions. By such zigs and zags, I managed to find Dan's village but not before a startlement.

Typical Libyan shepherd

As I was crossing a rock-strewn wadi a snake darted between my legs. I jumped, then realized I was lucky it wasn't some kind of venomous asp. I would be remiss if I didn't mention at this point that my getting lost in Libya and dealing with a snake echoed the same predicament encountered by Alexander the Great, some 2,300 years before. In 332 B.C.E., having founded the city of Alexandria, Alexander, believing himself to be the son of Zeus-Ammon (the combined Greek-Egyptian master deity of the day), decided he would march his army 170 miles across Egypt and into the Libyan desert to consult with the female oracle of Zeus-Ammon in the Siwa oasis to confirm he was a demi-god. However, the trek was no idle walk in the park. Historians recount that his army faced an ocean of sand, and as in my situation, "it is impossible to tell one's direction, as there are no mountains or trees or solid hills to serve as signs and guide the travelers on their way." (*Nota bene:* "Ammon" means "sand" in Greek!)

Unknown to Alexander (as meteorologists were in short supply in

332 B.C.E.), one danger facing him was the *khamsin*, a periodic great strong wind that can blow huge amounts of sand upon the unsuspecting. One such unsuspecting victim was Persian King Cambyses II, who, in 525 B.C.E., along with an army of 50,000 warriors decided to attack the oracle's temple at Siwa, and was promptly buried by a cataclysmic sandstorm.

Where I had the advantage of shepherds, Alexander was fortunate to have two speaking snakes that guided him accurately to the oracle. (My snake didn't say a word to me.) As far as the likes of Livy and Ptolemy can tell, the oracle confirmed to Alexander that he was indeed a son of Zeus-Ammon. From that point forward, Alexander was at pains to present himself with the rams-horn symbol of this god. And his bucket list included being buried at his death in Siwa.

**Silver coin from the third century BCE depicting
Alexander the Great with a ram's horn**

Reproduced with permission of the trustees of the British Museum

Back to the mundane. In El Khozeur, Dan and I shared dinner with his five roommates, speaking a mixture of English and Arabic. For some reason, Issa had taken a shine to the passive voice in English. Every sentence he uttered was passive. Instead of "I read the book," he would say "The book was read by me." Or, instead of "I opened the door," he would say "The door was opened by me." Instead of "I ate the apple," he'd say "The apple was eaten by me." He took great joy in this, as if this power of the passive bestowed upon himself a mastery of mystical knowledge. Much mirth to us.

On my return trip, on Friday, I used GPS ("Goat-Pointing Shepherds") in reverse to find my way back to Al Gala.

My socializing was all-male. The lack of female company was an increasing source of frustration as the months passed by. I was also aware of lack of human touch, and realized how important this is to our emotional well-being. I thought more and more about Jeanne, with a growing longing to see her. She wrote that she was going to spend the summer in the U.S. (I didn't know it at the time but she was heading for Bisbee to train at Libya III.)

Letters to friends and family continued to fly back and forth. At the time, I regarded all this as just writing letters. In retrospect, what I was really doing was reinforcing and refreshing relationships.

Chilling out with these male friends continued: going to Yifran to hang out with the French; Tom Weinz stayed at my place one night and we played many games of chess with the new, improved chess set, even working games backwards from checkmate to analyze the games; one night a long talk with very talkative, very funny El Haadi about the Koran. He used to tease me declaring, "Mr. Randy, *inta moosh mufiid*!" "Mr. Randy, you are useless!")

Without having lived in Libya, I never would have been alerted to one key concept in Middle Eastern politics whose debates rage to this day.

Inquisitions and Inculcations

If one exerts even a modicum of observation, one can glean insights. I learned that rather than a monolithic mindset, citizens of various Arab countries were oft-times jealous, suspicious or competitive with respect to other Arab countries. The Libyans were suspicious of Egyptians. Egyptians were seriously touchy even about Tunisian accents. I learned that different Arabs had different reputations: the Lebanese were the clever merchants. The Palestinians the smartest. The Egyptians speak the most precisely, while the Moroccans slur their speech.

In repeated discussions, I learned that Libyans—and by extension all Arabs—had no religious problem with the Jews. They claimed they were not anti-Semitic, but rather, anti-Zionist—against the political take-over of Palestine by the Jews. I initially regarded this with great skepticism. It seemed like splitting hairs. That this argument was a dodge, an excuse. After all, for decades the American media had pounded into the American psyche that Arabs were anti-Semitic. That the Arabs hated the Jews. A belief deeply inculcated into American public opinion. Furthermore, I had never even heard this notion of Arabs arguing that they were anti-Zionist rather than anti-Semitic. This Arab opinion was largely suppressed.

My Libyan friends claimed that for many centuries, the Arabs lived peacefully side-by-side with Jews. They said this was proof there was no inherent enmity between the two groups. They said it was only in the years around the establishment of Israel in 1948, and in the turbulent years following, that relations between Arabs and Jews became contentious, and that it was therefore a political issue. This, too, I was skeptical of. However, they seemed sincere and I, being of an open-minded bent, started looking into their claims.

So, I looked at the years from 629 A.D. (establishment of initial Arab power under the prophet Mohammed) to 1948 (the founding of Israel). The historical fact of the matter is that with some limited exceptions, Jews and Arabs lived together harmoniously for a full 1,319 years (that ain't just whistlin' Dixie!).

Jews held positions in all strata of Ottoman society including in finance, in handicrafts such as tannery, large scale commerce, governmental positions, as heads of customs houses, treasurers, secretaries and interpreters. In Tunisia Jews were assigned to be the keeper of the Bey's jewels and valuable articles. In Libya during this period, there was a thriving Jewish community in Benghazi. In Tripoli in 1941, 25% of the population were Jewish, practicing their faith in no fewer than 44 synagogues. According to Gina Waldman, who was born and raised in Libya, "My family came from an ancient Jewish community known as the Mizrachim. They had lived in Libya for over 2,000 years." The first Jews arrived in Cyrene, Libya in the 3rd century B.C.E.

Family in the Tripoli Jewish Quarter

It is richly ironic that a predominantly Christian country (the U.S.) has expended so much effort to tar the Arabs with enmity towards the Jews when the Jews' treatment at the hands of Christians has been demonstrably much worse. One could cite hundreds of examples, but besides the Spanish

Inquisition, there was an earlier Medieval Inquisition. In 1290 England expelled their Jewish population. Then France expelled their Jewish population in 1306. On August 2, 1492 King Ferdinand and Queen Isabella decreed the Edict of Expulsion of the Jews from Spain. (The very same day, by the by, that Columbus, directed by the self-same king and queen, left for his famous expedition.) This decree was executed by the notorious inquisitor-general Torquemada. In 1492, Jews were expelled from southern Italy. The Ottomans *invited* these Jews to their territory. In 1496, the Jews were expelled from Portugal. In that year, Moslem Sultan Bayezid II of the Turkish empire received thousands of Jewish refugees. There were widespread pogroms against the Jews in late 19th-century Europe and of course, there was the Holocaust.

It was only the onset of Zionism that sparked anti-Zionism among Arabs, with the 1948 Israeli-Palestinian War, the Israeli invasion of Egypt in 1956 and more generating enormous animosity in the Arab world, resulting in the elimination of Jews from all Arab countries in the aftermath.

In short, my consciousness was raised, as were most of my fellow PCVs. Exposed to facts of history, systematically suppressed by the U.S. press for decades, our volunteer world-view was permanently changed, better informing our view of the Arab-Israeli conflict for the rest of our lives. An unintended consequence of the Peace Corps.

It had always struck me that American frontier folklore "an apple for the teacher" was a tiresome cliché. But it feels much different when you're on the receiving end, and in Libya, to boot. Out of the blue, on May 24 at Um El Jersan, one student gave me four eggs, and others gave me a total of six apples. I was stunned and gratified by these gestures. As to education itself, the students in both schools were making solid progress. We had now breezed through all of the English for Libya 1 reader and were primed for the English for Libya 2 (which we didn't have on hand yet). Classes were better, and "they're all reading well now." There were pleasant surprises, e.g., some formerly poor students were forging ahead. However, on the disciplinary end, the split continued: "Al Gala murder again. Um sweet by comparison." One day in May: "Only 18 kids showed up for Al Gala. Mad-house." And on another day "One kid struck back at me today."

The inevitable fly in the ointment was the year-end exams on June 14. I helped the Libyan teachers administer the English exams. We were sand-bagged to discover the exams were going to be multiple choice! The kids had no experience with multiple choice. Had I known, of course, I could have familiarized them with this. The error was compounded by the Libyan teachers themselves, who were at a loss. That afternoon, I corrected the exams. Unfortunately, many flunked.

In Dave Munro's Ras Al-Hilal class the girls' names were Rebha, Nuwarah and Jamilah. This latter means "beautiful" but did not apply at all, sadly, to her looks. She was also, as Dave describes it "a major miscreant on exam days. I found her forearms heavily inked with words she thought might come in handy on the test. It didn't matter, she failed anyway."

According to Malcolm Travelstead, some of his kids cheated by writing answers on the cuffs of their shirts, on the soles of their flip-flops and even on the inside heel of their flip-flops.

One big deal for a special few of us in June of 1969 was the visit to Libya by the Peace Corps director, Joseph Blatchford. At the age of 34, at the time he was the youngest head of a federal agency ever. He and his entourage dropped in on Jim and Joyce Swanson's house in Tarhuna. Joyce prepared couscous and invited some of their local Libyan friends. Unfortunately, Blatchford, unaware of local customs, reached over and ate what was supposed to be others' portions. He also stopped by in Benghazi where Jeanne Maurey cooked him up a meal. He visited Phil Akre and Rich Thibault in Al Qalil. And in Homs, the Petersons served him camel burgers.

Libyan, Phil Akre, Peace Corps Director Joseph Blatchford and Rich Thibault in Al Qalil

In this May/June timeframe, I learned that a number of PCVs had left Libya (by the time we were done it was a 20% attrition rate). There was no one reason. At the end of the school year, Peter Hawkes and Frank Dauterich left. Peter felt that too many of his fifth-grade students would learn English, then after sixth grade would simply become shepherds, and all his teaching would be for naught. He was simultaneously torn on an issue of school choice for the next year. The powers that be said he had to choose between a school where he had been living in Salene to teach with four Libyan teachers he really enjoyed being with, or going to another school in the town of Shigran, where he loved the students. Finally, in the big picture, Peter didn't rank teaching English up there as noble as teaching agriculture or helping the sick or building hospitals.

Earlier, in March, Rufus Cadigan received a letter from his local draft board claiming he had illegally left the country and that he had to immediately return to the U.S. 50 years later I unearthed the relevant policy from the Peace Corps' 1968 Annual Report to Congress: "Despite the common belief, Selective Service regulations do not require a draft-eligible male to receive a permit from his draft board to leave the country." But in those Vietnam days, the word of draft boards was the word of God. Plus, Rufus, living in remote Azzizia and unable to consult with anyone, much less a lawyer, felt he had no choice. He had to suddenly desert his students, his Libyan friends and his Peace Corps friends. In retrospect, it is not clear exactly what had happened. It might have been that had Rufus informed his board ahead of time, all would have been well. The other explanation could have been that Rufus was the victim of an overstepping draft board. Two years earlier, Peace Corps Director Jack Vaughn complained to the Presidential Appeals board, "the problem of induction notices to overseas volunteers is becoming a major concern for us. Pulling a volunteer off a productive job at mid-tour is unfair to the nation, to the host country, the Peace Corps and the individual."

Mike Lee self-terminated after the first school year. His location was not in a village. The two schools he taught at were in the middle of no-where. There was no community to bond with. "There was no way to be a part of everything," he noted. John Legasey and Frank Nicosia left at the same time. Through a combination of extreme culture shock and with other factors, three volunteers suffered nervous breakdowns and left Libya. In one case, the volunteer was a brilliant but unstable individual who was obviously not adequately screened by Clearfield psychologists and D-group sessions. One of his endearing traits was, when angry, he cursed out fellow volunteers in Latin! In another one case, a volunteer's students were older. They would often not show up for school. They'd throw stones at his house. Dr. Coulson, the Peace Corps doctor, accompanied another PCV, to his eternal gratitude, on a plane all the way back to the United States to a medical facility. One perhaps unintended consequence of Dr. Coulson's hospitality—allowing PCVs in from the hinterlands to sleep in his office—was that some of the volunteers helped themselves to the "black beauties" (amphetamines cut with phenobarbital) in his unlocked medicine cabinet so they could stay up all night partying or riding Moto Guzzis. He also allowed PCVs to stay at his spacious house close to the Mediterranean.

In all, there were 28 defections: 13 for medical reasons, including a couple whose wife suffered repeated miscarriages; four due to pregnancies; three due to selective service problems; two due to family hardships such as an ailing mother; and six for various adjustment issues. This included a Jewish couple who resigned because of anti-Jewish feelings among Libyans;

two couples due to tough site situations; and one male volunteer who found the isolation, lack of intellectual stimulation and lack of feminine companionship as too much.

Bob Pearson relates that a number of his charges in Cyrenaica who were practicing Catholics experienced a kind of religious culture shock. They were used to going to Mass every Sunday. In Libya while there were a few Catholic churches, they were few and far between. The Catholic volunteers felt guilty, even though it was not their fault. They actually worried what their parents would say. Bob found himself in a parental role, listening sympathetically to these PCVs and counseling them to be aware of their feelings and fears, while reminding them that they were adults now and should be able to learn how to cope. "But it was difficult for them to accept the fact that they could live just fine without going to church." (Once more, no pre-counseling on this topic in Clearfield or Bisbee.)

I forgot to mention that I often noted in my diary how tired I was all the time. I don't remember why, maybe simply not enough sleep. I was also writing of the increasing discomfort of my hernia. And certainly, there was my growing trepidation of the upcoming operation.

I continued to be Protestantly busy playing guitar, trumpet, trying to learn speed reading, planting (for whatever reason) orange and spruce seeds in a tray of soil in the enclosure behind my apartment. At some point, much to my delight, three buds came up but I didn't know what they were and they never did much else.

Jeanne partook of a mini-adventure. One day in Benghazi she ran into two pilots she knew. They asked if she'd like to fly 650 miles to Sebha. She asked when they were leaving. "In 15 minutes." On a lark she said "OK!" She hopped into their empty DC-3 and right into the cockpit. In 125 degrees on the ground, they spent a couple of hours looking around, then flew home. Only this time the plane was filled to the gills with the Benghazi men's soccer team.

DC-3 Jeanne flew in to Sebha

Jeanne in 125-degree Sebha Airport

About the end of the first school year, many years later Bob Marshall wrote for a Peace Corps newsletter, "nine months in a Saharan oasis, without electricity or running water, without ever seeing a female was a time of solitude, beauty and learning that will affect my life forever."

We were not all bereft of female companionship. Closer to Tripoli, Ted Kelley at Gashir near Tripoli developed a relationship with a UN secretary. She would regularly visit him for the night, driving up in a high-profile red Triumph sports car.

The guys within driving distance of Benghazi, Derna or Tripoli regularly got to hang out with the single women PCVs in those cities. In Derna, Cathy Kaiser, her roomies Mary Buelt and Trudy Swartzentruber, plus six male PCVs from the area formed a cooperative. They bought a washing machine that could be wheeled over and hooked up to the kitchen sink. A real luxury! Alas, we more distant PCVs had to wash our clothes ourselves, by hand.

Living it up in Benghazi: Dave Munro, Frank Reese, Shirley Greuel, Mark Lepori and Angus Todd

On June 14, the very last day before I was to head off to Tripoli, I got a letter from Jeanne. Sent from Benghazi, she indicated she might be in Tripoli starting on this day for an undetermined number of days before going to the U.S. Wow! A chance to finally get together! My heart was astir.

Vittles

The surprise of Libyan food was an experience of extremes. On the one hand, food that was so unexpectedly wonderful. On the other hand, not-so-wonderful options. Like when you're with friends and how can you refuse something appalling?

Let's start on the positive side. When I was in Yifran, I'd patronize the bakery where they offered—piping hot and straight out of the oven— delicious French-style bread—about 18 inches long. Kinda like a pregnant baguette. And only six cents. I'd snarfle the whole thing down. No butter. No cheese. No fixin's. Best bread ever, universally adored by PCVs all over Libya.

At recess at the schools, they served a snack called *helwah*, literally "sweet." While scores of variations (and spellings—like "halvah") of helwah exist across North Africa and the Middle East, this small rectangular block was made up of layers of sweetened puff pastry. At many other schools around the country, as part of the national nutrition program, they served tuna fish with harissa and olive oil on a roll, washed down with Mirinda, Limoni or Pepsi.

In Al Gala, they often served me bazeen. It's boiled barley patted into a volcano shape. In the caldera of this volcano they would pour a warm hot sauce, spiced with cayenne, fenugreek, onions, black pepper, sweet paprika, salt and tomato paste. In my initiation to bazeen, they told me to eat it with my fingers. To dip it in the hot sauce. I popped a hot wad in my mouth and began to chew. Scrumptious! But I saw them watching with much consternation.

"Mr. Randy, you're eating it wrong!"

"What do you mean?"

"You have to swallow it whole!"

I was taken aback. First, swallowing anything whole was gross, plus the chewing/taste sensation was terrific. This was one case where I had to go against custom.

"I'm sorry, but I just love this bazeen, I'm going to chew it!"

Due to many years of Italian influence, spaghetti was often served in Al Gala, with, literally and figuratively, a Libyan twist. A large metal bowl. Communal consumption. Spiced with hot sauce. Eating with the fingers. But instead of rolling up the strands of spaghetti on a fork pressed against a large spoon, the Libyans replicated this by deftly twisting and spinning their fingers around the spaghetti before bringing it up to their mouths.

Then, the crowning glory of Libyan cooking, the Libyan national dish, couscous. No comparison to the slushy Moroccan couscous you may have had in the States. It is cooked in a cous-coussier, consisting of a bottom pan about a foot high, a steamer pan with many holes in the bottom that fits atop the bottom pan, and a lid to close up the top. The basic idea is that while the stew-like ingredients in the bottom are boiling, the steam gently moistens the grains of semolina in the pan above.

Before steaming, great care is taken to treat these light brown grains, adding spritzes of water and rolling them circularly by hand, continuing until the couscous is in discrete granules. Even after steaming, Libyan couscous maintains a firm texture. To keep it all warm, they place a beautifully-crafted decorative, woven couscous cover over the bowl.

Libyan couscous cover

Everyone surrounds the large bowl, sitting cross-legged. Meat is eaten first, and the Libyan hosts nudge the "best" pieces of meat to guests. One volunteer described Libyans' approach to meat in particular: "Libyans eat very quickly, tearing large portions of meat and fat off the bones and afterwards, breaking open the bones with their teeth to suck out the marrow. I had difficulty keeping up with their pace, especially when trying to chew the tough, stringy lamb." To offset the hot spiciness, on the side of the bowl the Libyans place long carrot-like red radishes, *fijil*, whose skinned peels reveal white flesh beneath. After a mouthful or two of fiery couscous, you grab a radish and gnaw off a piece, imparting a cooling effect.

Couscous is a complete meal, with all the food groups (starch, meat, vegetables). You enjoy a wonderfully varied set of textures: the firm couscous grains, the soft vegetables, the meat that falls off the bone and the snappy crunch of chick peas. Then mixed in, a symphony of spices—cumin, garlic, salt, turmeric, paprika, cinnamon and cayenne—that stew for hours infusing their flavors into everything. A perfect meld and balance of gustatory sublimity. My favorite meal.

On the how-boring-can-you get category, down in Qutta in the Fezzan, all Kevin Hunt ate morning, noon and night, with his four Libyan roommates, was pasta with spiced tomato paste. That's it.

On the how-to-cope side, there are, for starters, "picnics." On February 9, I experienced what most of my fellow Libyan PCVs experienced at one point or another. In the U.S. this a typical picnic was a wicker basket stuffed with ham sandwiches, deviled eggs and potato salad. A Libyan picnic involved hopping onto the back of a Toyota pickup truck with a live baahing kid. Then driving ten miles out into the sparse, semi-desertic countryside. Then witnessing (while trying to withhold a gag reaction) the slicing of the small goat's neck, watching it die, along with shaking legs, the draining of its blood and its evisceration. I had never seen any mammal killed in my life, quite a shock. They built a make-shift fire and cooked every part of the animal. This included wrapping the goat intestines on sticks and roasting them on open flames. This was my first goat and it was tasty-fine.

On the how-to-do-it-even-better category, Greg Strick was struck by the Libyan method of skinning sheep. They would poke a hole in the front leg, down near the hoof, opening a space there between the skin and the bone. Then they would blow into it to loosen it up which enabled the rest of the skin to come off easily.

On one occasion down in Samnu, some Tuaregs came through town. They presented an older, decrepit camel. While intoning *Bismillahi el ah-ram errahim* ("In the name of Allah, the all-beneficent, the all-merciful"), they slit its throat. Bob Gausman was grossed out when he witnessed the blood spurting six to eight feet in the air. The Tuaregs laughed mightily at Bob's reaction. Grossing out Bob further, within a minute thousands of flies buzzed in out of nowhere to infest the camel.

In Gara Bulli, the first time Neil McCabe and Roger Scott went to the butcher shop, they wanted to sample camel. But they didn't know how to order amounts. They had no idea what a kilogram was. So, when the butcher asked them how much they wanted, Neil shrugged and said "Eight?" They walked home with 17 pounds of camel meat.

One day in Yifran I stopped by a butcher shop. Hanging on a hook was a huge slab of pure fat. I asked the butcher what it was. He said it was a camel's hump. I had naively assumed a camel's hump was full of water.

In the Fezzan in Ubari, Ern Snook couldn't stand camel meat, so his gambit, when no one was looking, was to throw it over his shoulder to nearby feral dogs. With an even less palatable choice, in Tripoli, Don Leydig was served what was considered to be a delicacy—slabs of camel fat. In Benghazi, Jeanne Maurey reported, "I had camel meat the other night and it was terrible! It was tough and sort of grayish. Ugh! I almost vomited!"

Gary Dahlman and Tom Weinz once were served bazeen with sheep's eyes. Tom was somehow able to hide the eyes he was to eat. Gary ate one and said, "It tasted like a juicy grape." Jim and Joyce Swanson inadvertently stumbled upon a trick to acceptably refuse eating sheep's eyeballs that we all wish we had only known about back when. When the eyeball is rolled in your direction, you can say, "I'm sorry, I'm so full." You make sure you repeat this two more times, *then* they buy into your refusal.

The locals celebrated Kevin Hunt's arrival in Qutta with goat. Goat intestines stuffed with goat organs was considered a delicacy, and therefore, an honor for the guest. Determined not to offend, Kevin ate it. Then they handed him the most prized part of all—the goat's jawbone. The idea was to gnaw on it to get at the tender meat. Kevin did not offend.

In El Khozeur, Dan Peters wrote:

We killed our four goats with the goats facing Mecca. We ate all the intestines (not good) and the next day my roommates roasted the heads, including the hair. The smell was nauseating.

Down in the Tripolitanian Sahara, in the village of Edri, the Libyans would shoot doves and eat them. Chip Chandler frequently partook. Chip also ate sheep's brains. In the brains department Jeanne Maurey wrote, "For dinner we had stuffed stomach, brains and stuffed intestines. They were really pretty tasty." On another occasion she had *osban*, a traditional Libyan sausage stuffed with a mixture of rice, herbs, chick peas, raisins, chopped lamb meat, liver and heart. At a teacher's home in Azzizia, Rufus Cadigan recalls having camel brains one night for dinner.

Once, in Derna, Mark Lepori was running a fever that would not subside. A woman who cleaned the school gave him a drink. She said it would purge him of the fever. He drank it and asked, "What was that?" She replied, "Donkey milk."

Then there's Libya and the Scoville scale (measure of spiciness). On a number of occasions while in Sebha, Jack Seifert had chummed up a Taiwanese Dr. Soo and his wife, who tended their own pepper tree. (Turns out there were up to 100 Taiwanese doctors at the time deployed all over Libya. Go figure!) They were crazy about peppers. The first night he was invited to dinner at their abode, he started to gag on the fumes of the peppers the doctor was frying. The doctor was oblivious to the heat, standing over a big kettle filled with peppers, singing.

Early in his stint, Mike Lee naively thought a hot pepper would cool his mouth. He ate one whole and the "ungodly" hot pepper made him feel like he was dying. No amount of water would quench it away. When Bill Cagle first arrived in Bin Gashir, he came upon a group of people dipping bread into a two-foot-wide tub of what he thought was tomato sauce. They invited him to join in. It turned out to be ground up, super-hot red chilis. "It blew the roof off of my mouth."

And who knew that mere rocks you choose to heat up food can put you at death's door? At the Derna beach the Libyans would gather rocks and heat them up for cooking. Trying to emulate them, Mark Lepori and some friends gathered and heated up rocks, not realizing they were chunks of lava that contained air pockets. When these heated up, they exploded and shards of hot rock flew out. One of them embedded itself in Mark's radio.

Some food could be highly dangerous even to Libyans. Dan Peters wrote, "In my village they grow wheat and some beans. These beans have been found to cause blindness in some cases when they're eaten raw."

While in June I was naturally anxietized about my upcoming hernia operation, I had no idea that a circumcision would be cause for merriment.

Emaciations, Operations,

Immunizations

On the Ides of June, I hitched a ride to Garian, then grabbed a group taxi ride for Tripoli. The only fly in this ointment was an obnoxious passenger who insisted on trying to open a broken window in the car. This engendered a roaring argument between himself and the driver. We other passengers were much bemused. It ended when the driver diverted to a police station where the yeller was arrested, leaving us with a quiet ride the rest of the way to the nation's capital.

I was one of over a hundred PCVs from all over Libya converging on Tripoli—by plane, bus, taxi—at the end of the school year and on the verge of summer activities—vacations, projects or both. The requirement for summer projects originated in the very first Peace Corps program in Ghana, where Ghanian PCVs were all given 60 days' vacation. Not wanting volunteers to be gallivanting all over Europe for 60 days, Peace Corps Washington imposed 30 days of projects at the beginning of the summer.

This convergence was also a chance for Clearfielders and Bisbeeans to finally mix. That evening there was a party at what we dubbed "the girls' apartment," where the Tripolitanian Bisbee single women lived. (In my diary, in Bob Marshall's diary, in everyone's letters home, it was standard in the late 1960s to refer to fully grown women as "girls." In viewing old TV shows on YouTube, I've noticed the same usage. While we may cringe today, it was common usage at the time.) To my delight and surprise, Jeanne was there. Great fun to be with her, especially after eight months since being with her on that plane and all those letters flying back and forth. The party went way into the wee hours. I fell asleep on the floor at 5 A.M.

I must have only copped a few hours of z's because I got a room at the Royal Hotel, then had lunch at the Hollywood Restaurant with Jeanne. This became a day- and night-long date. We had dinner. We went to *The Magus* movie starring Anthony Quinn, Michael Caine and Candice Bergen at the Uaddan Hotel ("Uaddan" is a kind of Libyan mountain goat). We took as romantic a walk as one can in Tripoli. We shared a drink at the National Hotel. We sat and talked outside the women's apartment for a full three hours. My diary said the day was "*lots* of fun" and that she was leaving the next day for the States.

That next day Dan Peters and I hung out. We grabbed some bread, ham, bologna, cheese, yogurt and wine. We ate lunch on some steps. That evening we imbibed beer and spoke at length about Dan's experiences in India. I was impressed to learn he'd learned Telugu there. (What, in his modesty, Dan never told me and I didn't learn about until 50 years later, was that when Dan was at the University of Wisconsin Oshkosh, he took the only Indian student there, Kamal Shah, a brand-new freshman, under his wing. Dan helped him with registration, with selecting courses, on navigating which credits to get. In another coincidence, at that time the University of Wisconsin Oshkosh had a special program with Libya and there were about a dozen Libyans there. With no place to go summer times, Dan invited Kamal to his dairy farm home. Dan's mother became Kamal's American mother. They became best friends. Kamal went on to become Vice President at United Healthcare.)

Overlaying this, the whole day, smitten with Jeanne, I couldn't stop thinking about her, so pretty, so sparky. The following day it hit 114 degrees in Tripoli. ("An oven outside.") I ran into Mike Culkin, who had lost 60 pounds, perhaps from dysentery? Also ran into a Bisbee couple who had decided to leave. The precipitative reason was their house was ransacked. Torn apart.

The following day at the Peace Corps office, I met Dr. James Mayfield, the upcoming Program Director for Libya III in Salt Lake City. He wanted to tour my region and I felt privileged to be his guide. He drove an International Harvester Scout while I answered hundreds of questions. First stop was Jado, where we stayed with Bob and Ann Job. They had spent the two previous years as Peace Corps Volunteers in Ceylon (now Sri Lanka).

The next day I showed him around Yifran and Al Gala, then we drove back to Tripoli. "Tomorrow go to hospital. Can't say I'm not apprehensive."

June 23. A cloudy dusty day that weighed in at 111 degrees, but I was fortunate to be welcomed inside air-conditioned Wheelus Hospital. Everyone was friendly, the food fantastic. But I also had quite a frisson of culture shock that was upsetting. I had been so habituated to the plain, simple, electricity-less, running-water-less life in Al Gala, this modern environment was overwhelming. "Suddenly seeing U.S. as it is in Libyan eyes." No doubt the anxiety of the upcoming operation contributed to my sensitivity as well—I had to wait (how I hate to wait for such potentially painful events!) two more days for the procedure.

The next day, "Exceptionally nervous all day thinking about operation." They took a blood sample. They shaved off all my hair from my knees to my chest. "*Really* looks weird." Passed some time talking to some Air Force guys recuperating in my ward. I found a piano and super enjoyed playing it for a while. PCVs Kevin Hunt and Dave Munro were admitted today with dysentery. Emaciated, Kevin had lost 30 pounds. It wasn't just the dysentery (which he contracted by drinking his roommates' water that was neither boiled nor treated with iodine), it was also his all-macaroni-all-tomato-based diet. In addition, Dave was suffering from giardiasis (also known as "beaver fever"), a parasitical infection of the small intestine. Symptoms include nausea, vomiting, cramps and weight loss. He was diagnosed as badly malnourished. In retrospect, we were exceptionally lucky to have a first-class U.S. military hospital as our official Peace Corps hospital in Libya. Most other Peace Corps countries have to settle for much-less-than-perfect local city hospitals.

June 25. 8:20 AM, into surgery. Coming out I learned the incision was eight inches long with 14 stitches. The rest of the day I lay painfully in bed, mitigated by some Demerol. I got a postcard from Bob Marshall. Bisbeeans Kathy McLean and Trudy Swartzentruber were so nice to visit. "Now it's clamping down the teeth and pulling through." My lower abdomen was painful all the next day. Highly sensitive to coughing, sneezing or laughing. Dr. Coulson was kind enough to stop by and visit. The TV in the ward pulled in programs from the satellites. That evening hilarious comedian Jonathan Winters was on. I started to laugh and pain spiked me in the belly. I had to hold my hands over my ears the whole show in self-defense. I couldn't very well be in stitches while I had stitches.

On June 27, Dan stopped by for a long visit. We played chess with a chess set he had kindly brought me. Later, I started reading Henry James' *The American*. That evening, the mock-spy TV comedy *Get Smart* starring Don Adams was on. I had to hold my ears tight for another half-hour. Over the next week-and-a-half I was gratified to be visited by Dave Munro and Kevin Hunt (who fainted on his way out of my ward). Then Trudy again, with Dan, Glenn Curry, Phil Akre, Bob Marshall (who brought me a copy of *Europe on Five Dollars a Day* which I read in avid anticipation of our trip which would start in Greece), Jay Shetterly, Stu Magee, and Randy Simpson.

On the last day of June, I finished *The American*. Read *The National Observer*. Dr. Coulson delivered the mail call: letters from my parents, from Hajj El Haadi, and from Norma Salem, daughter of the Mr. Salem Bob and I were to visit in Cairo. That evening a new patient, Lt. Bloodworth, joined our ward. He was a party-guy, drunkenly swerving around the base on a tricycle when he was hit by…an ambulance! That shortened the trip to the hospital! They had to operate on his injured leg.

The next morning, he explained to me that just before they put him under, the surgeon said, "Well, son, I notice you're not circumcised. So long as we'll have you under, why don't we fix that, too?" He figured, "Whatever" and assented. He did not count, however, on two things. When you're an infant you cry it off and never remember the pain. But for an adult, *very* painful. The second problem was that babies don't get erections, so they had to give him special pills to take when things started to stretch to prevent the stitches from pulling out. This second problem was compounded by the visits to our ward by a most comely young nurse named Lt. States. Whenever she entered the room, he'd urgently reach for the pills.

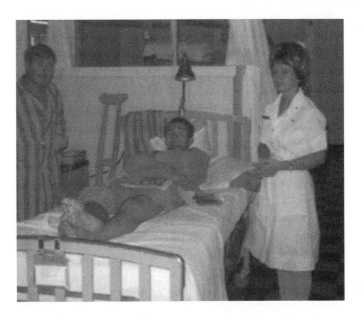

Air Force patient Dennis Ringler, unidentified and Lt. States

On July 2 they took my stitches out. "Didn't feel a thing." Started reading a book about Libya, *Children of Allah* by Agnes Keith. Another patient joined us this day. A Turkish teenager named Vacshy. He was in to have his left leg shortened, because it was an inch or so longer than the other. When Vacshy arrived, Air Force orderly Sgt. Moore hastened to my bedside. "Randy, you have to come talk to this guy, we have to explain some things to him."

"But I don't speak Turkish."

"Well, you speak Arabic, isn't that close enough?"

"Not really."

"Please, come on, you've gotta at least try."

"Well, maybe he speaks some other language I know." I ambled over and shook Vacshy's hand while Sgt. Moore and two nurses hovered expectantly over his hospital bed.

"*Tit-kellam al Arabi?*" (Do you speak Arabic?) He shook his head.

"*Parlez-vous francais?*" (No.)

"*Habla espanol?*" (No.)

"*Sprechen Sie Deutsch?*" (No)

"Do you speak English?"

"Yes."

I nodded to Moore and asked him what he wanted me to say to Vacshy.

"Tell him, this button here is for him to summon a nurse whenever he needs one."

I turned to Vacshy and said in English, "This button here is for you to summon a nurse whenever you need one."

The orderly added, "And...and...tell him that this bedpan is for him to urinate in after the operation when he can't walk to the bathroom."

I turned to Vacshy and said, "This bedpan is for you to urinate in after the operation when you can't walk to the bathroom."

Moore breathlessly continued, "And, and tell him this here button will move the bed up so you can be sitting upright to read or eat."

I turned to Vacshy and said, "Vacshy, this here button here will move the bed up so you can be sitting upright to read or eat."

I asked Sgt. Moore if that was it. He said "Yes" while vigorously shaking my hand, saying "Randy, thank you *sooo* much for translating!"

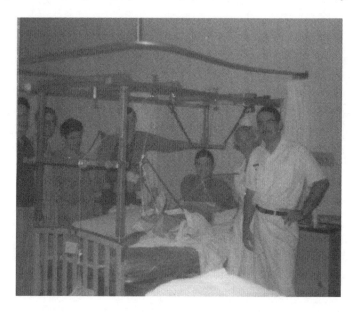

Lt. Bloodworth (third from left), Vacshy (in bed) and Sgt. Moore (far right)

On Independence Day, Wheelus staged a beach carnival. Walking slowly, I managed to visit. I ran into an old Air Force hand who told me a funny story about Libya and World War II. It seems at one point in the shifting attacks and retreats of the North African campaign, the British Army had to hastily abandon a major camp. They didn't have the time to haul their munitions with them, and they could not, of course, let the enemy get them. So, they placed dynamite charges on the various ordnance locations, then strung wires up to a battery of detonator plungers atop the crest of a hill well away from danger. The British general was about to give the order to blast away when an Italian Air Force bomber squadron appeared, obviously intent on bombing the camp thinking the British were still there.

"Wait!" he said. "Let's have some fun." He knew the Italian Air Force was famous for many of their bombs being duds. And from his vantage point, he would be able to see a bomb being released from each plane. When the first bomber dropped its bomb, the general ordered an engineer who was manning a detonator that would blow up some two hundred yards away from where the bomb was going to stand by for his signal. Exactly at the moment the bomb hit the ground, he said "Fire!" The Italian bomb didn't go off, but it appeared to the Italian bombardier that it went off—two hundred yards off target. He started to madly start to recalibrate his bomb sight. The next bomber dropped another dud bomb on another location, and the general ordered another simultaneous explosion far off from where the dud landed. This continued until all the munitions had blown up, leaving a cadre of Italian bombardiers completely befuddled, and a cadre of British soldiers laughing their heads off.

That day I learned that 33 Libyans were heading stateside to train Libya III Peace Corps volunteers, who in turn would be shipping out to Libya in September.

I also learned, to my dismay, after many conversations with Air Force people, that they referred to the Libyans as "ragheads."

On July 7, a sudden burst of urgency as five seriously injured men and women were shuttled into my ward on gurneys, with doctors and nurses swarming over them, inserting IVs, taking blood pressure, working on bleeding issues, etc. It turned out they were Peace Corps volunteers Al Nehoda, Jay and Nancy Corrin and Terry and Nanette Jones (now

Holben) who had been driving up and down sand dunes in a Land Rover. This group was on their way to the Ubari Sand Sea, a vast area of towering sand dunes, on a project for the Libyan Museum to photograph and research pre-Islamic cave paintings and their relationship to the primitive designs on Fezzani rugs. They had been skimming across the desert surface and came unexpectedly upon a steep "slip-faced dune"—too late to stop. The Land Rover fell 40 feet, hitting the ground hard, totaled. Jay and Al sustained severe cuts to the head. As Jay describes it,

> Nancy went down on the gear shift and broke her back and incurred internal injuries. Nanette went through the window, sustaining a deep slash on her throat and breaking her jaw. Terry and I had head wounds and concussions. And Terry sustained a compression fracture of the spine. We expected to die. Only Al was able to walk and after a long trek miraculously came across a local Ubari Sand Patrol, who drove all the Americans to a small first aid clinic in Sebha. Al and I were sewn up by a Taiwanese medical student who had no anesthesia. He splashed iodine on Nanette's throat wound. He then stitched her up with 10-pound fishing line. He began to stitch up Terry's head with fishing line, also with no pain killer. When I complained, the medical student took out a big needle and banged Terry's head with it. Then I got the same stitching treatment. The word of the accident swiftly spread to the locals who swarmed the hospital to watch the Americans die.

Nancy recalls, "The women began wailing lamentations for the dead. They were chanting and touching me as they walked around me in a circle." Somehow, in the gallows humor of the moment, Nanette remembers Terry and Jay managing to joke about their good fortune in not being stitched to one another.

A U.S. Air Force C-47 cargo plane arrived from Wheelus Air Base, carrying Dr. Coulson. They were so happy to see him they labeled him "an angel from God." They were immediately medevacked to Wheelus.

"When we arrived, there must have been a half dozen doctors who quickly took care of us, mercifully removing the stitches from Nanette's neck." Nancy needed a back brace, but because she was short, there were none small enough at Wheelus to fit her. Nancy spent over five weeks at Wheelus hospital waiting for that back brace.

That week I was released from the hospital. I had one week left before going on my vacay. In addition to travel with Bob Marshall, I decided to travel on my own in Europe for a bit, then join my parents who were going to visit me in Rome. Dr. Coulson was kind enough to pick me up. Happy goodbyes to everyone at the hospital. In order to get an exit visa, I needed permission from my principal, Belgassim. This was to be ready for me at the Ministry of Education Office in Garian. I grabbed a taxi, got my permission letter, and received what for me was a king's ransom for summer pay: $500.

Each PCV was expected to participate in a productive summer project. At one point I intended to do something involving "medicine." These projects were not assigned, it was up to each volunteer to figure out what he or she should do. I didn't end up doing a project; perhaps I was exempt due to my operation. For their project, Frank Nicosia, Mike Culkin, Paul Rhodes and John Meynink flew to Salt Lake City to help train the Libya III men's group on Libyan culture, customs, things to do, things not to do, etc. Bob and Anne Conway went to the Libya III Bisbee location to train. A cadre of PCVs trained Libyans in English. Angus Todd and Bob O'Keefe helped an archaeologist from the University of Michigan, excavating the Temple of Demeter in Cyrene, cleaning pottery, keeping records, etc. Dennis Carlson and a colleague developed and published an "English for Libya Workbook." Others created manuals and workbooks for use in the upcoming year.

Don and Lani Leydig's summer project was to teach young Libyan women who had never been to school at all and had never been away from home. Only two showed up. Both cried and cried. They left and never came back.

In the most impactful and ambitious summer project, Sam Cangemi, Roger Scott, Dick Kean and Walter Matreyek worked on the Misurata Medical Project under the auspices of the WHO (World Health Organization). They provided immunizations and stealing a step on me, treated Libyans for trachoma. They went to villages in the Misurata area in Tripolitania where doctors never go. In five weeks, they immunized 3,200 children—from the age of three months to 14 years—against smallpox and polio. For trachoma, they dispensed aureomycin to parents to treat themselves and their children. A Libyan nurse in the project, Miss Sooda, gave DPT (diphtheria-tetanus-pertussis) injections. And they planned to expand the project countrywide to include all Peace Corps volunteers. This was just four PCVs over five weeks. There were 38 times that number of PCVs all over Libya who could conduct the program over the next nine months. It would not be out of the realm of possibility that they could reach a half-million Libyan men, women and children in a country of only two million. An ambitious and deeply worthwhile effort that, un-fortunately would not come to pass due to the great interruption to our program that no one saw coming.

Back in Tripoli, I didn't go to a hotel. Bob Marshall's Occidental friend, barrel-chested Irv Welch and his wife Naomi, had a spacious house in the Giorgimpopoli neighborhood of Tripoli—an ex-patriate Western enclave. Irv invited Bob to stay at his house, along with fellow PCV and personable, fun Yalie, Jim Luikart. And Occidental employee Ellis Austin and his hospitable wife Ginny graciously invited me to stay at their place. The Welches' daughter Sandy and their son Tom were a lot of fun to hang out with, along with Sandy's friend Mary Alice Carlson. I only learned 47 years later from Bob's diary how much energy and time Bob had spent trying to find digs for Jim and me and for some Bisbee women, checking out apartments, the University of Tripoli dorms, communicating with the Welches and Austins and more. I had no idea at the time, but for me a quite gratifying entry in Bob's diary for July 16, 1969: "Having Randy around was a godsend. He's so outgoing that everyone enjoys him on first meeting and we get along perfectly. (I like him best because he laughs at my mediocre jokes but I like him least because he laughs at other people's mediocre jokes.)"

We went to parties. One night, Jim, Bob and I treated Sandy and Mary Alice to a delicious dinner at the Swan Restaurant. Picking up a third of the tab set me back a whopping $12. "Uproariously funny almost all night with banter ranging on all topics." I played on the Austins' piano. We watched the lift-off of Apollo XI on a satellite-fed TV. From the States,

I got a letter from Jeanne. Bob and I ran around getting travelers checks, visas for Lebanon and Egypt, exit and re-entry visas for Libya. We finalized the plans for our trip which would take us from Athens to Istanbul to Beirut to Cairo and then back to Libya. The plane fares were ridiculously low—$92.80 from Tripoli to Athens. Then a special deal made in heaven: Athens-Istanbul-Beirut-Cairo for only $140! Each day a plane from that airline would leave one of those cities, and you could choose any day to just hop onto the plane. No reservations required. The final hop from Cairo to Tripoli was $91.10.

■

Not remembering my elementary school math about converting from Fahrenheit to Celsius soon got me in hot water.

Maladies

Before venturing to a third-world country, you can get 11 injections for plague, yellow fever, hepatitis, typhoid, etc., as we did (including additional gamma globulin shots every four months) and still not be out of danger. For example, you can't vaccinate against diseases like malaria, schistosomiasis or Lassa fever. You can come down with medical conditions triggered by exposure to various vectors like insects, contaminated water, etc. Nor can you vaccinate against ignorance or circumstance. All manner of malady may befall you. Many of us doughty Peace Corps volunteers struggled with such assorted ills and ails.

One night I suffered from uncontrollable shivers, nausea and diarrhea. The next day, my fever spiked to 103°. I decided to visit the medical clinic down in the village. I realized that before I could go, I'd have to translate my temperature to the metric system. It took a while to figure out whether you subtract 32 degrees first, then divide by 9/5ths or was it multiply by 5/9ths? Or first multiply by 5/9ths *then* subtract by 32? The difficulty was exacerbated, of course, by my unfocused condition. OK, I finally figured it out. 39.4 degrees Celsius. Armed with this datum, I went down the steep hill to the village in the stifling Libyan heat.

At the clinic, I told the doctor that I had a fever of 39.4 degrees. Without taking my temperature, he declared, "You have no fever." Despite my objections, he insisted. Swearing up a storm, I marched back up the hill, hopped on my motorcycle and forced myself to motor all the way to the hospital in Yifran some six miles away. A Yugoslav doctor attended me. I spoke no Serbo-Croatian, but he spoke Italian and English. He had a male nurse who spoke Arabic and Italian. Due to the daily parade of Libyan patients, they'd fallen into the knee-jerk habit of the doctor speaking Italian to the nurse, the nurse speaking Arabic to the patient, then when the patient replied, the nurse translating back into Italian to the doctor. I thought it would be more efficient for us to speak in English directly with one another, but they just blindly followed their regular protocol, so I had to speak Arabic to the nurse who then relayed my input to the doctor in Italian. He took my temperature in a way I had never experienced before, slipping the thermometer inside my armpit. He declared that I did, indeed, have a temperature—of 39.4 degrees. (Duh!) He also diagnosed me as suffering from dysentery.

Dysentery hit a number of us. It hit John Maclean hard—he was doubled over in pain. More like tripled over. Also in agonizing pain was Maggie Brossoit, cramping badly. She made her way to the Peace Corps office where Dr. Coulson said, "Come on in, you look like hell."

Misdiagnosis in the third world is often a problem for the native population and for PCVs. Tom Weinz came down with inflamed gums. The local doctors had no idea what it was. It was only when he returned stateside that a bit of penicillin did the trick. John Lynch came down with what were diagnosed as "Baghdad Boils" on his elbows. The folk belief was these were caused by eating too much meat. In fact, Baghdad Boils are lesions caused by cutaneous leishmaniasis that come from sand fly bites. Baghdad Boils have bedeviled thousands of U.S. troops in Iraq in recent years.

Then, there was good old-fashioned malpractice. Joyce Swanson tells of how they had recently built a Turkish hospital in Tarhuna, staffed with Turkish doctors, interns and nurses. Apparently, it was incumbent upon the Turkish interns to learn how to remove appendixes, so whenever a Libyan came to the hospital for whatever ailment it might be, they ordered their appendix removed. Max Richardson went to this same hospital with a serious case of hemorrhoids. A Turkish doctor there just held a knife over an open flame to sterilize it, and went to work.

Having received a typhoid shot like all of us didn't do Bob O'Keefe any good. He came down with *para*typhoid (for which there is no vaccine). It's caused by ingesting salmonella and results in fever, headache, abdominal pain, malaise and anorexia.

One volunteer, who understandably wishes to remain anonymous, came down with bad cramps and diarrhea while on a local trip with his headmaster driving the car. He urgently needed to get off the car and take

care of things, so he started to shout *"Hammam! Hammam!"* ("bathroom")
But the headmaster didn't stop, despite repeated requests. Much to his
humiliation, the volunteer ended up going in his pants. The headmaster
had to open all the windows of the car wide. Later on, the volunteer found
out that he wasn't saying "bathroom" but rather "bath."

Stoney Bird, not as susceptible to anonymity, freely tells his diarrhea
story. On an eternally long bus ride from the Fezzan to Tripoli, he had to
periodically ask the bus driver to stop. He would run outside and gaze at
a flat, featureless, tree-less, vegetation-less, rock-less terrain all the way to
the horizon. There was no place to hide from the gaze of everyone on the
bus while doing his business.

On the heels of a trip around Cyrenaica Dave Munro and some Libyan
friends found they had depleted their water supply. So, they had to retrieve
water from ancient Roman cisterns that dot the Cyrenaican countryside.
Back at Athrun, Dave began to experience "galvanic intestinal gurglings
and contractions, accompanied by violent diarrhea and stomach cramps."
He went to the hospital in Derna, which, according to Dave "was the sort
of institution that would have made Charles Dickens feel right at home."
All the doctors—save two—were from China, the nurses were Italian
nuns and the patients Libyan. No one shared a language. The nurses
could communicate with the patients in broken Arabic, and then would
transmit a garbled account to the doctors in pidgin English garnished with
gesticulation. The long, dimly-lit wards were crammed with ancient metal
bedframes whose paint was yellow and peeling. The walls resounded with
groans and strangled cries of anguish."

The Chinese doctors gave him an assortment of pills, including charcoal tablets, to lessen gas pain. They were just throwing things against the
wall to see what would stick. According to Dave:

> No dice. None of it worked. I motorcycled back to Derna
> after a week and consulted the Chinese doctors again.
> They prescribed various alternative remedies, none of
> which brought any relief. Ultimately, I visited the hos-
> pital's one Egyptian doctor, who ordered lab tests and
> diagnosed me with amoebic dysentery and giardiasis (an
> infection caused by microscopic parasites). He prescribed

drugs which eliminated many symptoms, but still left me with stomach cramps and occasional diarrhea. In the process I went from 155 pounds to 120 pounds and decided to go to the Wheelus Air Base in Tripoli once school was over in June. Before hopping on a Peugeot 404 taxi for the two day-trip to Wheelus, the village elders instructed me that should I need assistance on the trip, to tell people I was a member of the As-Sha'ri tribe. I thought this a ridiculous notion. Who would believe a foreigner, speaking broken Arabic could be a member of a Libyan tribe? A boy who met the taxi asked if I needed help. I told him I was traveling in Libya and that I was a member of the As-Sha'ri tribe. He immediately took me home to spend the night with his family. They laid on food, tea, conversation and a comfortable bed for the night. I was grateful, if astonished. This was, indeed, the famous Bedouin hospitality. At Wheelus, I learned that the Egyptian doctor had, in fact, cured me. But I was suffering from malnutrition. The doctors told me to spend a week in the hospital and prescribed a strict diet of fried chicken, hamburgers, steak, French fries, pie and ice cream. A wonderful week.

Of course, in the big picture we volunteers were lucky. In Brak, the mother of one of Anne Conway's students had a baby that contracted measles and died. In Qutta, two of Kevin Hunt's students came down with the measles…and they also died.

■

Jalapeño peppers were soon to imperil the Libyan women of Libya III.

$\mathcal{B}$rot$\mathcal{h}$els, $\mathcal{B}$ras and $\mathcal{B}$lasts

On July 6, 1969 two Libya III groups, scheduled to arrive in Libya in September, started their training. 103 men from 30 states, the most, 14 from California, and, curiously over-represented, 11 from Ohio, along with 52 Libyans descended upon the verdant University of Utah campus in Salt Lake City A few weeks later, 53 married couples and 12 single women (from 27 states and Washington, D.C.) and 33 Libyan men arrived at the aforementioned gulches and gullies of Bisbee, Arizona. This new crop of Peace Corps trainees was fresh-faced, eager, idealistic, highly motivated to learn Arabic, learn how to teach TEFL, excited to serve their country in an exotic foreign land. There was nary an African-American among either Libya III group. Just like Libya I and Libya II Clearfield, there was but one Japanese-American trainee in the men's group, Randall Kawamoto. A Jewish volunteer, Ron Aqua, had spent his junior year from Hamilton College in Sweden where he learned that Sweden has its own Peace Corps. This experience inspired him to join the U.S. Peace Corps.

Dr. James Mayfield (whom I had escorted about my area of Libya) was program director. The Libyans at the University of Utah (UU) were to teach Arabic, dancing, culture. For living arrangements in the dorms, program management paired up Libyans with Americans. The very first night the Libyans arrived in Salt Lake City they all promptly visited a local whorehouse. UU's summer program was in full swing and because this was the Sixties, the co-eds wore short shorts and T-shirts. For the Libyans anyone sporting such attire must be a prostitute. As a result, they started going after the co-eds, speaking to them in off-color language as if they were hookers. Trainee Rey Sodini (University of Illinois) and other Americans had to take their roommates aside and explain. The Libyans were embarrassed by their behavior. They were also called in to get a talking to by Dr. Mayfield and then cleaned up their act. There were also many American college men walking around with long hair. The Libyans thought this meant they were homosexual.

The trainees and Libyans got on well. On weekends some of Libyans would frequent bars with trainees in Salt Lake City. However, the Libyans always sought out back rooms, as they didn't want to be seen drinking. For the straighter-and-narrower Libyans in the group, just the fact of the American trainees drinking in a room defiled the room: going forward, they couldn't pray in that room.

In the absence of D-groups, other criteria for deselection were deployed. One was health reasons. For example, one Salt Laker was allergic to iodine, and iodine is often used to purify the water in Libya. Another came from management sand-bagging the volunteers. At their weekly all-hands meetings, management encouraged these idealistic young men to be open. "Be honest, we're here to help you. Express your feelings, let us know what's right and wrong about the program." The trainees duly spoke up: about problems in the training, about Vietnam, about civil rights, about their drug use. The older-generation, more conservative management didn't like what they heard and several complainers were sent home. It didn't take long for the trainees to get wise and stop providing feedback. The tension between trainees and management festered throughout the summer. It reached such a pitch that at one point leadership abruptly shut the program down and told all the trainees to leave town and come back in one week.

A potentially terminal crisis almost squelched the whole program. One night a bunch of trainees got drunk and almost passed out on the lawn. The Libyans (presumably the ones who were not drinking in bars) called the Libyan Embassy to complain. The Libyan Embassy called the U.S. State Department. The State Department called James Mayfield and told him, "We're going to pull all the Libyans out of there." Mayfield ordered all the trainees to apologize to their Libyan roommates and the crisis was averted.

Unlike the Clearfielders, the Salt Lakers found the training itself—a mixture of Arabic language classes, Libyan culture and TEFL—to be well executed. The Arabic language classes were mostly written and coordinated by Pancho Huddle from Libya I.

These volunteers and Libyans also traveled to the Navajo Reservation in Arizona in August of 1969 to practice teach using TEFL.

Rey Sodini was assigned to Rock Point Community School in the northeast corner of Arizona. It was a boarding school for elementary school-age children. For five days a week these children were separated from their families. Rey and other trainees asked why such young children were in boarding school and did not get a good answer.

The first meal served to the Libyans at Rock Point included pork. No one in Peace Corps administrations had alerted the Bureau of Indian Affairs to the Moslem prohibition on pork.

The Libya III program in Bisbee (which one Libya IIIer likened to a "run-down ghost town") was once again run by Westinghouse Corporation, with Bob Kohls in charge. He delivered his welcome speech to the group at a dinner in the basement of the local Elks Club. The Peace Corps office was in a former mortuary. Their main meeting place was a local church. Every day at 3:30 PM a huge dynamite explosion would erupt from the Lavender Pit copper mine rattling windows throughout town.

Lavender Pit copper mine

Most of the couples were gung-ho about going to Libya. Libya II Bisbeeans Malcom and Brooke Travelstead, and Jeanne Maurey, plus Libya I John Giordano—an excellent, highly-valued teacher—and Franklin

"Pancho" Huddle (who trained for Libya I but went to Tunisia) came to train on culture. They taught how to cope with the highly distinctive Libyan culture. They taught about the food. About how to use the money. The women, about how to dress. They were advised how not to go braless. How they would not be allowed in stores or mosques. How they would face other specific difficulties in Libya based on Brooke and Jeanne's first-hand experiences.

Pancho took a shine to trainees Charles and Julia Marton Weber, who had amazing lives before and after Libya III training. Julia and her younger sister Kati Marton were born in Hungary and had a French nanny. Kati went on to marry famous broadcaster Peter Jennings, then high-profile diplomat Richard Holbrooke (Peace Corps director in Morocco, Ambassador to Germany, Ambassador to the UN, special representative to Afghanistan and Pakistan). Charles, who majored in math and Chinese at Harvard, graduated summa cum laude. When he took the pre-med test, he scored the best out of 300 students. An accomplished linguist, he quickly gained impressive proficiency in Arabic.

As part of the ongoing screening process, three psychologists on staff would meet regularly with all the trainees. The psychologists characterized Peter Eichten (College of St. Thomas) as "an angry young man." Peter describes himself as "passionate," not angry. Perhaps, again, the older generation was misinterpreting our rebellious baby boomer generation. True to form, the psychologists tried to get a rise out of Peter, but he didn't take the bait. One religious Texan couple were flushed out of the program. They were missionaries determined to convert Libyans to Christianity.

Mort Dukehart (Lafayette College) a self-described "protected, New-York-Episcopalian-Trinity-Pawling kinda guy," would talk to the Libyans between Arabic classes. In a series of conversations over several weeks between Arabic classes, the Libyans opened Mort's eyes to the plight of the Palestinians.

Group management held a meeting for the Jewish trainees, worried for their safety in Libya. After some role play, one Jewish couple decided to opt out.

At the end of the summer, the trainees were given an oral language test. The scenario is you're in Cairo and need to ask directions for a square you've forgotten the name of, but you recall it's got a fountain. The trick, as recounted by Julia Marton, is that they purposely did *not* teach the word for "fountain." They wanted to see how volunteers coped in the absence of that word. Most freaked out not knowing the word. Julia was praised for not panicking and for managing a work-around, describing it as "the place where the water goes up and down."

Like the Libya II Bisbee group, Libya III trainees went to Naco, Mexico to practice teach in the fourth grade in the sole school in town. The town was very poor, dusty, and had no paved streets. Many of the school's windows were broken. Mort and Dotty Dukehart found dead pigeons in the drawers of their desks. Other live pigeons perched on the rafters. One day, all twenty of Rick Umpleby's (Colgate) Mexican students threw everything they could at a perching pigeon—pencils, books, chairs—so they could have it for dinner. Another problem? As it was summer, the kids were out of school but had been forced to learn English by their parents. If a Peace Corps teacher turned his or her back on them, some would jump out the window and run away.

One day in Naco, all 33 Libyans suddenly disappeared. The Peace Corps management couldn't find them. It turns out that, yes, they, too, had all gone to Naco brothels. (Given the level of sexual suppression in Libya, this was not surprising. Bill Cagle relates that all his Libyan male friends would admit to whoring in Egypt.)

Again, in Bisbee III, the Libyan men and women ritually slaughtered a sheep. Rick Umpleby relates that the American women and Libyan women were cutting up jalapeño peppers for the meal, but the Americans failed to warn the Libyans about the effect on their hands. The Libyan women's hands swelled up enormously and turned red. Some were taken to the hospital with 3rd degree burns.

Towards the end of their training, both the Salt Lakers and the Bisbeeans got their posting assignments. Mort and Dotty Dukehart were given Derna. They were much excited about this, full of the JFK spirit, uplifted, and looking forward to making the world a better place.

In my upcoming barnstorming of the Mediterranean, while in Istanbul, I was to witness the most wondrous spectacle of my life.

Trips and Trip-Ups

For their 1969 summer vacation, most of the Libya II PCVs scattered themselves about Europe. To detail all these tales would steer me too far from my Libya narrative, but I must include one remarkable tale from a fellow volunteer and some of the most notable ones of my own.

On July 17, still sore from my hernia operation, but happy to end a satisfying school year, I embarked on a whirlwind tour of the Mediterranean. I began with a solo foray flying on Alitalia to Rome where I snagged a night at the YMCA for a mere $1.60. (Point of order. With a monthly salary of $168 plus a $70 monthly housing allowance, after ten months we had each accumulated the princely sum of $2,380. Keep in mind, a loaf of bread was just six cents and a typical dinner for me at home was 60 cents. So, a tidy sum we could sock away.)

On to Barcelona: I found the smallest hotel room in Europe. Four feet wide and six feet long. Put me back a whopping $1.14. The next day, my first bullfight. (Diary: "Why not make it a real sport and fight a rhinoceros?") I've since learned that *Olé* in Spanish comes from *Allah* in Arabic, deriving, of course, from the many centuries of Moorish occupation in Spain where to this day there are 4,000 words of Arabic origin. While visiting the Pero family, I witnessed the Apollo XI moon landing. The whole family was agog. As for me, I felt a great swelling of pride to be an American. (Diary: "INCREDIBLY UNBELIEVABLE!")

On to Madrid, Toledo and Nice, where I hooked up with a comely blonde named Jill who insisted on a platonic trip. (Oh, well!)

We visited Genoa, then Pisa. On the way to Florence, we hitchhiked with two monks who were chattering away...in Latin. On August 2 I visited the celebrated Ufizzi Museum. In the galleries I ran into Nick

Kourides, a Princeton varsity tennis player I knew somewhat. In astonishment, he said that the night before he'd had a dream about seeing me.

Back to Rome. I joined up with my mother, father and sister Bassett. Thanks to some deal with an advertiser from his radio station (WHWH in Princeton, NJ) my father was able to add me to his flight itinerary from Rome to Paris to London and back for only $36! (Another coincidence. When he started his radio station in 1963, because there were about 6,000 stations, there was only one call sign available for him: WHWH. HWH were my father's initials—Herbert Windsor Hobler.)

On to Paris and London. All the sights. In London, for the first time ate Scottish balls, hard-boiled eggs surrounded with sausage, loaf and fried breadcrumbs. On August 12, I bid fond farewells to my family and on to Greece to hook up with Bob Marshall for the third leg of my vacation.

Before describing my disembarkation at Athens, indulge me one story at the expense of Libyan PCV John Becker.

John prepared for his trip by purchasing Bank of Libya Travelers Checks. (Hey, we were all young and naïve back then.) At the conclusion of his first dinner in Rome, having heard those Italian pickpocket stories, John decided, before venturing forth, to outwit any potential pickpockets by *not* putting any of his valuables in any of his pockets. Instead, he slipped his passport, his Peace Corps ID card, his wallet and all his Bank of Libya Travelers Checks inside a map. He hopped on a bus. When he exited the bus, he realized *all* his carefully-concealed valuables were gone. (Hey, we were all young and naïve back then.)

He beat a quick path to the nearest police station to report the theft. Instead of processing his claim, the attending policeman said, "Young man, you have to have more respect for our pickpockets. They are very good!" So, John beat a quick path to the U.S. consulate to report the loss of his passport.

The very next day, the consulate called. "We have your passport. We have your Peace Corps ID card. We have your wallet. We have your Bank of Libya Travelers Checks." John rushed over. Turns out the Italian thief left all his items atop a garbage can behind the U.S. consulate. It seems he figured the Bank of Libya Travelers Checks were worthless, and by extension, all the other documents must have been, too.

While plotting our trip, Bob Marshall and I had agreed to meet in

Syntagma Square in Athens. However, we had no idea how large the square was. We didn't know of any landmarks there. It wasn't good enough to pick a date and time. How would we find each other? After some pondering and brainstorming we hatched a scheme. At 9:00 PM on Tuesday, August 12, Bob and I would both show up at Syntagma (Constitution) Square. Bob would start walking around the perimeter of the square in a clockwise direction. I would start walking counter-clockwise. So, at 9 PM on the dot, I dutifully showed up at Syntagma Square. It turned out, indeed, to be expansive with many trees obscuring lines of sight. So I began to circle the square—counterclockwise. It didn't take long to run into clockwising Bob. Worked like a charm! Speaking of charm, he was with his college girlfriend, Siri Swenson, a willowy, pretty blonde of decided Swedish descent. Also a sharp-as-a-tack Cliffie. (Radcliffe undergrad).

Bob Marshall, unidentified and Randy somewhere in Greece

On to Turkey.

Floating bridges. Spice bazaars. The incredible Topkapi Museum. On that day Bob and I somehow went separate ways. I thought it would be cool to visit the eastern edge of the Bosphorus waterway that divides Istanbul in two, and separates Asia from Europe. Just to take in the view. I stopped dead in my tracks. There was this enormous flock of birds. And not just any old birds, big ones with seven-foot wingspans. White storks. These beautiful, majestic storks were bearing down from the north. The flock was at about

9,000 feet, about a hundred yards across and about 15 storks deep. And this mass extended back to the northern horizon. I couldn't see the end of it. This was already breathtaking, but there was more.

Exactly when these storks reached the Hagia Sophia Mosque with its huge dome they stopped flapping their wings and silently and majestically glided in a gigantic spiral from 9,000 feet down to about 1,000 feet. Right above the dome. At that 1,000-foot level, they began once more to flap their wings, heading straight to the south. I had to turn my head now to the south to absorb the rest of this panorama. The storks extended as far to the south as I could see, beyond the horizon. I stood there, frozen, mesmerized, for what seemed like a half-hour, taking it all in. The most memorable thing I'd ever seen in my life.

In fact-checking this, I learned that these flocks are about 125 miles in length and they migrate to winter in Kenya, Uganda and as far south as South Africa. Based on ornithological studies, I had been witnessing a flock of about 17,000 birds.

In my observations, I have been struck by what most Arabs would conceive of as a common calligraphic conceit, wherein the flexibility of Arabic writing enables one to artistically stack words one upon the other in a beautiful, flowing script. I saw this rendered at the Suleiman Mosque in Istanbul and was so moved by it that I've kept it to this day. It doesn't really matter what it says, but it happens to be a central mantra of Islam: "None has the right to be worshipped, but Allah."

Ornate Arabic calligraphy

On to Lebanon.

Bob and I boarded a 707 towards an uncomfortably hot and humid Beirut. As Siri Swenson was friends with the Anschuetz family in Beirut we were able to crash at their elegant duplex apartment, replete with high-end artwork on the walls. The father, Norbert Anschuetz, a former Foreign Service officer, was an executive with Citibank.

Monday, September 1, 1969. This is in bold because this was the watershed date that impacted the lives of some 400+ Libyan Peace Corps volunteers.

On the way back from a long walk Bob and I saw Libyan King Idris' photo on the front cover of the local newspaper. That was highly unusual, as he was a rather minor king from a third world country. I'll let the diary tell it. "Libya overtaken by coup d'état! Idris in exile in Turkey! What happens to Peace Corps? To us? To me?" Needless to say, this changed the complexion of the rest of our trip.

In the newspapers, I avidly read news about the Libyan revolution. At this point in time, Libya was in the control of the "Revolutionary Command Council," a clever move that disguised who they were until they could be sure all resistance had been removed. We also learned that

Syria opened its border to Lebanon today, so we decided to visit tomorrow and add another country to our list.

On to Egypt.

We hopped on a Middle East Airlines one-hour flight to Cairo. We were met at the airport by Mr. Salem, Mrs. Salem and their son Badia. Since they spoke French in their household, Bob and I spoke French with them for our whole visit. They drove us to their modest apartment where we expected we would stay for just a few days.

After a few days of sight-seeing, I told Bob that next I wanted to visit The Black Market. I naively thought that there was such a section in town, with a big black banner straddling the street at the fourth-floor level with white lettering, saying "Black Market."

Over the course of my first days in Cairo large welts, the size of spider bites, multiplied and soon covered every square inch of my forearms and my upper arms. They itched like crazy. Of course, I wondered, hypothesized, struggled to figure out the cause. The Salems declared unequivocally that they were not from insects. (I was a bit dubious of his entomological expertise as his kitchen sink was crawling with cockroaches.) I then guessed that maybe it was the drinking water in the apartment which came from the Nile. I started drinking beer instead and after two days, the welts disappeared. I found out later that no one recommends drinking Nile water, as it contains a variety of insects, snails, and other contaminants. My ignorance. (Of course, the pendulum of caution can sway too far—one fellow PCV back in Libya was so wary of water that he brushed his teeth with Pepsi!)

Every day Bob and I trundled off to the Libyan Embassy. And every day no word on any travel options to Libya. On the way to the American Embassy a man snuck up next to me and said, very loudly "Jewelry, perfume, sir?" then, in a conspiratorial whisper, while glancing furtively about, he said, "You want change money?" (Egyptian money at that time was highly devalued and American dollars highly prized. But such street exchanges were illegal. So, *this* was the black market!)

We probed exhaustively to learn that every travel option to Libya was closed. Roads were blocked. Train tracks were blocked. No taxis. No flights. No ships, not even freighters. We figured if we were stuck in Egypt for some indeterminate time, and we had a place to crash at no cost, why not go up the Nile 300 miles to Luxor and the Valleys of the Kings and Queens?

We trained overnight to Luxor. Took in the mammoth Karnak temple, larger than some cities.

The following day we hired a tour taxi—a 1952 Chevrolet—driven by a wizened, wise, anecdote-spouting guide named Ghali Hanna. With his commanding knowledge of Egyptian history, he was able to relate it to the Bible, all the more to spark the interest of tourists. We noticed that all the other guide taxis were 1952 Chevrolets. Ghali said that Gamal Abdul Nasser had once heard that the 1952 Chevrolet was the most reliable car ever made, so he went on the used car market and bought hundreds of them for all the guides in Egypt. I should point out that the 1952 Chevy was pre-Ralph-Nader so the dashboards were made of metal, not cushioned as they are now. And there were no seat belts.

One stop was at King Tut's Tomb. Discovered by English archaeologist Howard Carter in November of 1922, it had lain undiscovered for over three thousand years because a large pile of stone chips from other tombs covered up the site. The topper for us was that Ghali was *there* in 1922 upon its discovery.

Ghali Hanna and Bob Marshall in the Valley of the Queens

On the way next to the Valley of the Queens, Bob hopped back into the front passenger seat of Ghali's '52 Chevy. About a mile from King Tut's tomb Bob suddenly slammed both hands on the metal dashboard, simultaneously shouting "Stop!" Ghali slammed on the brakes and we all pitched dangerously forward.

Bob leapt out of the car and ran pell-mell to a spot about fifty feet behind us. Ghali and I thought we had run over something. But Bob was not scouring the road, he was looking up. For four long minutes, up he gazed, then tranquilly returned. Since he didn't explain what it was all about, and since I knew him so well, I knew how to get his goat. He was dying to tell us what happened, but he wanted the satisfaction of my asking him first. So as Ghali resumed our drive, I said absolutely nothing for about 10 minutes, letting the tension fester. Finally, feigning a nonchalance I was *not* feeling, I said, "Hey Bob, what was that all about?"

He said, "Randy you won't believe this! On top of the telephone wire I saw a red-crested, black-billed, white-collared, tufted, blue-tailed purple-bellied plover! [or words to that effect]. So rare!"

I replied, "You almost killed us for a bird?"

Back in Cairo, we proceeded to visit no less than six airline offices. Kingdom of Libya Airlines was out—"no foreigners allowed." With all other means of transportation still blocked, Bob and I went into scheme-hatching mode again. Soon, Bob and I discovered an Air Tunis flight from Cairo to Tunis that *stopped* in Tripoli. Ka-ching! We'd simply pay the full fare to Tunis but get off in Tripoli.

The next day, rubbing our hands in anticipation, we arose at 6 AM, downed orange drinks for breakfast, then Mr. Salem drove us to Cairo Airport. We landed at Tripoli at noon, not realizing there was a fly or two in our ointment. As we got off the plane (no jetways, just mobile stairs) the stewardess warned us the flight was taking off in a half-hour. We said, "Yeah, yeah, sure, sure, don't worry." We noticed that all over were nervous, jittery Libyan soldiers with submachine guns and bandoliers of bullets criss-crossing their chests. The revolution was a mere two weeks old, and many were worried about a counter-coup. First, we went through passport control. No problem. But at the next station our first glitch—our visas had expired. We explained, as best we could, that we were victims of circumstance, that the revolution had prevented us from entering the country before our visas ran out. The control agent said he had to check with his supervisor. Luckily, he OK'd us and they stamped us through.

Then we went to a room where we had to show our yellow WHO (World Health Organization) cards proving we had received our smallpox vaccinations. There were two agents there and three Libyan soldiers with submachine guns eyeing us warily. Glitch #2: our WHO cards were in our suitcases. We experienced travelers had failed to have them upon our persons! The Libyans started to shake their heads. Jesus, we were going to be sent back to Cairo! Then they said they could give us smallpox inoculations right away. So, I stood, they gave one to me. Bob nodded to me, knowing I was acutely aware of his fainting predisposition. As they approached Bob, he said, "Catch me," so I moved quickly behind him to prepare for his fall. As they pricked him, Bob fainted full out. I caught him. However, the soldiers thought we were pulling some kind of counter-coup! They trained their submachine guns at us, moving in hostilely, fingers on their triggers. I immediately started babbling in Arabic to them (not knowing the word for "faint") saying things like, "No, no, it's OK, he's sick. No problem, no, he's just sick." They finally backed off. Bob came to and luckily, we could move onto baggage claim without being riddled with bullets.

Thinking all issues were now well behind us, we duly handed our luggage tags to the Libyan baggage handler. He handed them back to us.

"These are no good."

"What do you mean?"

"These tags are marked for Tunis. Your bags are going to Tunis."

Glitch #3! Here it was 12:15 and we only had 15 minutes to somehow get our bags. Our adrenaline was pumping. Bob and I weighed in.

"Well, we're getting off here. We live here."

"No, these bags are marked for Tunis, that's the procedure."

"We're in the Peace Corps, we teach Libyan kids."

"Sorry."

"I'm in Aujila. Do you know Aujila?"

"I live in Al Gala. You know in the Nefusa mountains?"

"I can't go against the rules!"

"The Libyan government is paying us to be here."

Blank stare. Suddenly, the ol' necessity-is-the-mother-of-invention-inspiration surged from somewhere deep in the depths of God-knows-where in my desperate brain. I blurted out, "But you don't understand! These baggage tags were filled out by an Egyptian!"

The handler brightened. "Oh, why didn't you say so?" He ran off. While he was gone, the clock passed 12:30. We watched our plane take off. Five more suspenseful minutes. Then he returned—with our bags!

Blissful indeed is ignorance when it comes to the future, which was soon to hold two memorable close calls for me.

Coup Copings

On September 1, Randy Melquist was apprehensive when he heard gunshots in the streets of Misurata. But it turned out it was only soldiers shooting rifles towards the sky to celebrate the overthrow of King Idris. A curfew was imposed. Randy tuned into Libyan Radio, but they were just playing martial music. It was only when he tuned in to the BBC that he found out what was actually going on.

Peace Corps Libya Deputy Director Rudi Klauss, on the day of the coup, shouted, "What're all the fireworks out there?" One day, when there was a brief four-hour lifting of the curfew, Rudi and Ed White went to a small shop to buy flour and tuna fish. They couldn't surmise why an old-hand Brit expatriate in front of them in the line was buying out all the liquor in the store. They understood when, on the very next day, the Revolutionary Command Council banned all liquor. Rudi found himself playing a major role in coordinating with Peace Corps Washington as to where all the volunteers would now go. He recalls there was considerable tension and stress because the Vietnam War was looming over everyone. Everyone was wondering, "What's going to happen to us?"

On the day of the coup, Ed White went up to the roof of his building with his eight-year-old son to observe what was going on. Suddenly, the roof door burst open and a young man in fatigues and a submachine gun cornered Ed, trained the gun closely on him and started barraging him with questions. He demanded Ed's passport. Ed said he didn't have it with him. The soldier, naively, said, "Oh, go get it." Of course, Ed and his son could've flown the coop. But they didn't. He returned with his passport and his visa. The soldier finally took his finger off the trigger of the gun.

Dianne Goode reports that Ed White was worried that a PCV could be hurt. Fortunately, the closest call was when a 16-year-old soldier with a machine gun struck a male volunteer across the face.

John and Rebecca Peterson arrived back in Homs before the coup, having traveled to Greece, Austria, Hungary, Yugoslavia and Italy that summer. During the coup, due to the danger, inspector Ed O'Shea moved in with them. Ghaddafi's army had set up a machine gun nest right across the street from their apartment. One night the machine gun nest came alive and bullets ricocheted off their building. After two weeks of this, John and Ed got cabin fever. They were tired of playing cards and reading books. Ed said, "Let's go for a swim!" John and Ed snuck out during curfew and began swimming in the Mediterranean. When they heard sudden gunfire. John said, "We'd better get back, Rebecca will be worried." They later learned that some people in town had been killed in the incident.

In Tripoli, Stoney Bird and another PCV were innocently tossing a football back and forth on the beach. Some soldiers observed them and started screaming "Bomba! Bomba!" It took a bit of hasty explaining to convince them it was not a bomb.

A group of revolutionary thugs charged Jay and Nancy Corrin's Land Rover while they were en route to Wheelus to get their final Peace Corps medicals. They began to tip it over. As Jay relates, "Fortunately for us, a U.S. tank was nearby and began to shoot at the zealots who soon fled the scene. It was a close call and without that tank we would have been killed by the mob."

When Lorraine Slawiak heard explosions in the streets of Benghazi she assumed it was firecrackers, celebrating Labor Day (September 1 was Labor Day in the U.S. that year). Then, she quickly realized Labor Day was only a U.S. holiday and that it must have been gunfire. She and all the other Benghazi volunteers were rounded up by consular personnel in armored military vehicles and consigned to the U.S. consulate. They had to spend weeks there, sleeping on the floor and passing time by playing cards, games, reading, talking. Finally, they were released to return to their apartments to retrieve their belongings and leave Libya.

Don Leydig remembers that Ghaddafi's soldiers' uniforms were not uniform. These forces had just grabbed whatever they could in a makeshift manner, ending up with different military designs and mismatched colors.

Ghaddafi's Revolutionary Army at the ready

At about 10:30 one night, standing by an open window of a Tripoli apartment he was sharing with six other volunteers who had all had to vacate their villages, Roy Douthitt watched the street celebrations. He heard the Libyans yelling, "We're free! Finally free! We can drink now! We don't have to go to Tunis to see movies now!" A Libyan in an apartment across the street saw Roy. He started yelling and pointing at Roy. "Jews! Jews! Jews!" Roy quickly closed the shutters. Ten minutes later, the doorbell rang. Roy went downstairs and opened the door. He was confronted by a young Army lieutenant and two 17-year-olds with Kalashnikovs. The lieutenant shouted, "Who are you?" in English. Roy said, "I'm an English teacher. I teach here in Libya."

"What are you doing here?"

Roy explained what he was doing there.

"Who's upstairs?"

At that point, Roy decided it would be wise to revert to Arabic, explaining that there were more English teachers upstairs. The soldiers barged upstairs with Roy leading the way. When Roy opened the door, the soldiers stepped forward and pointed their guns at the other volunteers. Roy recounts, "Their eyes got bigger than saucers."

"Can I look around?" asked the lieutenant.

"Yes, no problem, whatever you want. Can I help you?"

The lieutenant looked around, then said, "No. No problem here."

Bob and Anne Conway were clearing things out in Brak. Since there was no bank there, they kept all their money in a cloth envelope in the proverbial mattress. People were coming and going. Then, they discovered that all their money was stolen. They went to Tripoli along with their two cats and checked into a hotel on the edge of a big square at the entrance to the Royal Palace. Every night people were shooting guns in the air and a guy with a microphone was shouting, "Death to America!"

On coup day, George Carter was in his village. Two of his night-school students came to his door with guns shouting *"Thawra! Thawra!"* (Revolution!) The local authorities imposed the curfew that had been declared nationwide. Three hours later, they came by and said to George "You must be bored. What would you like to do?" George said, "I'd like to visit my friend Mohammed." So, defying the curfew, his two gun-toting students escorted him to Mohammed's where he had a nice two-hour visit, then escorted him back home.

The exact curfew invoked was 9:30 PM. (Wise choice, why decree 9 PM or 10 PM?) Country Director Ed White declared, "We have to get everybody ready to leave." He told everyone that the 5th grade TEFL program was being canceled. At one point, the Brossoits were in a car with Ed White when they came upon a demonstration. When the demonstrators started violently rocking the car, they were petrified. Ed said "Don't say anything." A soldier yelled at Ed, who pretended not to understand, even though he was fluent in Arabic. They finally got away.

Besides consolidating power, among the more immediate directives of the Revolutionary Command Council was the complete Arabicization of the country. All signs in English and Italian were banned, including storefronts and advertising signs. The word "Stop" in English on all road signs was removed, leaving only the Arabic *Guf.* "No Parking" and "Bus Stop" signs were taken down. Richard Massey noticed that tape was put over the English signs in Tripoli. The Roman alphabet was banned everywhere. At the Palace Hotel, the words "Ladies" and "Gentlemen" were removed from all the bathroom doors, turning nature's call into a guessing game for non-Arabic readers. On September 18, 1969, Premier Al-Maghrabi held a press conference and announced that Libyan grad school students would henceforth study only Arabic—no English.

All Libyan citizens had to go to the police station and have their identification papers re-stamped "Libyan Arab Republic" to replace "Kingdom of Libya." A communications blackout was imposed on all media, telephone, cable, telegraph, incoming/outgoing mail and radio. As a result, for my favorite Wheelus Radio DJ Howard David, his wife back home in the States had no idea if he was alive or dead. The Peace Corps Office of Volunteer Support fielded dozens of anxious communiqués from parents, as reflected in Parental Inquiry Logs. These ran the gamut from "No mail for nine weeks, where is she?" to "Concerned," to "Any plans to evacuate?" to "Parents heard that hostilities broke out in three additional cities," to "I would like some reassurance from you as to the safety of my son," to anger. "One father was very irate, wants to talk to someone who knows the whole story to call him back ASAP." And finally, to the inscrutable query of one son's mother smack-dab in the middle of the revolution who "Wants to send him some vegetable seeds."

More ominously, as 1970 rolled on, the Revolutionary Command Council proceeded to deport some 20,000 Libyan citizens of Italian descent to Italy.

Coming up: strikes for ice machines.

Post-Coup Strandings

At the time of the coup d'état, there were 100 PCVs outside of Libya. When PCVs Bill Cagle and two friends got to Rome, the coup hit. Once in country, they were not allowed to return to Bin Gashir, so they moved into an apartment in Tripoli. They were promptly put under house arrest.

On their summer vacation, Tim Vollman and Jack Seifert had first hitchhiked to Tangier, Morocco and Madrid. Blissfully unaware of developments in Libya, they ventured on to Portugal, where they heard about the coup. After hustling off to the U.S. Embassy, they then made their way to Barcelona, Marseille, Tunis, and eventually Libya. Jack was determined to get back to Ghat to retrieve his belongings and most importantly, give away his chickens. He hitchhiked 480 miles to Sebha. The only way to get to Ghat—another 350 miles—was to stand at a certain fork in the road and wait for a ride. This was a long shot, since only one or two vehicles *a week* pass by. After a whole day no one came. The next day a caravan of Libyan military jeeps and trucks came by. An officer sternly asked "What are you doing?"

Jack said, "I'm a school teacher in Ghat. I need to get back and retrieve some baskets and leatherwork I'd bought from caravans."

The officer didn't care. "You can't go back there."

Ever resourceful, Jack found a radio telegraph and dictated a message to his Ghat friends to give away his chickens, radio, stove, baskets and leatherwork. Luckily, Jack knew he could stay with Dr. Soo and his wife. Stoney Bird was there already. Dr. Soo fed them a wonderful meal. With everything settled in Ghat, and sated with dinner, Jack was looking forward to a comfy hot bath on the second floor. The water supply was attached to an old gas heater the workings of which Jack was totally un-familiar with. After some futzing around, he figured out how to heat the water and settled down to luxuriate. However, he didn't know that he was breathing in undetectable gas fumes. He passed out. Stoney heard a crash upstairs. (Hard not to notice when 235 pounds is dropped in a tub!) Stoney and Dr. Soo rushed upstairs, dragged Jack out of the tub and out of the bathroom, saving his life. A few minutes more and he would've been gone.

Speaking of Sebha, Peace Corps Libya Associate Director for the Fezzan Al Nehoda returned there during an anti-US. demonstration. The locals were vigorously chanting, "Down with Imperialism! Down with America!" Al passed a friend who shouted, "Down with Imperialism!," then in a normal voice, "Hi, Al." He then shouted, "Down with America!" Then, "Al, did you have a good summer?" Then, "Down with Imperialism!"

Over in Aujila, Bob Marshall wrote in his diary about his villagers' expectations: "Workers want the promised land now. There are strikes for more money, for air conditioning, for ice machines!!"

Trooping through Tunisia and Algeria were the McElhinnys, who remarkably ran into various Black Panthers, who were in exile in Algiers.

At the time of the coup, Cathy Della Penta was in Damascus, Syria with Barbara Forslund and Mary Slatt. They traveled back to Cairo, where they were marooned, out of money, and blocked from re-entering Libya. They went to the U.S. Embassy (which flew the Spanish flag due to the recent Six-Day War). Embassy officials gave them a measly per diem—one meal a day at a hostel. That lasted three weeks before they could get back to Libya.

Richard Massey, Victor Gramigna and Pat Hilliard ended up in Rome September 1 after visiting Athens, Nicosia, Istanbul, Beirut, Cairo, and two nudist beaches, one on Mykonos, another an island near Dubrovnik in Yugoslavia (I'm sure this was purely accidental!). Once he returned to his village, Victor noticed his villagers were stunned by the coup and were still nice to him, even helping him to pack up.

Richard Massey then went back to his village:

> I sold everything in my house that was sellable: my radio, tape recorder, etc. The village went wild and crowded in before I was really ready for them. I had my glasses stolen

and all my tapes. They rummaged through all my old clothes that I was throwing away, underwear with holes, old shirts, T-shirts, socks and took everything. It was kind of embarrassing to see them fighting over stuff like a rummage sale. For two days I had to sit in my village with no way to cook. So I had peanut butter for dinner twice.

PCV John Becker returned to his village of Gira in the Fezzan, gathered his belongings and hopped on a bus out of Sebha for Tripoli. Not long after leaving, two gun-toting soldiers stopped the bus and began aggressively interrogating passengers. Among all the swarthy faces, John's fair skin and blond hair stood out like a like a white birch in a stand of pines. The soldiers zeroed in on him and just when it seemed they might arrest him, a passenger a few seats behind him who, unbeknownst to John, was from Gira, told the soldier to stop bothering him, that he was a good guy, that he was a teacher who worked with the village children. The armed men moved on. Afterwards, John thanked the man profusely. To this day he feels a deep debt of gratitude for this Libyan he did not even know, who courageously faced down men with guns to protect him. And to this day he feels a deep sympathy for immigrants and others in the U.S. who are summarily and unfairly rounded up, jailed, abused, deported.

Unlike the rest of us, music aficionado Craig Owens lucked into one of the great jazz concerts of all time. It was the "Festival Mondiale du Jazz d'Antibes" in Juan-Les-Pins to the west of Nice. (I myself had heard Louis Armstrong play there just two years before.) Craig heard Chick Corea and the Miles Davis Quintet perform there for two nights. He described it 50 years later as "the most powerful music I have ever heard." Jazz historians labeled it "breath-taking." He arrived back in Libya just one day before the revolution, on August 31. Once back in Tripoli, he holed up in a Peace Corps apartment with other PCVs. Someone brought a ton of hashish. With all the door invasions, there was a fair chance they could've been thrown into the local hoosegow. "Looking back on it, I'm asking 'What in the world were we doing?' "

Jim Seroogy and Tony Watson, who had just traveled to Malta, Italy, Switzerland and Austria were in Germany on September 1. They went to the nearest U.S. consulate to see what was going on. Consular officials gave them a $10-a-day per diem for a couple of weeks. So they went to Yugoslavia, and of course, visited the same nude beach in Dubrovnik that Mssrs. Massey, Gramigna and Hilliard had no doubt also read about in *Europe on 5 Dollars a Day.* As Jim was leaving his village and taking photos of his villager friends, the police ordered him to take all the film out of the camera. They only relented when Jim explained that he had so many valuable pictures of Europe on the film.

The way Jay Shetterly and Dianne Goode found out about the coup was in a round-about game of language musical chairs. They were aboard a Bulgarian train on September 2 with a couple of Bulgarian soldiers who spoke no English, and an Indian who spoke Hindi and Bulgarian. Jay spoke Arabic and Hindi. The Bulgarian soldiers, pointing to their Bulgarian newspaper, started shouting, "Leebeeah! Leebeeah!" Everyone else in the compartment was shrugging, wondering what this was all about. So the Indian asked them in Bulgarian, then translated it to Hindi for Jay, who translated it to English for Diane.

When Angus Todd and Bob O'Keefe learned Libya was open, they stopped by the Libyan Consulate in Yugoslavia where they were told they couldn't go back to Libya. "Why not?"

"Well, you have a re-entry visa in your passport to 'The Kingdom of Libya' and there is no more Kingdom of Libya. So you can't go."

After much protest, the staffer relented and just scratched off the word "Kingdom of" on the re-entry visa.

Tom Weinz (who had been providing training at Libya III in Bisbee) hopped on planes to get to London where he had the strange experience of flying in a Kingdom of Libya Airlines plane on which the word "Kingdom" had been hastily painted over.

Frank Reese and Mary Buelt were in Beirut on September 1. They flew to Athens and joined Mark Lepori as they hopped on a ferry to Brindisi, Italy. They took a train to Naples, then a boat to Sicily, Malta and thence to Benghazi. In Benghazi, they were placed under house arrest and told they had to get back on a boat to Naples. Frank, Mary and Mark said, "Hey, all our possessions are in our towns. We have to go back and get them." A Libyan army lieutenant finally provided them with the requisite permission letters.

Before his departure from Libya, John Lynch sought out his student Elie Boudt and gave him a copy of the U.S. Constitution.

On September 1, Cathy Kaiser and Trudy Swartzentruber were attending the Pan-African Cultural Festival in Algiers, having already traveled to France, Switzerland, Spain, Gibraltar, Tangier, Rabat and Casablanca. In Tunis, they managed to wangle a room in the basement of the Catholic Cathedral to spend the night before forging on to Libya proper.

At the time of the coup, about fifty volunteers from Cyrenaica were out of the country. Bob Pearson, as Area Director in Cyrenaica, stepped up to the plate and escorted a sizable group of volunteers coming in on a ship from Piraeus to Benghazi. Rebuffed at the port, they were ordered to ship out to Tunisia. They then tried again to enter the port at Benghazi. They were confronted with what looked like 15-year-olds with submachine guns who refused them entry. Bob asked why not and they said, "You need permission to enter the country." Bob asked, "OK, who's in charge, then?" They told Bob he had to go to Ghaddafi's headquarters in Benghazi. So, Bob went there on his own and began asking another group of 15-year-olds toting submachine guns for permission for his volunteers to enter Libya. Finally, one of them said, "Oh, OK, I'll give you permission." He grabbed a random piece of scrap paper. In Arabic he wrote "Let the American teachers in." Bob took that paper back to the port, with no official stationery or seal on it, and gave it to the Libyan soldiers. They read the piece of paper and said, "OK, let them in."

Neil McCabe found himself at a hotel in Malta on September 1, but soon ran out of money. The hotel owner invited Neil to stay at the hotel, in return for working in the kitchen. That tided him over for the weeks it took before Libya opened up.

Next, a textbook case on how to carry off a bloodless revolution.

Backstories and Uncomfortabilities

Over time, the origins of the Ghaddafi revolution emerged. It turns out that Muammar Ghaddafi was born in a Bedouin tent in Qasr Abu Haadi just south of Sirte in Cyrenaica. His father was a goat and camel herder. Young Muammar had been plotting against King Idris from the time he was five, playing soldiers in the sand while fantasizing about overthrowing the king. By the late 1960s others, too, were plotting, including a shadowy character, Abdullah al-Abid al-Senussi, known as "The Black Prince" (who was literally black) and a group called "The Black Boots," headed by a Libyan army officer, Abdul Aziz Shalhi. And by then, Ghaddafi's view of the king had evolved to a more adult opinion that Idris was inept, anachronistic, weak and corrupt.

All these conspirators were waiting in the wings for their chance to pounce. On August 4, 1969, an ailing King Idris issued a letter of abdication to the president of the Libyan Senate, designating his nephew, Hassan El Senussi, as his successor, effective September 2, 1969. He then sallied off to Turkey for medical treatment, accompanied by a retinue of 100 (including concubines, of course). At the direction of the remote king, his circle of royal Bedouin tribal guardsmen planned to take over Libya on September 2, 1969, displacing his nephew in the bargain.

Unlike his behind-the-scenes competitors to power, Ghaddafi got wind of the September 2 coup, planning his own pre-emptive coup for September 1. He code-named his takeover "Operation Palestine." In the meantime, the Black Prince orchestrated a coup from Chad and The Black Boots missed their mark by planning a coup on September 5, 1969.

Perhaps a contributing backstory for Ghaddafi was the 1968 publication, just a year earlier, of a book by Edward Luttwak entitled *Coup d'Etat: A Practical Handbook*, which, while partly tongue-in-cheek, essentially encapsulated the best practices of coups d'état. Previous coups d'état were rather hit-or-miss affairs. Luttwak prescribed key elements of a perfect coup: take over all the radio and TV stations; take over all the newspapers; take over the post office; take over any foreign military bases; jail your opponents, etc. In this way you control all communications and consolidate power. The book's nostrums were immediately embraced by many across the world, including in the Arab world. One cannot say whether Ghaddafi had read Luttwak's book, but one could surmise he had heard of the lessons therein, because his takeover on September 1 was a textbook case of a coup d'état: he took over the radio station, he took over the post office, etc.

The coup turned out to be a largely bloodless one, because the king's forces, seeing that the coup was in motion, simply assumed that the king had moved the coup schedule up one day, so, they deployed side-by-side with Ghaddafi's people. It wasn't until a day or two later that they said, "Gee, this isn't our coup!" By then it was too late and Ghaddafi's troops clanked them in irons. There was some limited fighting in Benghazi, but with only several deaths involved.

Along the way, Ghaddafi also ringed Wheelus Air Base with tanks. The base went into immediate lockdown. They wheeled armed F-100 fighter jets at every gate. While Ghaddafi's soldiers didn't dare charge the gates shooting at the F-100's (which would have been suicidal) as Arabs, they had to save face. So their solution? Race down the road in Jeeps directly towards the main gate, while blasting their mounted machine guns into the sky. Once they got to the gate, they spun around and retreated, laughing their heads off.

In addition, to prevent any of the king's sympathizers from fighting back, Ghaddafi didn't even identify who he and his comrades were. It was announced over the radio that "The Revolutionary Command Council" was in charge. Kind of hard to shoot at a target you can't see. It wasn't until one week later that Ghaddafi identified himself, once he was safely in power.

Once arrived in Tripoli on September 14, Bob and I had no place to go but to the Welches' and Austins'. They welcomed us with proverbial open arms. The next day at the Peace Corps office, no one knew what was going on: the proverbial fog of war. I did pick up a letter from Jeanne but it was old. She did indicate she would be coming back to Benghazi around October 10. Of course, dying to see her, but having no notion of what the next few weeks would bring. I was free from work, so on a whim, I bought a plane ticket to Benghazi ($25!) somehow, I guess, to be nearer to Jeanne, even though she was 5,000 miles away.

So, I joined fellow PCV Richard Massey and Cyrenaica Director Bob Pearson, his wife Roz and their young son Eric, on a bus to Tripoli airport. A nervous Libyan soldier stopped the bus, and feeling his oats, inspected all of us. We laughed at this silly display of power, but that got his goat, as one might express it in Libya. Not a great move on our part, as he had a submachine gun and we did not. A proverbial mismatch of power. Luckily, he left the bus in a huff. I settled in a seat next to Richard Massey and we took off in a French-built Caravel airplane, the pride of Kingdom of Libya Airlines.

Kingdom of Libya Airlines Caravelle

For some inexplicable reason, when we reached a cruising altitude of 30,000 feet, the Libyan pilot decided to reverse the engines! The plane went into an immediate nose dive. Food and drink flew all over. As the plane shuddered mightily, I could imagine the pilot pulling back desperately on the joystick. People started screaming. Some got sick. The nose-dive continued. I had always imagined that in such a situation I would have panicked, screamed, prayed. But in reality, for both Dick and me, we felt totally helpless. I looked over at him and said "I guess there's nothing we can do." He nodded calmly. The pilot finally pulled the plane out of the dive and the rest of the flight was uneventful. For the rest of my living days, however, whenever a fearful airplane moment occurs, I remember those harrowing few minutes when I came "that close" and appreciate every extra year fate has blessed me with.

Richard Massey and I checked into Benghazi's Grand Hotel. I went to Jeanne's apartment and met her roommate Shirley Greuel, who later married a handsome Libyan electrical engineering graduate of UC Berkeley named Mustafa Shembesh. (She was the only one of us to marry a Libyan.) Richard and I wandered about the very pretty city. I took in a Dean Martin movie *How to Save a Marriage and Ruin a Life*. I went to the harbor and just calmly absorbed its beauty. Back at the hotel, I finished a letter to Jeanne and sent it. Abed reading an 800-page book, *The Sot-Weed Factor* by John Barth, which I had started on the plane before being so rudely interrupted. (Again, quite coincidentally, Bob Marshall and Bob Pearson had read this very book just five months before.)

Over the next four days, I went to much-revered Libyan resistance leader Omar Mukhtar's tomb and hung out at Shirley's. We played Scrabble; she baked a pie; I made a crossword-puzzle out of the Scrabble pieces for Jeanne. I left the bracelets I'd bought for her with Shirley who was quick to inform me that what Jeanne really wanted was an ankh—the ancient Egyptian symbol of life—oh, well. Went out to Cyrene, founded by the Greeks in 631 B.C.E. as the first Greek city in North Africa, to visit the ruins—very cool; I heard that school would restart October 10; got three rides to Derna and visited PCV George Carter.

Mark Lepori's detailed sketch of Cyrene ruins

Back at Shirley's I learned that, in fact, the Peace Corps was being kicked out of Libya—well, that changed everything! On a bench facing Benghazi Harbor, I sat for an hour and lost in thought. What to do next? Where to go? What about the draft? What about Jeanne?

Then after five days, out to Benghazi Airport, where the proto-soldiers in fatigues-cum-submachine guns were omnipresent. They frisked us before boarding the plane for Tripoli. When we landed, the soldiers proceeded to frisk us again! How could we have come into possession of firearms up in the air? When it came to my turn, although I thought the exercise stupid, I chided myself to stay calm in this potentially volatile situation. The inspecting soldier reached into my jacket pocket and pulled out my yellow WHO card. He glanced at it for a second, then dismissively tossed it over his shoulder. I stayed calm. From my front pants pocket he extracted my keys, then tossed them over his shoulder. They jangled as they skittered across the hard floor. I stayed calm. From my other jacket pocket, he pulled out my passport, tossed it over his shoulder. I stayed calm. From my back-left pocket, he lifted my wallet. Tossed it over his shoulder. Calm. From my back right pocket, he extracted my wad of toilet paper. He held it up quizzically, having, of course, no idea what it was. He tossed it over his shoulder. I shouted, "Nooooo!" while shoving the soldier aside and raced towards the toilet paper. I pounced upon it like a linebacker smothering a fumble in the end zone. I didn't care. I could do without everything else. But not this!

Of course, this greatly agitated the soldiers and for the second time in two weeks, heavily armed Libyan soldiers were shouting and training their machine guns at me. I don't know what I said, but was at pains to jam the toilet paper in my back right-hand pocket where it belonged. They returned my valuable documents without tossing me into the clink. (I guess they were at a loss as to what to do because there is scant mention of toilet paper in the Koran.)

The next day, a general meeting at the Peace Corps office. It was terrific to see all my fellow PCVs, especially Dan. We were briefed on the situation. On the day after the coup, all the buses in the kingdom were shut down. All post offices were closed. Physicians were required to write all their prescriptions in Arabic. A curfew was put in place except for the hours of 10 AM to 1 PM. They warned us of possible anti-American demonstrations. There were rumors about a counter-coup. The Libyans were upset that supposedly the Air Force had smuggled a Libyan Jew hiding in a military plane out of Wheelus. They informed us that Dr. Coulson was authorized to distribute Valium to PCVs who were freaked out. According to Jay Corrin, with all the stress they were facing, including the banning of booze, the Valium was most welcome. They reported on an unsubstantiated rumor that all PCVs would be put on trial in a kangaroo court and summarily sent to prison.

In this time, one of the women volunteers in Tripoli was being followed by soldiers who threatened to rape her. She ran to Dr. Coulson's house. He told her to run upstairs and faced down the group of soldiers.

Down in Samnu, Bob Gausman was told he could go to Peace Corps Nepal next. However, that would entail two more years and he knew that his colleagues were opting for one additional year in the Peace Corps in another country, or one more year in the Teacher Corps in the U.S. So he asked, "Hey, what about Tunisia; they speak Arabic there." They replied, "No, you have to speak French to go to Tunisia." Bob didn't speak French, but he figured, with his linguistic background, he could pick it up quickly enough once he got to Tunisia. So, figuring that no one would ever know, he declared that he spoke French.

A few weeks later, he saw, off in the distance, a cloud of dust on the horizon, signaling the arrival of a rare automobile. A Land Rover. Out hops an American guy. He dusts himself off and says, "I'm from the American Embassy in Tripoli and I'm here to test your fluency level in French." Bob stammered about, saying, "Well, I can say 'Eiffel Tower' and 'Parlez-vous français' but that's about it."

The Embassy guy blew a gut. "I drove 18 fucking hours from Tripoli only to find out you were bullshitting us?" He turned on his heel, gave Bob the finger and stormed off for another 18 hours of grueling desert driving.

In less than two months, another coup d'état shook some volunteers.

Dashed Hopes and
Whipsawed Whim-Whams

Meanwhile, the repercussions of the coup swept over to Salt Lake City and Bisbee where the Peace Corps Libya III volunteers had been preparing all summer to live and teach in Libya. Ghaddafi ordered all the Libyans home. When the coup hit, the Salt Lake City group was practice teaching on the Navajo Reservation. In an echo of the Libyan-Navajo brouhaha in Clearfield the summer before, upon returning to Salt Lake City, all 52 Libyans rushed out to buy guns. When asked why, they explained they needed to defend themselves when they returned to Libya. This time no one stopped them. (This was in the days when you could openly take guns onto airplanes.)

In Bisbee, everyone was summoned to a meeting in the gym and told that all American teaching contracts in Libya would be honored by Ghaddafi's government. Two days later, Ghaddafi issued a scathing, scorching denunciation of Peace Corps volunteers, calling us "capitalist pigs." Whoops.

Switching gears, Bisbee management told the assembled trainees they needed three days to create packages for what each volunteer might do next. Panic set in. In addition to the general draft threat, the men were on tenterhooks about the draft lottery, scheduled for December 1, that would affect so many men's fates forever. (The lottery would simply take all the 365 dates of the year, corresponding to each person's birthday, and randomly distribute them. If your number was low—for example 1–20—you were a shoo-in for the draft. If your number was high, like 340 to 365, you were home free.) Instead of sending everyone home and then all the way back to Bisbee, management sent half the trainees to the Grand Canyon for three days and the other half to Guaymas, Mexico on the Gulf of California. (I'd love to be a fly on the wall to see how they came up with these destinations.)

Charles and Julia Weber were offered Somalia in place of Libya. They had no idea if this was a good assignment and said they had to think about it a bit. Julia called her journalist father. He said, "Don't go to Somalia." Sure enough, just two weeks later the Prime Minister of Somalia was assassinated. So much for the Somalia option.

Having befriended Tom Weinz, who suggested they come to Iran, Peter and Jane Eichten requested Iran for their Peace Corps term of service and ended up being just a few miles from Tom.

In Salt Lake City, according to Ron Aqua, the trainees were surprised and shocked at the peremptory nature of how the Peace Corps handled them at this point. Libya Desk Washington staffers flew out to discuss each volunteer's options. They were brusque and impatient. "Hey, you've got these three countries you can go to." They wanted instant answers: "What are you going to do?"

They told Rey Sodini that it was mostly Korea that was available. Rey asked what the weather was like. They said "Cold in the winter." Rey asked how difficult the Korean language was. They claimed, "Arabic is a piece of cake compared to Korean." This wasn't Rey's cup of tea, so they offered him Micronesia. But Rey declined, deciding instead to go to grad school in Hawaii.

A few weeks into the revolution, the new Libyan government demanded we leave the country but they hadn't provided a mechanism for us to do so. But they were upping the ante to force us out. The government-controlled *Libyan Times* ran an article with the headline "Peace Corps CIA Agents." They wrote that Peace Corps volunteers were "spies in teaching clothes." Piling it on thick, the newspaper *Al Hakika* ("The Truth") headlined "Spies in the Form of Teachers," praising the new revolutionary government for eliminating Peace Corps English teachers, stating that all 126 of them had no qualifications and were CIA spies.

Peace Corpsmen Are Spies in Teachers' Clothes - Al-Hakika

UNDER the heading, "Spies in teachers' clothes," a columnist in the national daily Al-Hakika, yesterday launched a blistering attack against the U.S. Peace Corpsmen, who came to teach English in Libyan primary schools, early this year.

He said Peace Corpsmen "entered our country under the guise of education and learning, while they were nothing more than hidden spies who breathe poison in the minds of our children at the tender age when they are most susceptible."

The columnist said he is not against teaching modern languages to our youth. "On the contrary, we welcome efforts to have the country's

After the meeting, I talked about options with Martin Sampson. One was for me to finish out my Peace Corps second year in Tunisia. Another was to go home and join VISTA or the Teacher Corps for a year. In any case, at this point I arrived at the highly disappointing realization that I would not have a productive second year in my village; I would not be taking the students in Al Gala and Um El Jersan to greater heights in English; I would not be learning a ton more Arabic; and, perhaps most importantly in the larger scheme of things, I would not be ridding the population of Al Gala of trachoma. My greatest regret.

TRIPOLI MIRROR

PHILIPS
EBCO
ddat O. Muktar, 310-A
'EL. 36049
TRIPOLI - LIBYA

INDEPENDENT DAILY NEWSPAPER   (Temporarily three times a week)

] تريبـولى ميرور [جريدة يومية مسـتقلة تصـــدر ٣ مرات أسـبوعيا مؤقتـا

VIII (New series) — No. 626   Sunday, 23 Ragieb 1389 — October 5, 1969   Price: 25

New Selection of Oriens decorative Sandals. Ideal for Summer. Best for casual wear
AT
NEECHAMA]
74-80 Sc. 24 Dec — Tel. 2
- TRIPOLI

U. S. PEACE CORPS TO LEAVE

The United States Peace Corps Volunteers in Libya will be withdrawn except for a few, according to a New York Times report Friday.

In the report filed by the newspaper's correspondent in Tripoli, the paper said the Peace Corps would no longer be needed due to the cancellation of the teaching of English at the elementary level.

I learned that Jeanne might be coming back. I so wanted to be with her. Dan went back to El Khozeur to get his things. My turn to go back to Al Gala.

The danger in the air impacted me physically. "Each night when I think of the situation I'm in, juices start dripping in my stomach, it tightens up, like before the operation."

On Saturday, September 27, I took a taxi to Yifran and hitched a ride to Al Gala. After joining 30 villagers for lunch, I sold off my belongings, giving gifts to Tahir and Milaad. The next day Dan and I were at pains to visit Um El Jersan to bid our goodbyes. We walked most of the way. We were at double pains to visit the venerated Hajj El Haadi. The pains were also those of sadness.

Once back in Tripoli, I got a note from Jeanne saying she was there! In no time flat, I tracked her down. We shopped at the bazaar. We visited the Welches. We supped with inspector Tom Weinz and PCV Bill Fligeltaub. I walked Jeanne back to Peace Corps staffer Marguerite Kivlin's apartment where she was staying. We then went to the Austins' for the night.

The next day, Jeanne and I met at 2 PM at the Peace Corps office and talked non-stop for two hours. This is when I learned that the Libyans would make good on the cancellation clause in the Peace Corps' contract with King Idris' government and pay us all around $800. (Bob Pearson *never* thought the Libyans would make good on the contract, whose cancellation clause called for three months' salary plus 15% of the contract remainder in the event of cancellation. He was summoned to the Ministry of Education in Benghazi with a paper bag and they dished out $20,000 worth of Libya pounds in cash to him. He nervously walked this to the U.S. Embassy and turned it over to the comptroller along with a list of the names and addresses of all the volunteers who were scheduled to receive checks in U.S. dollars.) Dinner with Jeanne at the Welches. We both crashed at the Austins' for the night at 2 AM. "Wow, great day!"

On October 1 Jeanne and I partook of breakfast at the Austins. To the Peace Corps office, where I chatted with Dan Peters for a bit. Jeanne and I then lunched at Barbeque King. That evening, took Jeanne to dinner at The Lantern restaurant. She was going back to Benghazi the next day to collect her things. We made tentative plans to travel back to the States together via France, leaving on Air Tunis. We exchanged what we assumed were temporary goodbyes. That night, "I miss her already."

It is only in retrospect that I have realized the short-term nature of our in-person relationship. Since our first letters together in November of 1968, we had been together for only six days by the time October 1969 arrived. So many letters sent back and forth! So little time together!

On October 1, I had gotten a cable from my father telling me to call collect ASAP. Wondered what the hell that was all about. On October 2, I was whipsawed. "Called home. Dad says he thinks I'll be drafted now or in December, anyway. Stalked out of post office gloomy, heavy, serious. Felt like I've never felt before. Mad." Then, "At PC office a five-page and a one-page letter from Jeanne. *Love* letters. Left me riding the clouds and loving everybody, walking on air." October 3, I heard from my father that my best option was finishing up my Peace Corps term of service with the Teacher Corps in the U.S.

October 5. Sent a letter to Jeanne.

October 6. Got a telegram from my father—I'm on the Teacher Corps list. Got an official letter from the Libyan Ministry of Education authorizing my exit visa. Learned that Bob Marshall will be finishing his Peace Corps term of service with a year in Tunisia. No letter from Jeanne. "How long do letters take from Benghazi?"

October 7. A windy, cold, rainy day. The Welches drove Dan and me to Garian through the mud and rushing rivulets of water to go to the Education Ministry to collect our severance payments. Dan and I each scored $800 in cash! I didn't know it at the time, but this was to be the last time I would see Dan. Back in Tripoli I got vouchers at Air Tunis for Jeanne's and my trip to France. I bade Irv Welch goodbye—he was going back out to the field. No letter from Jeanne yet. "Fantastic day—I'm crossing my fingers for Jeanne and our plans."

This was Bob Marshall's last day in Aujila:

> If the farewells had been prolonged for more than their 30 seconds, I might have broken down. As it was, saying goodbye to Mr. Ali brought tears to my eyes. One old man came to my door touchingly hoping I'd be back someday. I shook a small row of hands in front of the coffeehouse. My exit from Aujila was less than majestic—with Irish electrician Terry on a tractor!

Barbara Forslund took a cargo barge to Sicily. Cathy Della Penta flew to Marseilles, then to Niger. Cameron Hume, Martin Mueller and Jim Luikart returned to Al Marj to retrieve their belongings. "the once friendly crowd became a taunting mob...yelling and tossing pebbles at the car. Nothing enough to hurt, more a sign of glee to celebrate 'the revolution.' "

In the maelstrom of disinformation were rumors that Ghaddafi would go after the American Peace Corps volunteers.

When Jay Shetterly returned to Tobruk, he was deeply moved when his *mudir* and several other teachers declared that if Jay were threatened by anyone, they and their families would die to protect him. Jay endured two contretemps while planning his Libyan exit. First, while waiting in line at the Tripoli post office, a Libyan man behind him began shouting vociferously, something about Jay's yellow Bic pen. He then escalated, screaming at the postmaster to arrest Jay. He claimed that Jay's pen was a transmitter and that Jay was sending secret messages to the U.S. Luckily, a teacher Jay knew interceded on his behalf and Jay was off the hook.

Then, at Tripoli airport Jay, feeling doubly safe because he and his baggage had been thoroughly inspected and that he was already on the tarmac a few yards from his plane, what do you know but he was intercepted by a 17-year-old with a submachine gun. This youngster hadn't quite gotten the idea of handling a gun because he was holding it on the wrong end, by the bayonet! He ordered Jay to open his bags again for yet another inspection. Among Jay's belongings was a notebook in which he had taken notes on learning Arabic. The soldier, who knew no English, started leafing through every single page, reading every single word. Of course, with so much at stake, Jay could do nothing but bite his tongue. All of a sudden, the soldier pointed to an Arabic word (*melik* meaning "king") in the notebook.

"We have no king in Libya!" he shouted in Arabic, ripping out the page and throwing it to the ground.

More pages. The soldier came upon the word *amir* ("prince").

"We have no prince in Libya!" Rip, throw.

More pages. This time he sees the word *gasr el melik* ("royal palace"). "We have no royal palace in Libya!" Rip, throw.

Mercifully, at least at first, he came to the first of 150 blank pages. Jay uttered a sigh of relief, knowing there was nothing more to see. The Libyan soldier, however, carefully examined every blank page, one by one. At the end he fumed, "Do you think we're fools? Do you think we do not watch spy movies? These pages are written in invisible ink!" He ripped the entire notebook in half and threw it, too, to the ground.

October 8. I tried to get my exit visa but the office was closed. "No mail. Starting to get worried about Jeanne. Didn't my letters make it? No word on Teacher Corps. I'm anxious and worried about plans with Jeanne. Here we are 1,000 km apart trying to make plans—jeesh."

October 9. A letter from Jeanne finally came. "I feel all reassured again." I handed in my passport and my official letter in order to get my exit visa. I would get it in three days. "Feel cautiously optimistic. Only thing that can shoot me down now is an early necessity on Teacher Corps." I was so looking forward to a romantic European trip.

October 10. "To Peace Corps office. Accepted by Teacher Corps! But they said I had to show up by October 15! Marshall at office—funny as usual, but he had lost 10 pounds from sickness. He told me Jeanne said go ahead and make plane reservations. I sent a rushed letter off to Dad asking for a few days' leisure on October 15th ruling."

October 11. "No mail. Moped about. Made reservations for Jeanne and me for October 13 for Tripoli-Rome-Paris-Strasbourg." (I had suggested Strasbourg because not only is it a beautiful, canaled city, peppered with half-timbered buildings, but it is a Hobler ancestral home. I was hoping Jeanne would come in the next day. Caught in a time squeeze by the Teacher Corps, I wrote, "Will I be cheated again and again until I desperately cheat myself? Agonizing." I was stampeded by the Teacher Corps. (It's only after decades of experience that I now know I could have shown up a couple of weeks later without a problem.)

October 12. PCV Randy Simpson and I went out and got our exit visas. "Only one ingredient my luck hasn't taken care of—Jeanne. If she comes in tomorrow's Benghazi plane, I might be able to get tickets at the last second—don't know. Getting incredibly uptight every extra second I'm here. Being pulled at both ends." The Welches served us a farewell dinner and I bade them a tentative goodbye. It was precisely our 365th day in Libya. Bob: "Randy and I did some after-dinner singing to celebrate."

October 13. "Got tickets for trip home. Went out to airport. Jeanne didn't come on those two planes or another later today...so I won't leave till Wednesday but then I'd better go, Jeanne or no Jeanne—bitter as that decision may seem. Letter from her via Jim Luikart—I'm so depressed."

October 14. "I am so frustrated. Jeanne didn't come in but got a letter from her saying she was coming. I am going to cry myself to sleep tonight. Made reservations for Jeanne and me for tomorrow. Will I have to cancel hers? MADMADMADMAD."

October 15. "Ride from Mrs. Austin to bus stop. $8 to airport in taxi—waited for Jeanne again, to no avail. So left. Rome (one-hour layover). Paris (six-hour layover). Plane to Strasbourg. Strasbourg in the mists is stunningly beautiful." Over the next two, lonely foggy days I consoled myself as best as I could by visiting the Archives where I was delighted to find many ancestors, including an Abraham Hobler born in 1672. I wrote a three-page letter for Jeanne that I intended to leave for her at the American Express office in Paris.

Saturday, October 18, 1969. When it was time to catch the plane for Paris, the fog was so thick, I had to bus it to the Basel-Mulhouse-Freiburg airport some 90 miles to the south on the Swiss border. From the Paris Airport, I called the American Express office. No letter for me from Jeanne. No Jeanne. So nothing else to do but to hop on the next flight to the U.S. Took a cab from JFK to Princeton. "Dad and Mom glad to see me." It felt so comfortable to be home. As if I had never left.

I had come full circle.

Freedom Birds

A codicil to our homecomings were the very final days of Peace Corps Libya. When it was time for Jim and Joyce Swanson to leave their village, Jim said, "It was a sad time to say farewell to our village friends knowing full well we would never see each other again. As we left in our taxi I looked back once more at our village. In a small field I saw a group of boys, using an old broom handle as a bat, playing baseball. Whether introducing this American sport was my greatest accomplishment in this small Libyan village, I do not know, but it's given me a wonderful memory."

Jay and Nancy Corrin faced suspicion in Misurata. Some people called them names and some spit on Nancy as they walked into their apartment. "Eventually, a man came along driving a donkey cart with some bags and sheep in the back. He gave us a ride to the next town there we caught the bus to Tripoli." They and Bob Albertson managed to escape by sea.

At the Peace Corps office, in front of some other volunteers, the Swansons duly turned in their Peace Corps medical kit to Dr. Coulson. The kit was still full. Dr. Coulson asked why. Joyce said, "Well, we were never sick." The other volunteers erupted in laughter and started rolling on the floor. Jim asked, "Why are you laughing?" One replied, "Hey, I've been high for a year because they have opium pills in the kit." (50 years later this was news to me, too.)

Nervous about going to the airport, they consulted with Ed White, who told them, "I don't know if they'll let you go at the airport. You've got your tickets, just go!" On the way to the airport, they were halted just about every kilometer by young teenagers in camouflage brandishing semi-automatic rifles. They would board the bus and rifle through everyone's luggage. It was illegal to take any checks out of the country, so Joyce and Maggie taped the checks with their separation pay to their stomachs, knowing that Arab culture would not permit any man to conduct body searches of women. However, one set of items did not escape the notice of the Libyan customs inspectors. In ransacking one woman PCV's suitcase, the inspectors were alarmed when they espied a pack of tampons. They thought they were bullets! (All the watching PCVs bit their tongues for fear of being thrown into prison or worse.) The inspectors unrolled the tampons, asking what they were. Their solution, at the end, was to confiscate them.

Joyce and Jim made it through customs, but then, just a half hour before their flight, the airline desk announced over the intercom that Jim Swanson should come to the desk. They declared the Swansons couldn't leave Libya. Mark and Maggie immediately joined the fray and said, "If the Swansons can't go, we won't go either." Somehow, this unexpected response made the Libyans back down. Mark, Maggie, Jim and Joyce boarded the first plane to escape Libya.

Like a captain leaving the ship, the last Peace Corps person out was, Bob Pearson, who left Benghazi with his wife Roz, and his young son Erik on November 1,1969.

The personnel at Wheelus lingered on until May 1970. They were evacuated in a series of flights dubbed "Freedom Birds." The very last plane to leave Wheelus was a C-130, lifting off at 8:41 AM on May 24, 1970, and flown by, yes, Martin Mueller's father, Rudy.

Hopefully now, some non-trivial food for thought.

Ruminations

"Peace can have its heroes, too."

—*The Great Books*

You never understand your own country until you've left it.

Peace Corps Advertisement

You never understand how subject you are to forces beyond your control—wars, revolutions, government policies—until you detach yourself from your home country and experience these forces firsthand.

You never understand the citizens of other countries until you have immersed yourself into their lives.

Julia Marton-Lefèvre felt the Peace Corps should have facilitated discussion groups to help volunteers decompress when they returned to the U.S. And it was Julia who asked why—if the United States is so serious about "Peace"—there is no cabinet position designated "Secretary of Peace."

For John Ziolkowski, "The Peace Corps changed my life for the better. It was—and still is—a wonderful idea. I'd grown up in a farm town and all of a sudden I was traveling all over the world."

For John Forasté, "Our presence in our communities was a positive one for the Libyans, the expatriate Arabs and, for sure, ourselves. It gave us a worldview that has remained a fundamental part of us to this day. We appreciated and enjoyed the simplicity of the Libyans' daily lives. While our American identity and citizenship were intact, we also identified as citizens of the world."

For Jay Corrin, "Serving as a Peace Corps volunteer in Libya was a seminal personal and cultural experience for Nancy and me. Certainly the challenges of getting through all this gave us the requisite confidence to take on new challenges without giving in to the fates. As Nietzsche said, 'out of the hottest fire emerges the best-tempered steel.' "

To live in a Muslim country had a most profound effect on Craig Owens. When he came back, he considered converting to Islam, despite the fact it was not the thing do. He didn't want to do the Christian thing, as Christian churches were saying that the Muslims are all going to hell. So he became Bahai, because they see all religions as being essentially the same from a spiritual standpoint.

John Farranto appreciated the unexpected consequences of participating in international volunteerism. "The exposure to other sides of arguments, of realizing other valid points of view. The realization that in the U.S. on some topics we can be as close-minded as any ignorant person in a third-world country. For just one example, I understand the Palestinians."

For Dave Goff, "The Peace Corps is the best way in the world to find out what you're made of."

Jane and Chuck Beach: "We came away with a realization that beauty, goodness, intelligence and wisdom are pretty evenly distributed around the world, even if healthcare, education, opportunity and freedom are not. We know that Islam is not a religion of intolerance and violence. We know that terrorism is not characteristic of Arab culture."

For Kathy Lamoureux, "Fifty years ago I started an adventure which has taken me around the world, introduced me to other languages, customs and people, and broadened my perspectives on just about everything."

One would think that the Peace Corps volunteers having it the easiest would have had the most satisfying experiences, when in fact, just the opposite was the case. Deprivation from running water and electricity, remoteness from Westerners, lack of Western food, little opportunity to speak English, the absence of movies, television and restaurants combined with deep immersion in small villages, being forced to speak Arabic most of the time and other hardships resulted in the development of close Libyan friendships, a more meaningful appreciation of Libyan culture and much greater command of Arabic.

The vicissitudes of Dan Peters' El Khozeur experience counter-intuitively boosted his morale. While my situation was not as tough as his, I, too, had a satisfying experience. Dan wrote home, "I found that the guys who have it a little rough and who have a lot of contact with the Libyans are most happy. The volunteers who are living with other Americans are the most dissatisfied although they eat American food and have nice houses. Generally, these men are bored whereas I am constantly challenged with the language."

Over the years, a number of Peace Corps Volunteers around the world have been murdered or wounded in their host countries. Notably, this never happened over three years in Libya. The worst? Alan Frank got a bang on his head. This is a signal testament to the Libyans' peaceful attitude towards us. And, of course, some of them went beyond this and pledged to protect, for example, Jay Shetterly with their lives should he be attacked after the revolution.

As for me, thanks to my consciousness being raised about media bias in the U.S., only discovered when I went overseas, it has left me forever careful and skeptical of what I read in the press.

Having been so immersed, a portion of me, a slice of me, feels forever Libyan. Ginny Austin, who hosted us in Tripoli during the coup, offers a saying that captures it nicely, "You can get the sand off your feet and shoes but you can't get the sand out of your heart."

I believe the Peace Corps made us better citizens of the U.S. and in fact made us citizens of the world.

From observation of not only Libyans but folks from many countries I realized that wars are never started by citizens. They are always started by leaders. An ordinary citizen of any country has no quarrel with any ordinary citizen of any other country. It is only when leaders decide to make war (always for illegitimate reasons—no wars are necessary) that they immediately demonize not just the leaders, but the people of the other country in order to justify ordering their young people to go out and commit murder. For just one example, imagine if FDR had told the truth and said, "Hey, it's the Japanese leaders who are the culprits here. We have no quarrel with Japanese citizens. Now get out there and murder as many of them as you can." Of course, the very fact that we can turn on a dime and move from hatred of the Japanese to being friendly with them today illustrates the illogic, because the Japanese are no different today than they were yesterday, than they will be tomorrow.

Up until 1961 the U.S. government had thrust young people into war for almost 200 years. John F. Kennedy was the first one to thrust them into peace.

In 1970, after Peace Corps, Teacher Corps and Air Force basic training, I expressed my opinions at the time in my journal about not believing in serving in the military:

> ...but I do believe in serving what this country stands for. This is patriotism for mankind, not narrow selfish patriotism for only one small artificial division of land and people on this globe. You can call people, like they do in our cherished military, anything you like, like 'gooks,' 'sadiiks,' 'geese,' 'commies,' 'niggers,' 'honkies,' but that doesn't change the fact that they are all people. Wherever they are in the world, let them be helped. Whatever their nationality, let them be fed. Whatever their beliefs, let

them be educated. Whatever the color of their skins, let them be freed from disease. If even Americans can't free themselves from their own narrow parochialism, how can Americans honestly say "Let there be peace"?

Let's wrap things up with highlights of what happened to some of us over the last 50 years. And what happened to Jeanne, me and Dan.

Epilogues

On the heels of the Ghaddafi revolution, 411 of us were summarily scattered out of Libya and out of Libya III training to the four winds and into 411 different life trajectories, entering much wider worlds than we had heretofore imagined. Some of us went to Tunisia, some to Iran, some to Afghanistan, to Korea, to Morocco, Kenya, Niger, Turkey, Nicaragua, Guatemala, Ceylon, Nepal, Ethiopia, Mallorca, Liberia, Thailand, Egypt, Saudi Arabia, and other countries. Others of us went to the Teacher Corps, to Conscientious Objector work in the U.S. and even the Army. Others just terminated.

In our careers, we ended up as lawyers, non-profiters, advertisers, teachers, financiers, thespians, artists, business people. Those who roamed the world ended up living, as citizens-of-the world, RPCVs without Borders. Many garnered advanced degrees in various languages. I am not worthy! Time and space do not allow for everyone's post-Libya career stories, but some highlights warrant recognition.

The most degree-intensive among us was Greg Strick. After Peace Corps Iran he eventually earned a master's degree in Arabic and Middle Eastern Studies at the University of Utah. His next step was to get a master's in education at the American University in Beirut. He then got a Ph.D. in Sociolinguistics at Georgetown. Not being shy, he went on to acquire an MBA at Pepperdine.

Angus Todd transferred to Peace Corps Tunisia, and later became a flight purser on TWA. To date, he's been to Cairo over 200 times. One of his job responsibilities was to announce—in Arabic—over the plane intercom on the approach to Cairo Airport, the usual "We are now approaching

383

Cairo Airport. Please put your seats in the upright position, close up your trays, etc." To this day he delights us all by rattling off this four-minute spiel in his flawless Arabic. He shipped his Peace Corps trunk back home in 1969. But unlike the rest of us, he has yet to get around to opening it!

Dave Munro alit in Iran and taught English for two years, along the way picking up Farsi. He then spent two years studying Arabic at the American University in Cairo. He then attained a masters at Harvard in Middle East Studies and History. After a banking career, he moved on to financial consulting. Over the years he's worked in Bangladesh, the UK, Sri Lanka, Iraq, the West Bank, the Sudan, Yemen Nigeria, Bahrain, Mongolia, Russia, Uganda, Saudi Arabia, Kenya, Jordan, Egypt and Thailand, where he now resides.

Martin Mueller, one of my favorite fellow PCVs, got a certificate from the Sorbonne in Paris. He then achieved a masters in French Literature and Linguistics at NYU. He then served as Chief of Africa Operations at Peace Corps headquarters in Washington. After serving in the 1990s in the office of the CFO of the National Science Foundation, he became Peace Corps Country Director for the Ivory Coast, then in the same capacity in Haiti. He remained in Haiti for three more years as Director at the Center for Disease Control and Prevention. He's currently president of the Miami Beach Botanical Garden Board of Directors.

Marcus Wood led a colorful life. He taught English for Raytheon in Saudi Arabia for five months, spent five months on a kibbutz in Israel. For 15 years he led tour groups around the world, where he visited 100 countries.

After working at the Peace Corps Martin Sampson acquired a master's and a Ph.D. in political science at Indiana University. He taught at the University of Minnesota from 1977 to 2014, interspersed three times with stints in Istanbul.

Libya I, the Old Guard in 2016: Dave and Mary Nygaard, Marcus Wood, John LaViolette, Bill Tsukida, Alan Frank, Martin Sampson and Steve Canfield

Julia Marton and Charles Weber went to Peace Corps Thailand. Along the way, they were divorced. She ended up heading up a Rockefeller program in Zambia. Then became Executive Director of the International Council for Science. Later in her career she was at Yale as a distinguished Visiting Environmental Scholar. And along the way, she was conferred the *Chevalier de l'Ordre National de la Légion d'Honneur* by the French Ministry of the Environment. It's the highest recognition in France available to a foreigner. She currently lives in Paris.

Cameron Hume remembers, on the heels of the coup, watching Libya disappear behind him for the last time on the deck of an Italian ferry, vowing he would never have anything to do with Arabs again. Upon his return to the states, he went immediately into the foreign service. Besides eventually becoming U.S. Ambassador to South Africa, Indonesia, and Algeria, and also served in Tunisia, Syria, Lebanon and The Sudan. (So much for vows.) He did reflect afterwards that all the people in these Arab countries were friendly and courteous. He has penned two books, *Ending Mozambique's War*, and *Mission to Algiers: Diplomacy by Engagement*.

Franklin "Pancho" Huddle from Libya I. He had perfect pitch and only took up classical piano when he was at Brown. He became so accomplished he once played with the Toronto Symphony Orchestra. He was a University Fellow at Columbia's grad school. Somehow along the way, he learned Arabic. After a stint in Tunisia and Morocco, he returned to the States, earning an MA in Middle Eastern History from Harvard. He also taught Freshman English at Harvard where one of his students was Bill Gates. Later, he got his Ph.D. from Harvard.

He found his way into the foreign service. He became Consul General of Bombay (currently Mumbai) India. While there, he and his wife Pom decided to fly to Kenya for a safari vacation. On November 23, 1996, in Addis Ababa, Ethiopia, they boarded Ethiopian Airlines Flight 961, a 767, bound for Nairobi. After Pancho and Pom boarded, they got a free upgrade to business class.

The flight was hijacked by three Ethiopians seeking asylum in Australia. The plane took a severe ditch and catapulted just 500 yards off the Comoros Islands. Pancho, Pom and everyone in their row, although injured, were alive and floated to the surface. Of the 175 people on the plane, fully 125 died. Pancho was operated on at the Comoros Islands' main hospital, without an anesthetic. The story was so dramatic it was featured in *People* magazine. And it is the only incident in aviation history of a wide-body jet ditching in water that included survivors.

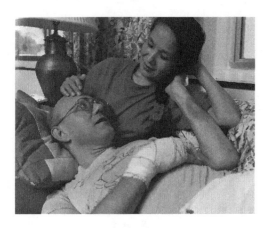

Pancho and Pom Huddle in *People Magazine*, 1996

Pancho later served as U.S. Ambassador to Tajikistan from 2001 to 2003. He was voracious in picking up languages. He says that while he's fairly fluent in Arabic, Russian, German, Burmese, Nepali and Thai, he admits his Hindi, Hungarian, Italian, Farsi, Welsh and Cebuano are "poor."

David Kalis from Libya III went on to Peace Corps Thailand. He became so fluent that he was able to moonlight as an actor on a Thai soap opera and became well known. He always played the part of a rogue who in the end loses the girl. In business, he worked his way up to Senior VP Worldwide Communications, RJR Nabisco, then later was VP Communications at IBM.

Having previously served in the Peace Corps in Afghanistan and trained volunteers for Morocco and Albania, after Libya, Deputy Director Bob Pearson got a Ph.D. from the University of Massachusetts. He went on to teach at Lafayette, Swarthmore and Muhlenberg. He managed a project in Romania for USAID aimed at bettering the lives of children in orphanages. Along the way, he co-authored a book *Through Middle Eastern Eyes* that was used in high schools for over 30 years.

Howard David, the Wheelus Air Base radio station on-air talent that I had so often listened to, came back to the United States in April of 1970 as part of the final evacuation of all Wheelus personnel from Libya. He'd finished his Air Force tour of duty. Looking for radio work among the 6,530 radio stations in the U.S., he sent out scads of resumes. On May 4, 1970, I happened to stop by to see my father at his radio station, WHWH in Princeton. I sat down in the anteroom outside his office. I struck up a conversation with this other young man. "So, hi, who are you?" The young man replied, "Howard David."

"Wait. You wouldn't be the 'mean old Howard David' from Wheelus Radio would you?"

"How in the world do you know that?"

"I was in the Peace Corps in Libya. I used to listen to you all the time!"

"So who are you?"

"I'm Randy Hobler, my father, Herb, is the president of this radio station."

"You're not going to believe this, but I just interviewed with him and he just hired me!"

Bob O'Keefe, considered one of our great teachers, went on to Peace Corps Thailand for three years. In Bangkok, Thai and Peace Corps staff developed a *Sesame Street*-type program on ETV called "Meet Mr. Maytree."

He starred as a bicycle repairman who bantered with two lizards. He soon became so famous he was greeted gleefully by children all over Bangkok.

Thai kiddie superstar Bob O'Keefe

Harold and Ellen McElhinny hold the distinction of being the only Libya volunteers to return not only to Bisbee, but also to Libya. In Bisbee, they visited the Philadelphia Hotel where they had stayed. Hotel management had preserved strange markings on wooden chairs, tables, etc. The mystery surrounding these added a certain *je ne sais quoi* to the hotel. They asked the McElhinnys if they knew anything about it. "Oh sure," said Harold, "those markings are Arabic words for the items they carved them on, for example, the Arabic word for 'table' we carved into the table."

Jay Shetterly married an Indian woman named Indira. They got married in a ceremony that included fellow Libyan PCVs Tom Weinz and Frank Reese, white horses, and yes, there was an elephant in the room. Jay went back to Harvard Law to finish his degree. Indira wanted to join Harvard's Sanskrit and Indian Studies program—a seven-year commitment. The professor in charge laughed at her, declaring her Indian college degree did not qualify her. She pressed him. He said, "OK, if you're serious, go to night school for a year and gain fluency in one more language." The following year, she not only gained fluency in French, but also in German. And top it off, she proceeded to finish the program in four years. As for

Jay's languages, when all was said and done, Jay ended up with Hindi, Arabic, Farsi, Spanish, Italian, French and a little Oriya under his belt.

The codicil to Jay's story involves his entomological focus on tiger beetles. He had collected 50,000 of them. At one point, he teamed up with a fellow entomologist in Australia. After Jay helped him out on his travel expenses from California, his friend discovered a new species of tiger beetle. In honor of Jay, he named it after him. The official name for this exotic-looking insect is thus "rivacindela shetterlyi."

Rivacindela shetterlyi

John Lynch's student Elie Boudt used the copy of the U.S. Constitution John had given him as the basis for continuing to learn English, rebelling against Ghaddafi's banning of all English in Libya. In 1979 he enrolled in Kalamazoo College, in Michigan. During college he worked in a wine store, studied wine lists, sampled wine, talked to many restaurateurs about French wine. Along the way he kept refining his oenological knowledge. In 2018, Elie's store was named by James Beard's online *Punch Magazine* as one of the Top Five Consequential Wine stores in the US.

On April 3, 2018, Elie, remembering his teacher John Lynch, posted the following on the Peace Corps Online website: "I have fond memories of Peace Corp Volunteer Mr. John Lynch. He served in Derna, Libya in 1968 as a fifth-grade teacher. I was one of the lucky students to be in his class at that time. Any information?" Your humble servant did, of course, have John's information, having already interviewed him for this book. I promptly got them both in touch with one another.

John Lynch: "Tomato Sauce" no more

Elie Boudt

Bob Marshall went on to Peace Corps Tunisia, later roomed with me and another guy that attended Columbia Law School. Later he married long-time sweetheart Siri Swenson who graduated from Yale Law. Along the way, in 1981, Bob published a book *Diary of a Yankee Hater*. Turns out Bob so disliked the New York Yankees he'd go to the trouble of flying out to Kansas City just to root against them. Recently, my girlfriend Alexa Smith and I had dinner with them at a couscous restaurant in Manhattan, leading to yet another coincidence. Bob and I were having dinner with Siri and Alexa!

Bob Marshall

Pray tell, did Ghadaffi leverage all that water under the Sahara? As much as I hate to give credit to someone of his ilk, he did. He spent $25 billion to excavate three billion cubic feet of rock to form a water pipeline from the heart of the Sahara to coastal Libyan cities to the tune of 6.5 million cubic meters of water a day—the largest irrigation project in the history of the world. He called it "The Great Man-Made River." (Not such a great name.) There was a hiccup or two along the way. For example, when this massive amount of water arrived in Tripoli, its old sewer system couldn't handle it and pipes burst out over half the city. The second hiccup? During the 2011 Libyan uprising accompanying the "Arab Spring" NATO warplanes destroyed most of the system's major pumping stations. ("The best laid plans…")

Sections of massive man-made river pipeline

King Idris? Exiled twice (from 1922—1951 and from 1969—1983), he died in Cairo May 25, 1983. He was buried in Medina, Saudi Arabia.

Libyans? As of this writing, they were writhing in a stalemated civil war among the Tuareg militia, the Tabu militia, the Government of National Accord, and the Libyan National Army, compounded by random vicious attacks from ISIS. Rufus Cadigan sums up what is now a violent, chaotic situation there, "It's very sad to think about the Libyan people now, people whom I knew as loving, peaceful and kind."

And what about Al Gala? It's much larger and thriving, including traffic jams. On the sad side, at the tail end of the Arab Spring in June of 2011, when Ghaddafi was on the run, his forces fired missiles into the village. Then his security forces mounted a counter-attack on Al Gala after it had already been liberated. They detained, tortured, then summarily shot 34 villagers and burned another one alive.

Funeral of 35 martyrs from Al Gala

Resting place of the 35 martyrs at Soffit Cemetery in Al Gala

Note that the cemetery is overseen by the Roman watchtower I previously mentioned that I could see from my apartment, and which I once visited. Upon learning of this massacre, I was worried that someone I knew might have been killed. Tragically, it turned out to be one of my own 5th grade students, named Said Ali Othman.

Thanks to Facebook and the villagers I was able to get a contemporaneous photo of Said. Needless to say, this was quite a shock to me.

Said Ali Othman in 5th grade

Said Ali Othman in the early 2000s

What about the Peace Corps itself over the last 50 years? While still thriving, what is not known is that in addition to their two-year stints, RCPVs are involved in no less than 157 Peace Corps chapters deploying thousands of community projects around the world—assisting refugees, building schools, etc.—a two-generation tidal wave of avocational benevolence. For just one example, Friends of Thailand alone supports 109 such projects a year. And our own Libyan RPCV, Maggie Brossoit, has toiled at community projects in Uganda four times.

Maggie Brossoit in Uganda

And what about Jeanne and me? While I began teaching French in the sixth grade of the inner-city, all-black Jefferson Elementary school in Trenton, New Jersey, applying the TEFL method to French, Jeanne was in Chicago. We stayed in close touch, vowing to make up for lost time by getting together in New York City. On October 30th, Jeanne flew in. We met at Skiff's Restaurant, then checked into the Penn Terminal Hotel for a whopping $12 a night. We crammed in as much as you could in a long weekend. The next day we went up to my best friend's law school—Columbia—and attended two classes. We went to the Guggenheim. We saw the movie *Midnight Cowboy* with Jon Voight and Dustin Hoffman. The next day we slept in till 2:30 PM. And that evening, we talked our heads off until 3 AM.

The next day our last morning in New York we shared a serious discussion. Later she wrote, "You told me that to be in love with a woman you would want to write her poetry and write poetry about her. And that you did not feel that way about me. I remember not being upset, but just sad as we had had a very good relationship. We had an outrageously fun, dramatic and intense short relationship." We kissed goodbye as she hopped in a cab for the airport.

Jeanne went to Peace Corps Thailand training in Hilo, Hawaii. There she met George Antonaros, with whom she became close. Thence to Thailand for more training on the heels of which Peace Corps Thailand wanted her to be a roaming TEFL teacher in Bangkok. She later married George, with Angus Todd, Barbara Forslund and Shirley Greuel in attendance. She and George had two sons, John and Sky.

**Jeanne Maurey, Angus Todd, Barbara Forslund
and Shirley Greuel at Jeanne's wedding**

They later divorced, and Jeanne then got a certificate in Interior Design at UCLA and practiced corporate design. In 1987 she married Milton Schlemmer, an intellectual property attorney with three sons. She is happy, visiting frequently with three of her own grandchildren, three stepsons, four of Milton's grandchildren and four great grandchildren! She now lives in Bodega Bay, California.

As for me, after the Teacher Corps, I joined the Air National Guard. Later, 13 years with IBM, then basically marketing consulting till the present day. Along the way, three wonderful children, six even more wonderful grandchildren and one unwonderful divorce.

Now I'm settled in with my soulmate, Alexa Smith. As one of many bonding elements of our relationship—in this case the Arabic part—she played dumbek, a Middle Eastern drum, in an Arabic band. The name of her band? Nasser, Nasser, Nasser, Mirhij and Smith. (On top of that, in her twenties she performed as a belly dancer twirling around with a sword stationary on her head. What's not to like?) Stemming from the writing of this book I was able to organize three Libya II reunions. Seven of us showed up in January, 2018.

Libya II reunion January 13, 2018. From lower left: Randy Hobler, Dave Munro, Alexa Smith, Lucy Freck, Peter Hawkes, Angus Todd, Ed Quinlan, Jack Seifert, Jim Luikart

And what about Dan Peters? Upon his return to the U.S. he began teaching Economics and History at Random Lake Community School, Wisconsin. In another case of coincidence, one of his students was one inspector Tom Weinz himself had taught two years previously at Random Lake. Tom had graduated out of college in Nebraska so the choice of Random Lake was literally random.

In October of 1969 Dan bought a Ford Torino. He started dating the woman he had so much corresponded with from Libya, Betty Klasen. They were soon engaged.

Dan and fiancée Betty Klasen with pet Lady

On February 21, 1970, after talking to their pastor about their upcoming wedding and on their way to see a movie in Appleton, Dan's car skidded on the ice, smashing into a tree. Betty was killed instantly. Dan was taken to Theda Clark Memorial Hospital in Neenah, Wisconsin and died two days later. They were buried side by side in Hillside Cemetery in Chilton, Wisconsin. I wrote in my journal:

> He had the hardest assignment in Libya and stood up to it remarkably. The fact that anyone's life can be poofed out like a candle is frightening. Plans shot. The future extinguished. Just life and then boom—nothing. I knew Dan better than anyone in Libya. I deeply cared for the guy, was interested in everything that happened to him, since we had gone through so much together. His interest in Arabic tied us together, too. Poof! poof, poof, poof, poof, poof. It makes all our daily pettinesses seem so little and meaningless. Also makes us resolve to be more kind, attentive to others, as Dan was.

Dan Peters at Random Lake High School, Wisconsin

Dan Peters, casualty of Peace.

In Memoriam

Peter Augenthaler
Dean Bliss
Mark Brossoit
Phillip Denney Brown
Dennis Carlson
Michael Crowley, Jr.
Dominic Dinardo, Jr.
Mary Buelt Froehlich
Kristi Carrie Christopherson-Clapp
Kathrine Colleen Ehart
Henry Farrar
Catherine Grace Friberg
Raymond Daniel Gumbrecht
Patrick Hilliard
Richard E. Johnson
Terry Jones
John Lundin
Randall Lee Melquist
Daniel Peters
Mary Richardson
Max Wayne Richardson
Barbara Ann Riggle
Walter "Chuck" Smith
Robert Suzuki
Angus Todd
Timothy Vollman
Charles Weber
Thomas Wilson

⨍ppendix

Abdullah 1

Abdullah 2

Abdullah Nakou

Abdusalaam

Ahmed   Ahmed Magroba

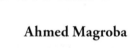

Ali Kamal   Almahdi Krura

Altahir Khalefa Abdullah Karish   **Altahir Sraba**

Aribi 1   **Aribi 2**

El Haadi 1   El Haadi 2

El Haadi Almiza   Hussein Aka'arud

Hussein Albouseifi   Hussein Mohammed Masoud

Ibrahim Solliman   Kamal

Khalifa   Mahamid

Mohammed 1   Mohammed 2

Mohammed Shaaban   Mohammed Solliman Alsweai

Omar Altahir Aribi Grada   Said Ali Othman

Solliman 1

Solliman 2

Solliman Emhemed

Solliman Hussein Algedbad

Tahir   Yosef Abdullah Alezzabi

Zakri Alezzabi   Unknown

Acknowledgements

To the late Dennis Carlson for his engaging Libya memoir, *Volunteers of America: The Journey of a Peace Corps Teacher*; to my soulmate Alexa Smith for proofing my first draft, for extensive proofing, insisting (in the face of my reluctance) on re-checking for facts, omissions, etc., with all 101 interviewees, resulting in hundreds of important corrections; for her inspiration, creation of the lead book title, and for her forbearance, patience and unwavering support; to Bob Marshall, for his 76-page diary, plus his insightful, demanding, resourceful and rigorous editing of this book; to Jim Seroogy for loaning me his copy of the 1997 Peace Corps Association Directory; to Raymond Cosma who provided me with copies of the entire biographical directories for the Libya III Salt Lake City project; to Chuck and Jane Beach, who scanned and sent me the Biographical Book for all the Libya II Bisbee trainees, newsletters and other key information; to Jim Putnam for photos, letters to home and for scanning and sending me the entire Libya III biographical sketches for the Libyan teachers and Peace Corps Trainees; to Alan Frank not only for his stories and connecting me to other members of Libya I, but for sending me hundreds of pictures he took in Libya; to Lorraine Slawiak Adcock for loaning me the two textbooks we used—*English for Libya 1* and *English for Libya 2*—and for photos of Bisbee; to Susan Glover for stories and photos; to Jeanne Maurey Schlemmer for 135 colorful photos and 20 of her letters to her parents; to Don and Lani Leydig for their anecdotes, photos and Libyan newspaper headlines at the time of the revolution. Also to Martin Sampson for his stories, input and research; Bob Pearson for many e-mails elaborating on the behind-the-scenes procedures of Peace Corps staff; Richard Massey

413

for stories and 26 detailed letters to his parents; Catherine Kaiser Krebs for her extensive input and for scanning her framed copy of Mark Lepori's wonderful drawing of the Greek columns in Cyrene; Tom Weinz for stories and photos; Paul Peters for photographs of his brother, PCV Dan Peters and for sending me dozens of letters Dan had sent to his parents; Andrea and John Murphy for stories and photos; Ern Snook for photos and stories; Margaret Brossoit for remembrances and scans of Libyan newspaper articles; Kathy Lamoureux for her stories and careful proofreading; Peter Crall for sending me a copy of editors Cathy Della Penta and Rosalind Pearson's 77-page collection of PCVs essays, *East of the Marble Arch*; and John Sheehan for multiple inputs for facts about the island of Kwajalein.

Special thanks to those who took time out of their lives to pre-read and pre-review my manuscript: Nicholas Craw, The Honorable Robert E. Gribbin, III, The Honorable Cameron Hume, Paul Sully, Tom Seligson, Jeff Wing, The Honorable Edmund Hull, The Honorable Niels Marquardt, the Honorable Deborah Jones and the Honorable Gene Cretz. Invaluable!

Thanks to James Voris for his story from his book *A Helluva Ride*, and to Melanie Jex of Village Lane Publishing for invaluable story advice.

Thanks also to the following for sharing their wonderful stories: Phil Akre, Bob Albertson, Ronald Aqua, David Benson, Stoney Bird, Karen Blanchard, Bill Cagle, Sam Cangemi, George Carter, Chip Chandler, Joe Connor, Robert Conway, Jay Corrin, Nancy Corrin, Charlie Cross, Glen Curry, Howard David, Mary Slatt Davis, Cathy Della Penta, Rich DiGeorgio, Dave Dittman, Roy Douthitt, John Doyle, Dotty (Dukehart) Hanson, Mort Dukehart, Peter Eichten, Diane Forasté, John Forasté, Tom Furth, Bob Gausman, Dianne Goode, Victor Gramigna, Trudy Swartzentruber Hartzler, Peter Hawkes, Nanette Holben, Franklin "Pancho" Huddle, Cameron Hume, Kevin Hunt, Ted Kelley, Rudi Klauss, John LaViolette, John Lawson, Mike Lee, Mark Lepori, John Lynch, John Maclean, Stuart Magee, Peter Mayberry, Neil McCabe, Harold McElhinny, Walter Matreyek, Randy Melquist, Julia Marton-Lefèvre, Martin Mueller, Dave Munro, Ritchie Newton, Frank Nicosia, Dave Nygaard, Bob O'Keefe, Craig Owens, John Peterson, Rebecca Peterson, Frank Reese, Paul Rhodes, Jack Seifert, Charlie Sellon, Kamal Shah, Randy Simpson, Othman Shemisa, Jay Shetterly, Stephanie Smock, Rey

Sodini, Greg Strick, Jim Swanson, Joyce Swanson, Angus Todd, Malcolm Travelstead, Louis Tremaine, Bill Tsukida, Rick Umpleby, Gary van Graafeiland, Marcus Wood, Tom Ziebell, and John Ziolkowski.

Thanks also to Adul Ajal, Malak Al Taeb, Mustafa Ayad, Osama Ben Sadi, Naji Elmabul and Mouner Essa for on-the-ground information in Al Gala. Also for Ali Said ElSeddick for general information about Libya. And to Elie Boudt for his life story.

About the Author

RANDOLPH HOBLER is, in no particular order, a perspicacious marketer, a fastidious author, a voracious reader, a tenacious researcher, a conscientious objector, a curious observer, an industrious composer, a gregarious world traveler, a punctilious musician, and a prodigious anthemologist.

Photo Credits

Photo of Janis Joplin by Brian C. Record

Photo of Leptis Magna by George Steinmetz

Photo of Norman Rockwell Painting, "JFK: Bold Legacy", licensed by IMG Worldwide

Photo of Bob O'Keefe by Michael Schmicker

Photo of Vice-President Lyndon B. Johnson in Libya by James Voris.

Photo of Aerial Photograph of NSD Clearfield from "The Supply

Depots", used by permission, Utah State Historical Society

Photo of Lyndon Johnson in Libya, used by permission from James Voris.

Multiple Personal Photo Credits:

Phil Akre

Maggie Brossoit

Bill Cagle

Chip Chandler

Alan Frank

Bob Glover

Cathy Kaiser Krebs

Don Leydig

Bob Marshall

Richard Massey

John Murphy

Bob O'Keefe

Paul Peters

Jim Putnam

Jeanne Maurey Schlemmer

Lorraine Slawiak

Ern Snook

Greg Strick

Tom Weinz

Sketch of Cyrene ruins by Mark Lepori

Arabic Calligraphy by Faraz Khan

Map of Libya by Aly Ollivierre

Calligraphic Book Title by Elinor Holland

Made in the USA
Columbia, SC
15 February 2021